FROM STONE TO STEEL

From Stone to Steel

ECONOMIC CONSEQUENCES
OF A TECHNOLOGICAL CHANGE IN
NEW GUINEA

R. F. SALISBURY

Assistant Professor of Anthropology
University of California

<pre>MELBOURNE UNIVERSITY PRESS
CAMBRIDGE UNIVERSITY PRESS
London and New York</pre>

Printed in Australia by Melbourne University Press

First published 1962
by Melbourne University Press, Parkville N.2, Victoria
on behalf of The Australian National University and
in Great Britain and in the United States by
Cambridge University Press

FOREWORD

From Stone To Steel deals with the changing life of a vague congeries of native people who inhabit part of the Eastern Highlands district of New Guinea. Now known as 'the Siane', formerly they had so little sense of identity or unity that to call themselves by a name evidently never occurred to them. The first explorers sighted them in 1933 but—such was their isolation—no other Europeans did so until after the war. Anthropologists knew nothing of them until Dr Salisbury's study began in 1952.

He had been a postgraduate student of the late Professor S. F. Nadel, a master of the theory and practice of his subject and a stimulating teacher whose ruling passion was a rigorous conception of research, who impressed on all his students that facts have to be collected for theoretical significance, not empirical interest, and that it is a moral as well as an intellectual duty to give inquiry as sharp a *Problemstellung* as knowledge and theory allow. But he also taught that sovereignty is with the facts. If they fall out in an unexpected way under study then there is only one thing to do with a provisional formulation that makes nothing of what is turning up: throw it away. The most critical stage of inquiry thus comes when facts start 'to unfold their inner rationale' for assuredly, he said, there is one. The logic of fruitful concepts—and that is where imaginative flair and a well-stocked mind come into their own—must be followed through, lead where it may. That teaching had much to do with the development of Dr Salisbury's study.

When Nadel arrived in Australia in 1951 to take up the foundation Chair of Anthropology and Sociology at The Australian National University, he set as a primary aim the reduction of the almost unknown ethnography of the Highlands. He declined to allow an inevitably small number of research-workers to spend themselves on piecemeal studies throughout Melanesia: research was to have a strategic aim, not become a scatter of raids and forays. In those days 'the Siane project' was part of the wider plan. Nadel had formulated it tentatively as 'a study of social structure and religion'. In the event, Salisbury turned it into a study of the consequences of technological change. Nadel did not live to see the completed work but I believe that he would have thought the metamorphosis a good example of how to take up the challenge of unfolding facts.

v

The Siane are a robust, vital people numbering perhaps 15,000, a very small part of the total population of the Highlands, which has been estimated at 700,000. The ethnographic divisions among them are still not very clear. Dr Salisbury's account is a useful addition to a growing store of knowledge. The Siane appear to have a familiar variety of segmentary organization but without persistent structures—in particular, political structures—of large scale or range. Their society, looked at in broad, lacks the definite anatomy and hierarchical build that many anthropologists have described from Polynesia and Africa. Inwardly, it has its own kind of structural intricacy. That aspect would have made a worth-while monograph in itself. But I doubt if it could have been combined effectively with the primary aim of *From Stone To Steel*.

The Siane social system, being relatively open, has a potential of development. An accident of history—the arrival of steel axes—exhibited that potential to the Siane themselves before Europeans visited them. They exploited it with zest. Steel drove out stone; the new cutting-edges saved men's working-time; and, from those beginnings, the whole design-plan and dynamism of their way of life changed. The external developments of the 1930s did not reach them; the war surrounded but did not touch them; and although peoples a comparatively short distance away went through devastation in 1942-3 and, later, civil commotion and upset, the Siane district lay as quiet as Sir Thomas Browne's Norwich under the drums and tramplings. Over that whole period the changes wrought by steel went on ramifying to fields of custom having no direct connection with technology. When Dr Salisbury arrived in 1952 he became aware of those circumstances and saw that they presented a unique opportunity of study. But the intended formulation 'social structure and religion' was clearly unsuitable. So he transformed the study into one of 'the consequences of technological change in a society . . . isolated from the world-wide market system, operating without money and . . . relatively self-contained'.

The acceptance of that challenge entailed a decision to limit the extent to which, on the one hand, the details of ethnography and, on the other, the complexities of social structure could be followed through at the same time. However, the wide range of topics on which, by customary standards, a social anthropologist is expected to give high detail, especially when a hitherto unknown people are the subjects of study, were not neglected. Salisbury has met well, within the limits imposed by the main task, the obligation to inform his readers on the fundamental matters. But with each such study the wisdom of Nadel's strategic conception becomes more apparent. Anthropology exists *for* comparative research.

We still know all too little of Melanesian society and culture on a comparative basis. The wide morphology of social organization, the varying styles of life and thought, the distribution of great institutions—especially the ritualized institutions—are not well understood even as regional phenomena. The search for valid comparisons is much less intense than for virgin ethnographic fields. A synoptic mind like that of the late A. R. Radcliffe Brown, which transformed our understanding of the social forms of the Australian aborigines, could do the same for our understanding of Melanesia. When that happens some classical texts may need revision and some famous peoples, about whom we may have supposed we had heard the last word, will need restudy. Recent research, especially in the Highlands, suggests that many impressions of the ethos and modality of Melanesian life left by the work of Rivers, Seligman, Malinowski, Williams and of those who followed them now need a long second look. Some remarkable variations now appear even in restricted localities. Typologies are hard to construct and the dynamics of social life elude clear statement. To give one illustration only, two such peoples as the Kuma and the Kunimaipa, studied respectively by Dr Marie Reay and Miss Margaret McArthur, could scarcely be more unlike in two important features —the psychology prevailing among women and their status in marriage—while being not very far apart in general style of life or, for that matter, in space. The progress of comparative anthropology will greatly change a general picture that had come to seem much of a muchness all over. Dr Salisbury's book has suggestive value from that viewpoint, not least because of its penetrating analysis of an economic system that must have much in common with others in Melanesia.

The main concern of the book is a *voluntary* process of *autonomous* development. It throws a helpful light on many practical problems—of both policy and administration—that arise in attempts to lift the material standards of native peoples by schemes for *induced* development and *directed* growth. Hence the stimulating force of a well-reasoned account of 'how a simple technological innovation can, given time and the free play of both the human desire for power and the randomness of innovation, eventually produce a new organization of society and a new standard of life'. We have no reason to suppose that the Siane changes were an isolated phenomenon. They must have had many parallels else-

where. A full understanding of Melanesian economic voluntarism
may have profound importance for all those who wish the native
peoples well in their difficult struggle with modernity.

Dr Salisbury could not find among the Siane any empirical entity
recognizable as *the* economy. But he distinguished three sets or
collocations or 'nexuses' of activity each associated with distinct
attitudes, customs, groupings of people, and types of commodities.
Two are the stock-in-trade of most accounts of Melanesian life:
the humdrum activities of subsistence, and ceremonial exchange.
The other—the production and use of inessential or 'luxury' commodities—has often been subsumed under one of the others because
it is less obvious.

On the basis of the distinctions, the account raises three sectors
of Siane life in both economic and sociological aspects: within
clans, the life of mutual help and sharing; within and between
clans, the life of diffuse friendliness and calculating personal interest;
between clans, as corporate groups using wealth to create and discharge obligations, the boastful life of self-esteem and public reputation. The first shows self-sufficient clans at work independently
but each organized to give its members equal access to the factors
and products of subsistence. The second reveals the self-serving use
by individuals of luxury-items, jealously held as personalty, and
doled out in lively hope of reciprocal favours to come. In the third,
the highly materialist ethos of the Siane is revealed in the public
transfers—mainly between corporate, intermarrying groups—of the
most prized valuables, which change hands in an excited atmosphere amid great shows of ceremony and rhetoric. The florid, self-
seeking transfers express in a material symbolism 'the more general
relationships between clans of opposition or hostility, alternating
with calculating politeness and alliance'. The segmentary social
structure expresses itself in a more or less continuous tension between the components whose members have to do with each other,
in the imprisonment of interdependence, by marriage, gift, presta-
tion, trade, insult, violence, feud, and war. Except where temporary
and usually very expedient friendships exist, the tension may range
from formal opposition to outright violence, according to the run
of ever-changing circumstances.

It is a well-drawn picture of ebullient materialism. A picture, not
of that rather abstract 'material substratum' of which Malinowski
wrote, but of the principled materialism of a whole way of life.
Not of the externals of savage covetousness, but of the substance
of a people's dynamism, old and new. Not of a naïve charade of
economy, as Europeans understand it, but of an authentic system,

bizarre but veritably human, of getting and spending and laying waste of days.

Dr Salisbury saw that his data set some true problems of theoretical interpretation, problems from which it has often been easy for anthropologists to turn away, sometimes from lack of interest, sometimes from a mistaken belief that the issues lie beyond their province. The productive, distributive and sumptuary plans of Siane life, as of any other, rest on calculations of regular outlays of time, resources, and effort, and of the yields and their disposal. How were traditional Siane modes affected by the time-saving steel axes? Within the autonomous revolution, the potentials of demand and supply were free to change. Did they change, and in what regular ways? Each nexus involved classes of non-substitutable goods of incommensurate values with traditional uses towards competing ends. Were the categories, values and allocations broached by the new goods, ideas and standards of valuation after 1933? Many such questions suggested themselves and *From Stone To Steel* goes some distance towards answering them. Other questions, less clearly asked or answered, provide food for thought in relation to the information provided. Doubtless, some will provoke controversy. For example, if increased leisure but no measurable increase of goods resulted, was the whole process truly one of 'development'? And where is the evidence of the continuously progressive recasting of all the outlays of material life that constitutes development in a European context? Dr Salisbury may not have provided all the information for which specialists, economists in particular, may look, but the imaginative span of the wider study should not be forgotten in the search for conclusive detail. Some of the more technical discussions—the nature and course of capital development during change, the anatomy of demand over the same period, the matter of values and the influences of change on them—seem to me adventurous and ingenious. When one takes into account the character of the material, and the circumstances of its collection, one will see that the concepts and numerical procedures have been handled with care. The freshness of the whole attack is illustrated by the author's decision to set up as a virtual monopolist of supply in order to work out empirically the types, scales, and elasticities of demand.

The conception of a social system as a demand-structure is fully in keeping with an anthropological approach. By working out that conception more fully, Dr Salisbury might have done anthropology a signal service. Twenty years ago, in a memorable controversy with Professor Melville Herskovits, the late Professor F. H. Knight

criticized what was then becoming known as 'economic anthropology'. The central criticism was that theoretical economics is a
principled discipline, whereas theoretical anthropology is not. The
force of Knight's contention may not have been fully grasped even
yet. The anatomies of theory in the two disciplines are not at all
alike in structure or plan. Anthropology cannot show, as economics
can, a lucid body of general or central theory in organic connection
with an interrelated set of branch and topic theories. The differences
between them have little if anything to do with subject-matters.
They are due rather to distinct logical foundations, types of conceptual development, and historical traditions of study. The main
intrinsic difference is that economics has taken as its central intellectual concern the problems of the determinations of its subject-
matter, which are the price-quantities of specifiable things at times
and places. Anthropology increasingly has taken the problems of
determinations for granted. Dealing mainly, by tradition, with
institutionalized relationships—those that, having been determined
in the long ago, can be regarded as standardized—it has not seen
at all clearly the need of even an abstract analysis of the processes
of institution-making, preferring to deal with consistency-studies
between determinate institutions. In the upshot, the two disciplines,
unlike in theoretical structure and plan, are taught in virtual dis-
connection, and whether they are kin, kith, or strangers is a question still inadequately examined. But *From Stone To Steel* sets up
an anthropological inquiry correctly in those respects in which it
seeks to examine the *re*determination of institutional modalities
consequent on a specified change in something basic to them all.

In such circumstances, to speak of 'economic anthropology' is at
least ambiguous. Any such phrase suggests a belief that anthropology can grow additively. A theoretical science cannot grow,
though it may swell, in such a manner. If anthropology is rightly
conceived as a discipline that eventually will generalize all social
relations of whatever kind then it may not simply borrow from
particular sciences and leave the borrowing at that. To do so is to
act like a bower-bird among bright objects. It has also to integrate.
But an intellectually-satisfying integration between the two academic
disciplines has yet to be attained. Those are matters for the arm-
chair and Dr Salisbury, rightly, has not let field-study wait upon
their solution. His duty was to bring the facts of a primitive socio-
economic system—and a developing one, at that—into focus as best
allowed by the state of theory in his subject. He did that duty as
well as anyone whose work I have read. The book adds force to the
statement by Professor Raymond Firth in the revised edition of

that classical study *Economics of The New Zealand Maori* that '. . . in order to understand the nature of a particular social system, it is usually necessary to understand the nature of the particular economic system related to (or embodied in) the social system'. Salisbury's work is no vague acknowledgment of the link between economy and life: it reveals the indivisibility in terms of categories and principles.

The aspect of *From Stone To Steel* that will make it of wide contemporary interest is its apposite commentary on what purports to be a universal theory of development. The book, fundamentally, is a study of growth. But the character of that growth is fascinatingly unlike the types of development which, in wisdom and conscience, Europeans widely feel are in the interest of native peoples unavoidably embroiled in this kind of world. The Siane realities—relationships, institutions, values, rewards, hopes—belong to a world distinctively their own. Dr Salisbury has shown that it is abstractly possible to find something like common terms with the European counterparts. The human prospects of bringing the counterparts to a true commonness of life are left in suspense.

For many years Western nations have experimented with plans and projects to induce development among native peoples. Usually the aim has been to match methods and ends with needs according to a European conception of all three. The failure, partial or total, of many essays has left an uneasy feeling. Has the work been with or against the native human grain? The question is less one of means and methods—about which, surely, there is little mystery—than of the European art of using them in situations only half-understood. The projects so far mounted do not seem very ill-judged against the ends and needs we postulate, especially in the light of our own familiar life-experience. But a hard fact is there: in the widest perspective things seem out of phase or gear. Native peoples resist or give their own twist to priorities and procedures that we feel are essential for true growth. They prefer their own approaches at their own speeds. In such situations it is as easy to despair of their initiatives as to feel suspicious of all European conceptions of development. The work of such anthropologists as Dr Salisbury has much importance at those times. Their studies increasingly document the positive plans of life by which many contemporary native peoples prefer, and try, to live. They make more clear the European postulates that need examination. And they help in those ways to build and strengthen the two necessary pillars of a bridge of understanding.

W. E. H. Stanner

PREFACE

THIS BOOK is one outcome of fieldwork conducted in New Guinea in 1952-3, as a Research Scholar of The Australian National University, under the direction of the late Professor S. F. Nadel, whose writings (together with those of Professor Raymond Firth) have stimulated much of the present analysis. He was a most methodical and tireless fieldworker, and his example and sharp criticism tended to force his students to emulate him, no matter how unmethodical they might be. Under his direction I had the advantages before I went to the field of learning pidgin from Dr Peter Lawrence, of being stimulated to collect economic statistics by Dr Cyril Belshaw, and of being introduced to field conditions by Dr K. E. (Mick) Read. My study was primarily of the social structure and religion of the Siane people, and was written up in 1954 in a manuscript report, although the economic statistics I had incidentally gathered remained unanalysed. In the summer of 1955 I had discussions with Drs John Pelzel, David Riesman and Howard Roseborough which stimulated me to write the bulk of the present work in the winter of 1955-6. At this time I had the good fortune to join a group headed by Drs Talcott Parsons and Neil Smelser, working on the final revisions of their book, *Economy and Society* (Glencoe, Free Press, 1957). It immediately became apparent that the substance of my study was an independent confirmation of many of the analyses contained in their work. It was arrived at inductively from the consideration of the economic concepts used by the Siane, whereas their analyses had been deductive starting from Dr Parsons' general theory of action. In the body of the present work I have not referred to *Economy and Society* but have left the convergences to appear of their own accord.

Dr Douglas Oliver, Dr Walt Rostow and Dr W. E. H. Stanner read the early drafts of the work and gave invaluable criticism after Professor Nadel's untimely death allowed him to comment on only one chapter. In 1957 the book was submitted as a doctoral thesis at The Australian National University, at which time further criticism was given by Drs Raymond Firth, George Foster, Gunder Frank, Bert Hoselitz and Sol Tax. The work was then revised for publication taking into account these criticisms, which have been of the utmost value in reformulating many problems, and drawing on comparative material available up to the middle of 1959. To all the people named above who have contributed to the writing of this book I would wish to express my thanks.

Nor could the book have been written without the help of those who made the fieldwork so pleasant. Everyone I met in New Guinea, officials of the Administration, private individuals and members of missionary groups, was unfailingly hospitable and helpful, from my first welcome to the Territory by Mr Dick Tebb to my send-off feast at Goroka provided by Mrs Ellen Pitt. My regret is that my friends in the Territory are too numerous to mention, while to thank some and not others would be invidious. Thanks must be given, however, to those who provided information used in the text, particularly Mrs Buchanan, Messrs Snow Blakely, Bob Cottle, John Foldi, Cherry Lane, Joe Searson, Jim Taylor and the Rev. Robert Hueter. Too many Siane helpers gave me information and hospitality for me to mention all by name, but I could not fail to acknowledge the help of Yawe, Kono, Famti, Yofantena, Noimfanu and Wemini.

I should like to express my gratitude to The Australian National University, which financially supported the fieldwork; to Harvard University, since the original drafts were written as an Arnold Fellow and Research Associate of that institution; to the University of California, which supplied funds for the preparation of the manuscript; and to Helen Winsor and Jan Seibert who typed and improved drafts of the manuscript, and Richard Roark who helped with bibliographical work.

Lastly, I wish to thank all those whose contributions were more diffuse: the instructor in H.M.S. *Cabbala*, who introduced me to the study of economics, my anthropological teachers at Cambridge, Harvard, and The Australian National University, and my wife, who has contributed intellectually, psychologically, and extremely practically, both during the fieldwork and during the writing.

Berkeley, California

R.F.S.

CONTENTS

ILLUSTRATIONS

FIGURES

TABLES

In the text

GLOSSARY OF SIANE TERMS

aigavo	payment made at birth
ainke	then; next; the second item in a series
airo	other; over there; third and later items in a series
amene	a shadow
amfonka	the absolute owner of personal property
ankuramfo	an edible plant with shiny yellow-green leaves
atana	a green-snail shell
atanefo	the 'eldest sister' of my lineage
aunefo	my grandparent
awoiro	courting visits by youths
ekanefo	my parents-in-law, new wife speaking
emona	his sister (see also *nemona*)
faivya	in vain; unimportant; of no account
faivya neta	a matter of no account; goods not accounted for
fine	fighting with clubs
firinka	a boundary mark
gerua	a decorated board, representing souls
gimaiye	to give a formal presentation; to present
gimito	given
hentaiye	to give birth; to beget; to look after
hentenamo	looking after; begetting
homu	first (in a series)
homaiye	to precede; to make an advance payment
horaiye	to hear
hori we	a man who hears; a skilled man
hovanum	a men's house
inkere	theft
kafo	the wild fig tree
ka mafo	yam taro; First Fruits ceremony
-kere	a collective suffix; 'and others'
kevora	small
kifana	a stone; a coin
koinanefo	my age-mate
komonefo	my sister's son; child of my clan
korova	spirits of the dead
kumfa	shoots of wild sugar cane, eaten like asparagus
kunanefo	my sibling of the same sex; my brother
makana	the land of the dead

mea	the long poles used to divide up a garden
menefo	my father
merafo	his father; its owner, guardian or trustee
meranefo	my father's sister
mika	ground; land
minkuri	growing crops in gardens
momonefo	my mother's brother
mona	the base; the trunk of a tree; the root; the original cause
mone	my penis
moka	your penis
montu	a hard wood used as roof timbers
muruna	my liver
naiye	to eat
no	eat! (imperative)
nakunefo	grandchild
namfa	big; a variety of edible green vegetable
namo	me; my
nanefo	my son
ne	there is; it is; they are
nemona	my sister
nemona we	my sister-man; my trade friend; my sister's husband
nenta	close
nenta wenena	close people; my phratry
neta	something; a thing; an affair; a valuable
niamfa	my close affinal relative
nitofa	my distant affinal relative
nofonefo	my cross-cousin
numuna	a house; the territory of a clan
ofia	a black palm-wood
oinya	the soul of a living person
onawaruma	edges of a garden plot
onefo	my mother
oraiye	to do
orufero	what a person has to do; his job
orunefo	my daughter
orune irofo	my wife; my married daughter
otova	a hard wood used for arrow heads
rafa	red
rako	one
ramfi	a hard wood
roi	the *marita* pandanus

rono	work; often applied to mean a garden
rowa	warfare
ruru	a shell
ruruafo	bride-price payment; the generic term for payments
sene	my bowels
sia	buttocks
sia ne	'there are buttocks'
turiye	to be mad; to be possessed
turimo	possessed by spirits
uma	shoot or tip of a plant; a tally
umaiye	to help; to give freely
umuto	given
umutoko	things which are given
wane irofo	my husband
we	a man
wenena	people
wena	a woman
wene	my mouth
wera	his mouth
wera neta	food
wo	go
waiye	to go
uto	gone
ya(ro)	there; where you are standing; nearby
yaroma	that (emphatic form)
yafo	pig
yafo koiya	the Pig Feast
yanefo	my eldest brother
yarafo	his eldest brother
yowo	smooth; level

1

INTRODUCTION

In FEBRUARY 1933 the first parties set out for the systematic exploration of the New Guinea Highlands, an area thought to consist of uninhabitable mountain peaks until its eastern fringes were first crossed in the epic journey of two prospectors, Leahy and Dwyer, in 1930. As the exploration parties passed through Siane territory they encountered peoples who used stone axes and who were completely ignorant of the existence of steel. From 1933 until 1945 no Europeans crossed Siane territory, since an easier route to the north had been found, and the Siane natives had no direct contact with Europeans, their governmental methods, or their teaching. Yet during this period steel axes found their way into Siane territory along the channels of indigenous trade and exchange; their use in the native system of production became universal, and, directly or indirectly, all other aspects of native life were affected by them. By 1952, when this study was undertaken, the few stone tools still in existence were preserved as keepsakes by old men, yet any man over 25 years of age could tell of how matters had been when stone tools were still in use, and could indicate when present-day practices diverged from what was current before 1933.

The change from a technology using stone tools to one using steel tools occurred in western Europe many centuries ago, and the social arrangements needed for the full exploitation of the new technology developed over a long period. In other parts of the world the same technological change occurred rapidly when, from the sixteenth to nineteenth centuries, Europeans conquered native peoples or settled near them.

Often, when Europeans settled near native peoples, other changes were effected at the same time—trade stores were established, land was taken over by Europeans, peace was imposed by European administrators—and it is difficult to isolate the effects caused by the changes in technology from the effects of other innovations. In other places, where Europeans were not present to record the history of the period, the details of the process of change have been irretrievably lost, although (as for example in the studies of the north-west coast of America by Codere [1950]) the general out-

I

lines may be reconstructed by scholars. The Siane, however, had time in which to work out their own social adjustment to the new tools. For twelve years they received steel axes from other tribes with whom they had long-standing exchange relationships; they had no direct contacts with European government, trade stores, missionaries or miners. The use the Siane made of their new tools, and the consequent changes in their society, can be seen as direct results of the new introductions placed in a setting of the pre-existing Siane society. Although the new tools originated outside Siane society, the subsequent changes can be interpreted as occurring autonomously following the technological change from stone to steel.

The Siane changes are not merely curiosities, interesting only to archaeologists who wish to understand social processes in the distant past. They provide a unique opportunity to study the consequences of technological change in a society isolated from the world-wide market system, operating without the use of money, and relatively self-sufficient. The purpose of this study is to show the way in which such a change affected the social arrangements of a simply-organized society so that eventually it was able to exploit the new techniques to their fullest advantage. Analysis of the changes in such a simple system may contribute to the understanding of the more complex changes occurring in many parts of the world today, changes which almost invariably include technological change as one component.

The reconstruction of the events of the twelve years from 1933 to 1945 in Siane is simplified by the fact that all men over 25 could describe both these years and the years when only stone was used. In fact, activities in the stone-using times differed little from those of the steel-using times, though the relative importance of many activities had changed profoundly, and the organization of those activities in terms of each individual's time and in terms of the co-operation of many individuals had also changed. The Siane described these differences impressionistically, and it was possible to collect some numerical data to support these impressions. In 1953 it was possible, by talking with natives who came from areas bordering on the Siane, who still used some stone tools, and who had seen only one or two white men, to confirm many of these reconstructions. The Siane description of their way of life ten years earlier was like the way of life of these uncontacted natives, while the exchange transactions between the Siane and the others re-sembled closely the descriptions of trade between natives living near European centres and the as-yet-uncontacted Siane of the early 1940s.

Since 1945, when Government patrols first entered the area, many other influences have been at work in Siane society. A Lutheran mission has been established in a neighbouring area. Administrative, medical, and agricultural patrols traverse Siane territory three or four times a year. Siane men have spent time on the coast as indentured labourers, and they sometimes visit trade stores at the European centres to buy goods. Nevertheless, the changes resulting from these influences are the continuation of processes of change already under way in the indigenous society. The bringing of peace, of manufactured goods, and of European skills have accelerated changes already in progress. They have allowed natives to select solutions to their problems from the gamut of ideas and goods presented by Europeans, rather than leave them alone to solve these problems by trial and error. Thus, when more valuable goods became needed for use in ceremonial exchanges, it was possible to obtain manufactured goods for the purpose, instead of having to create a completely new type of 'valuable' using native resources. In this way the presence of manufactured goods has contributed to the increase in the number of ceremonial exchanges. Needless to say, such a use of goods obtained from trade stores will draw the Siane more and more into the world system of monetary trade, and this involvement will have effects in its own right, but in 1953 they were not yet important, and will not be treated in this book. They will be the subject of later study.

In studying the processes of economic change in Siane society I shall take first a descriptive approach, and shall then describe a series of activities in which the people engage, and in which they appear to organize their behaviour in terms of a rational calculation of the quantities of goods or services produced, exchanged, or consumed, in such a way as to allocate scarce means to meet competing ends. Many of these goods and services have no immediately obvious connection with the production of the goods needed for subsistence or the satisfaction of bodily needs in the society, yet the organization of the activities related to these goods and services has close parallels with the activities of brokers and merchants in our own society. In short, the behaviour would be classed as 'economic' by common parlance, although it would not appear to be part of the economy, if we take a limited definition of a society's economy as 'that part of the total activities of the society concerned with the production, distribution and consumption of the material requisites for well being of members of the society' (Marshall 1925: 1). However useful the concept of the 'economy' may be for other purposes, it does not correspond to any single empirical entity in Siane society, and in this, a descriptive study, it will be discarded in favour of a consideration of 'the economic aspects of Siane behaviour'—those aspects in which there is allocation of scarce means, based on a rational calculation in terms of quantities of goods and services, and in which goods are produced, exchanged, or consumed (cf. Robbins 1935: ch. 1).

One of the aims of this study will be to isolate some of the principles in terms of which these rational calculations are made. This will primarily involve analysing the way in which natives themselves approach their exchanges—the concepts and terms they use, their rights to land and other property, and their means of transferring property from one person to another—the way in which they organize their work and distribute the fruits of their labour, their attitudes to work and the expenditure of time, and the desirable ends they hope to accomplish through their work, their exchanges, and their leisure activities. I shall attempt to abstract the principles in terms of which the natives themselves make their calculations, rather than to demonstrate that the Siane use the principles of calculation familiar to us from the science of economics. Such demonstrations are no longer needed, following the pioneering work of Malinowski, Barton, Firth, Richards, and others who, at the same time as they demonstrated that non-western peoples did use the forms of calculation we use, also demonstrated that these forms of calculation do not exhaust the types used.

After describing the economic activities of the Siane peoples during stone-using times, in so far as these activities can be reconstructed from the data obtainable in 1952-3, I shall describe the activities then current and reconstruct, using both direct testimony and inference from it, the process by which the changes took place. Beginning with Chapter Six, however, simple description and immediate analysis of the data give way to a deeper level of analysis: an attempt to see how far traditional western economic concepts assist in understanding the process of change in Siane, and to see whether any distinctive Siane economic concepts can be isolated from the first level of analysis—concepts that might be of use in the analysis of economic change in other societies, even in Western society. The traditional western economic concept potentially most applicable and useful in understanding the Siane material is that of 'capital'. I shall attempt to provide a measure (since the usual measuring rod of money is absent) by which the levels of accumulated capital and of annual capital investment in stone-using times can be compared with the levels in steel-using times, and shall then examine how far the changes in level of capital investment can be seen as *the* crucial changes which start the process leading to a higher real income *per capita*. The fact that the level of capital investment in activities producing goods actually remained steady, or even declined, led me to reject the proposition as stated in such simple terms, and to look for other interpretations. The stocks of goods used in materially *un*productive activities increased, as did the amount of time spent in such activities, and thus led me to consider applying the concept capital to these other activities, and to consider the 'services' they produce.

There is also the problem of why *demand* for these services should have increased, although they had little direct connection with the change in technology. Changes in demand on this macro-economic level of long-term aggregate trends are made easier to understand by considering, on the micro-economic level, how the demand patterns of individuals changed during the twelve-month period I was present. For this period full figures are available on the effective demand for many types of goods, since I was the only source of supply of manufactured goods for an area of several hundred square miles. Analysis of these figures reveals that the general pattern of change in demand in response to an increased potential supply is the same on an individual level during the period of a year as it is on an aggregate societal level over a long period. One category of goods, in which any article may be purchased as a substitute for another, has a demand of great initial elasticity that increases many times as the supply increases but then remains relatively constant. Another category, within which a similar substitution may occur but no goods of which can be substituted for goods of the first category, has a demand pattern which increases only when the demand for the first category levels off, but later it also appears to level off. After a lag there appears a small but steadily increasing demand for a third category of goods, which also may substitute for each other but may not substitute for goods of other categories. Yet a fourth category shows an unchanging pattern of demand regardless of changes in the supply. These categories, established by analysing elasticity of demand and by the behaviour of native consumers in demanding specific articles in place of others momentarily out of stock, correspond to the native categories of goods as analysed in the chapters that describe indigenous economic activities and the patterns of thought concerning them.

Closer analysis of the behaviour relative to these categories of goods indicates that each category is valued in terms of its contribution towards the attainment of different ends. Goods in the fourth category—those for which the demand is relatively unvarying—are subsistence goods, valued in terms of how far they enable individuals to perform their recognized roles in society. Goods in the first category—that showing the greatest initial elasticity—are valued in terms of the power they enable an individual to acquire, over and above the authority he may have from his recognized social status. The next most elastic demand is shown by goods valued in terms of their use, either in entertaining visitors, or in directly gratifying an individual whose idiosyncratic desires are not gratified in the performance of his recognized social role or by the accepted methods of acquiring power over others. The remaining category—goods demanded after a long lag, when demand for luxuries or power-bestowing goods is satiated—consists of capital goods the use of which would produce goods or services over and above those needed to maintain the existing level of subsistence and the current amount of power-seeking and leisure activities. A comparison with some other non-monetary societies for which there are relevant data shows the same categorization and also that changes in these societies follow somewhat the same pattern as in Siane.

The last chapter of the book attempts to organize into a coherent conceptual scheme these descriptive generalizations. It relates the generalization about the existence of several disparate standards of valuation within any one society—standards allowing a certain range of goods to be ranked, though not themselves ranked in any overall order, as is implied by the economist's calculus in terms of money—with the pattern of changes in demand and thus with the increase in standard of living and the establishment of an economic organization capable of supporting that standard. Implicit in this conceptual scheme is the idea that standards of living do not increase evenly; they increase by jumps. If the scheme were more generally applicable it would imply that the presence of money, although it 'rationalizes' choices by apparently forcing disparate sets of values to be ranked, also acts to confuse the process of change by permitting activities to take place out of the order in which they necessarily occur in non-monetary societies. It would also imply that the different patterns of demand empirically discovered by economists in Western society, and described by different 'demand curves', could perhaps be systematically related to each other by breaking down the concept of marginal utility into at least four components.

2

THE SIANE: ENVIRONMENT AND
SOCIAL ORGANIZATION

THE SIANE, whose economic behaviour forms the main topic of
this book, are a group of tribes comprising some 15,000 people
who live in the New Guinea Highlands between the meridians of
145° 10' and 145° 20' E. and between the parallels of 6° 0' and 6° 20' S.
(Fig. 1). In the Australian administrative divisions of the Territory
of New Guinea they were in 1953 the major group of tribes occupying the Western census division of the Goroka sub-district of the
Eastern Highlands district. Physically they are a dark-skinned
people ranging in colour from a light brown to an intense purplish-
black. Their hair is dark and wavy or curly, and many of the men
sport dense beards. There is an immense diversity of lip form, nose
shape, and bony structure, including almost the whole range of
'types' found anywhere in Melanesia, but in body build the people
are relatively homogeneous. They are well muscled and athletic-
looking—fat Siane are almost non-existent. The men average about
5 feet 4 inches in height, the women are about two inches shorter.
The language they speak is non-Melanesian.

The term 'Siane' was not a term used by the people for themselves as a whole in pre-European times, since the largest grouping
feeling any sense of unity and having a common name was the
tribal group which varied between 400 and 2,000 individuals. The
Administration used the term 'Siane' to describe this group of
tribes, since the word is the characteristic form of greeting in the
area. As a consequence of the administrative usage, people who use
the greeting are now beginning to differentiate themselves from
their neighbours, for whom the Administration has other names—
Gahuku to the east, Bomai to the south, Chimbu to the west and
Sinesine to the north-west.[1] I shall use the term Siane here to
designate the members of the sixteen tribes, the names of which
appear on Fig. 1 and are listed in Appendix A.

This usage is not meant to imply that the behavioural patterns
of these sixteen tribes are clearly distinct from those of other tribes
in the Highlands, or that they interact among themselves in such

[1] See Read (1954) for a description of these other groups.

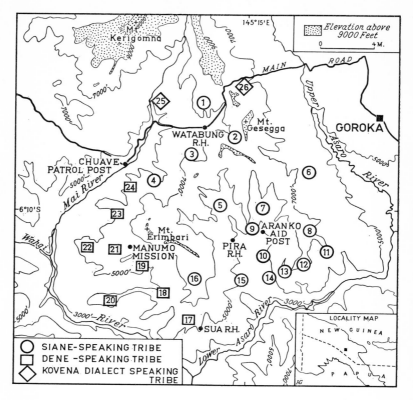

FIG. 1   Siane-speaking and Dene-speaking tribes in the New Guinea Highlands.

(Nos. 1-16 Siane-speaking; 17-24 Dene-speaking; 25-6 speak Kovena dialects)

1	Komenkaraka	7	Aranko	13	Nivi
2	Yamofwe	8	Omena	14	Wanto
3	Komunku	9	Fowe	15	Namfayufa
4	Raya	10	Ramfau	16	Yantime
5	Emenyo	11	Yaviyufa	25	Ono
6	Rafayufa	12	Urumfa	26	Korefa

a way as to form one social system with clear boundaries dividing the Siane from other people. Geographically, it is true, the area in which the Siane tribes live is well defined. To the west there is a clear boundary: a mountain scarp, on the other side of which live the linguistically different Chimbus. The east and south are bounded by uninhabited mountain slopes covered with tall *kunai-*

grass[2] (*Imperata arundinacea*). To the north and north-east the mountains become higher and covered with dripping moss forest, making a geographical divide. But culturally there is no sharp boundary between the Siane and the neighbouring peoples; instead, there is a cultural *continuum* from the far north-east to the far south-west that over-rides geographical and linguistic boundaries. Between neighbouring villages the cultural differences are imperceptible and become clear only when one travels rapidly from a village at one end of Siane territory to a village at the other end. Nor are there any large native political units to give unity to the Siane area by politically opposing the Siane to other peoples. The settlement pattern, of villages of 200 individuals scattered evenly over the land to give a population density of about 80 to the square mile, continues on both sides of the Siane area.

Out of this seemingly amorphous collection of villages it is necessary to specify the unit on which the present study is based, and for convenience I have selected the unit that can be most easily defined. The Siane form a linguistic group using the common greeting 'Siane', they live in a geographically well-defined area whose boundaries are recognized to some extent by the Administration, they have a culture that is relatively homogeneous throughout the area (though not exclusive to it), and now—as a result of governmental measures—they are beginning to feel some degree of group unity in opposition to other groups of a similar nature.

The Environment

The Siane live in an area of the Highlands of New Guinea that is relatively level, with an altitude varying between five and nine thousand feet, and that is situated between two chains of extinct volcanic mountains which rise to about 13,000 feet and which run from east to west. In some places to the east and west of the Siane the 'relatively level area' does become a flat plain, where once there were large lake beds, 5,000 feet above sea level. These plains—the Wahgi and Goroka plains—were the sites of first European settlement. Between them is the Siane territory, and there the 'relatively level area' is composed of deeply eroded valleys and razor-backed ridges, where to journey from one ridge to the next—a distance

---

[2] This is the pidgin (Neo-Melanesian) term for the coarse grass which grows to a height of three feet wherever the original tree-cover of the mountain slopes has been removed and not been allowed to regenerate itself. *Kunai*-grass produces a thick root system which is almost impossible to remove, using stone tools, and which effectively prevents the growth of most other plants. For the spelling and general connotation of pidgin terms see Murphy (1949).

of perhaps a mile as the crow flies—involves a scrambling descent down a thousand-foot slope with a gradient usually steeper than one in five, and then a tiring climb up a similar slope on the other side. In wet weather the slopes are covered with a film of liquid clay on which only heavily nailed boots or bare feet can keep a footing, so that travel becomes a nightmare in any direction except along the ridges. It is only to the geographer or air traveller, who can compare the Siane ridges with the massive forested mountains to the north and south, that such country appears relatively level. To the traveller on foot the main impression is of a confusion of ridges and an unending series of precipitous climbs.

In this confusion there is in fact some regularity, dominated by certain main geological features. To the west there is a steeply-tilted limestone slope whose scarp faces west in a sheer cliff several thousand feet in height and culminating in Mount Erimbari—a landmark visible for a hundred miles to the westward. North of the Siane area stands Mount Kerigonuma, round which numerous streams flow in a westerly direction, in deeply cut, rocky valleys. The chief of these streams is the Mai River, whose valley was made in 1953 the route of a road running the length of the Highlands, but which in pre-European times constituted a major barrier to communications north and south. The bulk of the Siane area is composed of sandstone ridges which radiate, fan-like, from a centre near Mount Gesegga in the north-easternmost part of Siane territory. The general direction of these ridges is from north to south. The eastern ridges are the steepest—in fact the easternmost ridge, which one climbs from the Goroka Plain, is 8,000 feet high, while the bottom of the plain is at an altitude of 5,000 feet—and the steepness of the ridges decreases as one travels westward, until one comes to the great tilted slope of limestone leading to Mount Erimbari. The rivers between this fan of ridges flow to the south and join to form one river basin, which drains into the Lower Asaro River just above its confluence with the Wahgi.

A pattern of vegetation can be discerned in the area. To the east the steep slope down to the Goroka Plain is dusty, waterless, and shadeless, and is covered with *kunai*-grass. To the south also, where the rivers and ridges come close together, there is an uninhabited area covered with *kunai*-grass. Elsewhere the whole area is forested. Even the summit of Mount Erimbari, 9,000 feet high, has its cover of dense, dark-green moss-forest, normally shrouded in clouds and dripping with moisture. Below about 7,000 feet the dark-green is replaced by the greyish-green of pine-like casuarinas, interspersed with smaller bushes and cleared, cultivated areas. In the midst of this grey-green there are small areas where the trees seem closer than normal, and the bright yellow-green of bamboo and bananas is visible; here people are living. These are the signs of villages, and are to be found on the minor ridges of the mountains, at heights between six and seven thousand feet. The valley bottoms are usually narrow, stony, and uninhabitable, while the few flat low-lying areas are swampy and liable to flood with the frequent heavy rains. Here are found damp-loving trees, such as certain varieties of pandanus, or dense stands of *pitpit*—the pidgin term for a variety of wild sugar cane (*Saccharum spontaneum*)—which rise some eight to ten feet tall.

The climate strikes the European visitor as ideal. Throughout the year there is little change in temperature—80 degrees by day and 50 by night are limits that are rarely exceeded.[3] The prevailing wind is from the south, varying between south-east and south-west. Usually, a cool breeze blows, but occasionally sudden, violent, chilling squalls do occur. Most remarkable is the consistency and predictability of the rainfall. Less rain falls from June to September than falls in the months from December to March, but there is rarely a day without rain in the evening, and over a hundred inches falls during the year. And almost every day starts with mist rising from the valleys where clouds have settled at night, and with the sky overhead clear. By mid-afternoon the clouds have built up, and in the evening it rains and clears the air for the next day. Provided that one can arrange to be indoors by 5.30 p.m. one need have no fear of the weather, and can count on warm, sunny, clear days that are never hot and humid, although during the rainier season a few days may be dull and drizzly. At night the temperature drops, so that blankets may be necessary, but it is never too hot to sleep.

Social Groupings

The Siane who inhabit this 180 square miles of ridges, forested slopes, and abrupt valley bottoms number some 15,000. Population density is thus about eighty persons per square mile, and the birth-rate, the age-sex composition of the population, and the genealogies I obtained suggest that this figure has been relatively stable for some time.

The people live mainly in villages stretching along the minor ridges of the mountains. A typical village stretches some 500 yards along the ridge, and contains three, or possibly four, 'men's houses'

[3] The absolute extremes I recorded in my house at 6,200 feet were 99° and 40° F.

and a 'street' of about fifty low-walled huts where the women and
children sleep. The women's huts, with roughly conical thatched
roofs, are separated from each other by a small fence. These huts
flank both sides of the street which is barred at intervals by the
strong fence which encloses each large oval-shaped men's house.
A badly kept path leads round each enclosure. The men's houses
may be as much as thirty yards long and twenty feet high in the
centre. Inside them sleep the men and boys who have been initiated.
In front of them are clearings which form the centres of village
social life. About 200 men, women and children live in a village.
Two miles away along the same ridge is the nearest village, while
two miles away on parallel ridges are other villages. This is the
typical picture; in fact, many villages are closer together; others are
farther apart.

The area between villages is not completely deserted, even at
night, for most men build 'pig houses' there. These are the same
size as women's houses, but they are built close to the gardens so
that the women who live in them can conveniently tend the crops
and look after the pigs, which forage freely in the uncultivated
bush or fallow land. But while everyone does not sleep in the
village every night, every member of the village group *does* have
a house in the village, and 70 per cent of the village members
sleep there on any average night. The settlement pattern changes
as the triennial Pig Feast approaches, for at that time all houses
in the village are rebuilt and all members of the group congregate
there. After the feast is over there is a steady drift out from the
villages to the 'pig houses' until a fluctuating balance of 70-30 per
cent, town-versus-country residents is reached once more. The settlement pattern is thus one of compact villages, with a tendency to
periodic dispersal into isolated homesteads, though this tendency
never becomes dominant.

The obvious residential group of the village is also a significant
social group, comprising, typically, one patrilineal virilocal clan,[4]
together with its wives and minus its adult daughters who marry
out into other villages. But there are other larger, less obvious,
residential groups, which also have definite social significance.

The whole assemblage of the people I have called Siane live in
a well-defined area, but never act together as a social group. It is
only a recent phenomenon that they have begun to differentiate
themselves from other assemblages of people, equally large and
amorphous, and to have some feeling of group entity.

[4] Except where specifically noted, my use of anthropological terms follows
that recommended in *Notes and Queries* (RAI 1951).

The largest unit normally recognized by the natives is the tribe. Each tribe has a name although there is no native term meaning 'tribe', and the sixteen tribes in the area are each composed of from two to nine clans. In a sense the tribe is a kinship unit, since kinship terms *can* be used to describe all the members of one's own tribe. But such terms are rarely so used, unless an individual wishes to emphasize his nearness to a tribal 'brother' as contrasted to his distance from a member of another tribe. This extended form of kinship is often validated by claiming common descent from the mythical tribal ancestor, who emerged from a hole in the tribal land and created the original clans of the tribe, but genealogies are not kept in support of this claim. On the other hand, many clans who call themselves by the tribal name and who call their fellow-tribesmen 'brothers' have traditions of migration to the territory on which they now live. They may be recognized as 'kin' by members of a distant tribe, from which they migrated. Nevertheless, since they were once granted permission to settle on tribal land and now live on it, they call themselves by the tribal name. In short, tribal membership is indicated by the use of a tribal name, members of the tribe think about its internal organization in terms of a kinship idiom, but the effective determinant of who shall call himself by the tribal name is residence on the tribal land and the possession of certain rights over that land.

If the tribe is a small one of two or three clans, as it usually is when there are no immigrant clans, it is coterminous with the group within which marriage is prohibited and which I shall call a 'phratry'. There is a native term—*nenta wenena*[5] (close people)— to describe such a group, but phratries do not have proper names. In the larger tribes there may be several such groups, each composed of two or three clans, which now live next to each other, even though they may have immigrated from widely separated tribes.

The phratry group has other functions besides the regulation of

[5] The spelling of native terms is phonemic, and is described in Salisbury (1956c). The writer spoke serviceable Siane at the end of his stay, and could maintain conversations on most simple topics with natives who could speak no pidgin. He could follow the drift of conversations between natives but not the detail. Even at the end of his stay about 80 per cent of his questioning was done in pidgin and only 20 per cent in Siane, since he was more accurate in pidgin and most natives by then understood pidgin. Replies by informants were about 50 per cent in pidgin, 45 per cent in Siane and 5 per cent in Dene. Similar bilingual conversations are perfectly normal in native life. Formal interpretation was dispensed with after about two months, except to obtain translations of texts, since by then the number of pidgin speakers had risen from about 1 per cent to 20 per cent.

marriage. Within it, all warfare is forbidden, although fighting with non-lethal weapons such as clubs is common when disputes need settling. 'Warfare', which can result in death and is forbidden, is called *rowa* by the natives; 'fighting', which is non-lethal and permitted, is termed *fine*. The phratry group does not combine together to wage war. However, a clan involved in a war against outsiders can be sure of the neutrality of the other clans of the same phratry. In the great religious ceremony that occurs every three years—the *Yafo Koiya* or Pig Feast—the clans of a phratry co-ordinate their ceremonies to honour the ancestors, and perform special dances that emphasize their 'brotherhood'. The occasion thus stresses the kin ties of the group, as well as being the one occasion when groups larger than the clan combine for united action.

The clan is normally the largest effective unit in Siane society, occupying one village and comprising about two hundred individuals. It is an exogamous group within which marriage is forbidden; it is a kinship group, where everyone uses either kinship terms or personal names for everyone else;[6] it has a clan name. There is, however, no native term for 'clan' as such. When referring collectively to all the members of the clan, its proper name is used: thus, 'Waifo are killing pigs' denotes that the men of Waifo clan are preparing for a ceremony. When referring to the area occupied by a particular clan, the word *numuna* or 'house' is used: one says 'I am going to Waifo house'. To express the idea of clanship, the phrase *we rako* or 'one man' can be used in certain contexts; thus 'Famti and I are one man' means we are clan-mates.

All men belong by birth to the clan of their fathers, and this normally means that they belong in the village where they live. The clan of the mother does have some claim to a child, but this claim is liquidated by a series of payments made by the father's clan. On the other hand, if a mother deserts to a different village taking her children with her, there is a conflict of claims between the clan of the father and the village of residence. Again, if a man takes up residence with his wife's clan at marriage, there is a similar conflict. Such exceptions to the rule of descent and locality are few, and for one clan comprised 2 per cent of all residents. There is a tendency for such people to be absorbed into membership of the clan with which they live, but this does not vitiate the general statement that clan membership is defined by birth.

[6] As distinct from the use of clan or tribal names. Members of other tribes might address a man as 'Man of Komunku (tribe)', for example; members of another clan of Komunku tribe would address him as 'Man of Roanti (clan)'.

The clan-village is the unit in the blood-feuding that follows a death. All members of the clan of a dead man combine to exact vengeance, while the death of any member of the killer's clan is felt to wipe out the debt. The clan is the normal unit for religious ceremonies; in the Pig Feast it performs its own ceremonial, but co-ordinates the performance with the other clans of the phratry; at other times it performs religious ceremonies independently, although representatives of 'brother' clans may attend; in rites of passage, although the main body of participants is the immediate kin of the principals, representatives of all sections of the clan participate. The clan also combines as a work unit: in such tasks as working for the Government on road-building the whole clan assists; and representatives of all sections of the clan attend the rebuilding of any men's house, even though the major portion of the work is performed by residents of that house.

The clan-village is divided into smaller residential segments or 'wards', each of which centres round a men's house, or *hovanum*. The men's houses, with their associated clearings, *tanket* bushes,[7] bamboos, trees, and thick fences, are situated some hundred yards apart along the ridge. About twelve or fifteen women's houses or *wena numuna* belong to the wives of the men who live in the *hovanum,* and these houses line the street on either side of the men's house. There is, however, no definite boundary separating wards, and women's houses attached to one men's house may be surrounded by houses attached to the next men's house. Each of these wards or men's house groups is typically composed of about thirty males over 10 years old, twenty-three married women, and eighteen unmarried girls and young boys.

Boys normally go to live in the men's house of their fathers when they are initiated, between the ages of seven and ten. They may go to a different house, to live with friends or to obviate over-crowding, but they normally live with their fathers. This means that the men's house is usually a kinship group. The fact that it is primarily a residence group, however, is brought out by the native usage of calling the members of the group by the name of the plot of ground on which the house is built. Thus, to say 'Maunori is building a new *hovanum*' means 'The men who live on the plot of ground called Maunori are building themselves a new house'. If they build on a different plot of ground they lose

[7] *Tanket* is the pidgin (Neo-Melanesian) term for *Taetsia fruticosa.* The bushes and their leaves are extremely hardy. The bushes are used as boundary marks in both forested and cleared land, while the leaves are used for tying bundles or as a rear covering for men, inserted in their belts.

the name of Maunori. The term *hovanum* is not used to describe the membership of the group.

Another method of referring to the membership of the group indicates another organizing focus of the men's house. This method is to call the group by the name of the most important man in it, and then to add the collective suffix *-kere*. Thus *Kaumfa-kere* means 'Kaumfa and his men' and refers to the men's house of which Kaumfa is the most important man. This usage also emphasizes the fact that personal preference can affect an individual's place of residence. If a man decides that Kaumfa is a better leader than Yofantena, or has built a more waterproof house, he can always take up residence in Kaumfa's house, instead of in Yofantena's where his father lived.

Counteracting this potential division of the village into isolated men's house groups is the tie between boys who are initiated at the same time. Four or five boys are initiated as a group every three years. They are of almost the same age, they have grown up together, they remain living together throughout their lives, as bosom friends, and they refer to each other by a special term *koinanefo*—'my age mate'—which closely resembles the term for brother. In many ceremonies age mates are considered socially identical (in the sense in which Evans-Pritchard 1940:7 uses the term 'social identity'), and an age mate is a first choice as the 'leviratic' inheritor of a widow.

The men's house group or ward can be observed as a discrete social unit in disputes, where all members of one ward stand on one side of a clearing, opposed to all members of the other ward on the other side; in rites of passage, when all members of the group attend; in work situations, when the clearing of large gardens is carried out by ward groups, each clearing a different area, although the work of different groups may be synchronized throughout the clan; in the consumption of food, when all men present in the men's house clearing give portions to all other members who are present. Within the men's house no disputes remain unsettled, although there are no organized sanctions for enforcing settlement. Living under the same roof with someone with whom one has an unsettled dispute is so uncomfortable that one either comes to a settlement or moves to a different men's house and continues the hostility from there. The ward group also tends to have rights in common over certain areas of territory, as do the clan and the tribe. However, these common rights largely derive from the rights which individual members have over areas of adjoining land. It is only when the plots of members of a ward are contiguous that it is possible to speak of rights vested in the ward group. This topic will be treated later at greater length.

A smaller size of grouping than that of the men's house may be recognized, although there is no native term for it,[8] and such groups have no proper names. This group can be isolated by the observer as soon as he starts to collect material on kinship, land tenure, and inheritance, and, although it has no traceable common ancestor, I propose to use the term 'lineage' to describe it.[9] Within this group, kinship terms are always used in both address and reference, and a form of genealogy relates all members; there is always one member of each generation who is referred to as 'eldest brother', in whom are vested the lineage rights to property. The lineage is associated with one particular pair of the sacred flutes, which are played in the major religious ceremonies; it owns a traditional design representing the souls of dead members of the lineage, and this design, when painted on a board and called a *gerua*, must be carried in the clan dance at the Pig Feast; it has the right to repeat certain traditional monitory speeches when everyone is assembled round the fire in the men's house during the evening. Since it is the 'eldest brother' of the paternal generation who exercises these rights, it will be seen that his position is crucial to the organization of the lineage, just as his existence defines the grouping. The rights and duties of his office will be discussed later, as will the mode of succession to it.

The lineage, although not explicitly recognized in native terminology, is an important economic unit. It is the work group for building women's houses or for clearing lineage land; the wives of lineage members live near one another and co-operate in preparing food for their menfolk. It is not a residential group, since its male members sleep in various sections of the men's house and may even sleep in different men's houses, while its women's houses are not necessarily contiguous. Typically there will be about five such groups in a men's house, each composed of one old man, four married adults, and two unmarried youths. These men will support two old women, four wives, and five children.

The elementary family hardly functions as a unit in Siane. Men

---

[8] Among the Gahuku-Gama to the east a similar grouping is called a *dzuha* (cf. Read 1951 : 154).

[9] This is contrary to the usage prescribed by *Notes and Queries* (RAI 1951) which restricts the term 'lineage' to groups possessing a traceable common ancestor. However, since the Siane 'lineage' bears so many resemblances to African lineages described in the literature, and is cognate with the Gahuku *dzuha*, which is a true lineage, I prefer to retain the term. For a fuller discussion of Siane lineages see Salisbury (1956a).

and women live apart, and husbands only visit their wives at night. Wives cook food outside their houses and eat with the young children, while the men and adolescent boys eat what the women bring to them in the men's house clearing with other men, the wives waiting outside. The division of labour is such that a man rarely works in the same garden in which his wife is working; men work with men, while women work with women. After a relatively short period when young children are looked after exclusively by their mother, and when they visit their father for fondling and affection, the training of children is undertaken by males and females generally, rather than by the elementary families. As soon as boys are old enough to talk and to understand, they are toilet-trained by their father and by older boys; after their ceremonial weaning between the ages of 3 and 6, their principal companions are other boys. The general lack of importance of the elementary family as a unit in Siane society does not mean there are no bonds of affection between spouses and their children. In individual cases husbands may work with wives, and of eighty-two husbands in one village, fourteen were living with their wives in pig houses on one typical night when I made a census. The fourteen tended to be older men, however. Thus, in a discussion of economically significant units the elementary family may be ignored.

Kinship

Kinship has often been mentioned as one of the organizing principles of the Siane groupings, and it is now necessary to consider the way in which a Siane individual, through his use of kinship terms, classifies the people with whom he comes into contact (see Fig. 2 for a schematic presentation of these terms). Within his own clan-village he divides people into generation groups, paying some attention to seniority with generations. He calls all men two generations senior to him *aunefo* (my grandparent);[10] all men one generation senior *menefo* (my father); within his own generation he calls the senior member of his own lineage *yanefo* (my oldest brother),

[10] All kinship terms are given here in their first person possessive form (if they have such a form) including either the suffix *-nefo*, or the prefix *n-* as the case may be. In later sections I shall have occasion to use them in the third person form, i.e. with the suffix changed to *-rafo* and the prefix either omitted or changed to *r-*. Thus *yanefo* (my oldest brother) becomes *yarafo* (his oldest brother), *menefo* (my father) becomes *merafo* (his father), *nemona* (my sibling of opposite sex) becomes either *emona* or *remona* (his sibling of opposite sex). In Siane the plural form of a noun is the same as the singular, but to make the sense clear to non-Siane speakers I have added an English *-s* where the plural is meant.

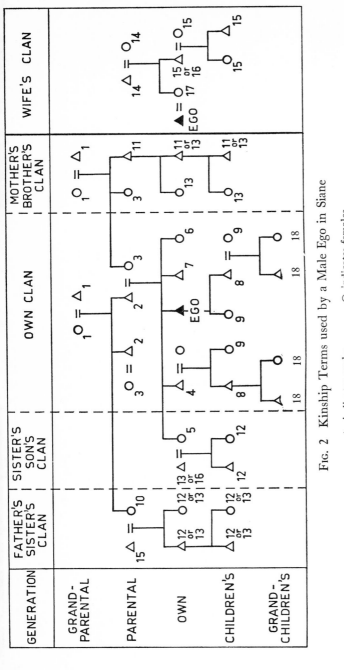

FIG. 2 Kinship Terms used by a Male Ego in Siane

△ indicates males   ○ indicates females

1 *aunefo* (my grandparent)
2 *menefo* (my father)
3 *onefo* (my mother)
4 *yanefo* (my oldest brother)
5 *atanefo* (my oldest sister)
6 *nemona* (my sibling of opposite sex)
7 *kunanefo* (my sibling of same sex)

8 *nanefo* (my son)
9 *orunefo* (my daughter)
10 *meranefo* (my father's sister)
11 *momonefo* (my mother's brother)
12 *komonefo* (my sister's son)
13 *nofonefo* (my cross-cousin)
14 *niamfa* (my close affine)

15 *nitofa* (my distant affine)
16 *nemona we* (my 'sister-man', or trade friend)
17 *orune irofo* (my wife)
18 *nakunefo* (my grandchild)

and all other males *kunanefo* (my sibling of the same sex). He calls
all males of the first descending generation *nanefo* (my son), and
all of the second descending generation *nakunefo*. A man divides
the women residing in his village into those who are the wives of
his *aunefo*s, whom he calls *aunefo* also; those who are the wives of
*menefo*s (fathers), whom he calls *onefo* (my mother); those of the
same generation as himself, be they wives of 'brothers' or daughters
of his 'fathers', whom he calls '*nemona*' (my sibling of the opposite
sex);[11] those of the first descending generation, be they children of
brothers or wives of 'sons' whom he calls *orunefo* (my daughter),
and those two generations below him whom he calls *nakunefo*. While
a girl is living in the village of her birth she uses the same terms
for other individuals as do her brothers, with the exception that
for her the term *nemona* (sibling of the opposite sex) refers to her
brother, while the term *kunanefo* refers to her sister. When a
woman is married and has borne children in her husband's village
she uses the same terms for other members of that village as does
her husband, again with the same exceptions. She calls her husband
wane irofo (my married man), while he calls her *orune irofo*
(literally, my married daughter). Before she has borne children to
her husband's village a woman uses the terms which a man uses
for members of foreign villages, to whom he is related affinally
(these terms will be discussed later), plus a special term *ekanefo*
for the true parents of her husband. During this period her name
is taboo to members of her husband's village, and they call her by
a newly bestowed nickname or by affinal terms. Her husband avoids
her and there is no communication between husband and wife until
the taboo on communication is ceremonially removed—normally
about nine months before she bears her first child, and between
three and six years after marriage.

As well as distinguishing the senior member of his own generation and lineage by a special term, for some purposes a Siane man
also distinguishes the members of his lineage of the generation
above him by seniority, although all are 'fathers'. Thus his true
father's *yarafo* (lineage eldest brother) is his *homu merafo* (first
father); the next oldest member of the lineage is his *merafo ainke*
(next, or second father); all other lineage brothers of his true father
are *merafo airo* (other fathers). In normal speech he will refer to
all these people as 'my fathers' without distinction, but when pressed
or in the appropriate situation he does distinguish. Similarly, he
always knows who his true father, his *merafo hentenamo* (his be-

---

[11] Except for the oldest female member of his own generation and lineage
whom he calls '*atanefo*' (my oldest sister).

getting, or caring father) is, but although this physical relationship is an affectionate one, it is the lineage relationship that is important in matters of succession and inheritance.

The patterns of behaviour between categories of people are clearly prescribed. 'Grandparents' and 'grandchildren' have a friendly, equalitarian relationship to each other; a 'father' must 'look after' (*hentaiye*) his children, male and female; a 'mother' must feed any person whom she calls 'child'; everyone has the duty of 'helping' (*umaiye*) anyone addressed as 'father' or 'mother'; boys and girls have a relationship of equality with their 'siblings of the same sex', yet have obligations of 'helping' them; boys must 'look after' and also show respect for their 'siblings of the opposite sex'. (The implications of the terms *hentaiye* and *umaiye* will be discussed later at greater length; here they are given merely as the native idioms and concepts for referring to interpersonal relationships. Their importance should be noted.)

There is a further pattern of behaviour—that expected of a *yarafo*[12] or 'eldest brother' towards his younger brothers of the same lineage—and it merits a fuller treatment than the patterns described above. The lineage *yarafo* holds the title to all lineage property owned by his generation, and he can decide when work is to be done on that property; he must pronounce the prescriptive speeches, which are the hereditary property of the lineage; he makes the *gerua* representing the lineage dead and carries it in the Pig Feast dance; he controls the marriages of his younger brothers, since he controls the valuables they need for their bride-prices. On the other hand, he must 'look after' and protect his younger brothers by taking their part in disputes, and by seeing that they are fed, especially when food cooked by a newly-married wife is taboo to them; he is responsible for entertaining any visitors to the lineage, and he must contribute to clan payments on behalf of the lineage; he must ensure that all members of the lineage receive adequate shares of cleared lineage land and of gifts made to the lineage. In other words he must act as a quasi-father towards his younger lineage brothers and sisters. This is shown symbolically when a sister of the lineage marries. Her *yarafo* may still be only a youth, and the pigs and gifts given during the ceremony will in fact be provided by the girl's father. Nevertheless, when natives describe the gift-giving they will always state that the gifts are given by the girl's *yarafo*. Even though he be only a youth, the *yarafo* does distribute the bride-price he receives from the groom's father; he

[12] I shall use this Siane form throughout the remainder of this book, since the English translation is clumsy and inexact.

it is who makes a small *gerua* representing his sister's soul and who guards it in his house; he it is to whom she will run if she is ill-treated by her husband.

When a *yarafo* dies, the next oldest member of his generation succeeds him, the succession passing down by seniority through all the lineage brothers. This continual expectation of succession, and the knowledge that the present *yarafo* is acting on behalf of his lineage brothers are accompanied by a general lack of sibling rivalry. I found little evidence of rivalry in behaviour, and only one myth where brother killed brother, but I saw many examples of a warm, protective attitude by 'eldest brothers', and of a hero-worshipping dependence by younger brothers.

The head of the lineage at any one time is the *yarafo* of the parental generation, who is the 'first father' of the children. If he dies, the previous 'second father' becomes head of the lineage—a *yarafo* to his own generation and a new 'first father' to the children. At the same time there is a rearrangement of the 'other fathers', the oldest of whom becomes 'second father' to the children. When all members of the parental generation have died or have 'retired', the *yarafo* of the next generation becomes head of the lineage.

For the *yarafo* this does not imply much change from the quasi-parental role he has already been playing towards his younger siblings. In addition, since he is likely to be about the same age as the youngest member of the parental generation, there is no discontinuity in the lineage leadership; no case of a youth succeeding a mature old man. The *yarafo*'s quasi-parental role also makes it easy for considerably older members of one's own generation to be accorded the status of 'father' and to be called *merafo*, or for members of different generations who are about the same age to refer to each other as 'eldest and younger brother', or *yarafo* and *kunarafo*. In short, the native division of the lineage into 'generations' is actually a form of age-grading, and frequently does not correspond with the division we would make in terms of a true genealogy. The dividing point between generations is arranged so that the *yarafo* of the rising generation is a capable person, and anyone younger than he is his 'younger brother'. If this is expressed in terms of the formal statuses present in a lineage it will be seen that there is a lineage head in the parental generation who is the *yarafo* of all men who are less than twenty years younger than he is; and that he is 'first father' to men more than twenty years younger. The men near him in age are 'second father' and 'other fathers' to the young men and are potential successors to the lineage headship if the *yarafo* dies before they all 'retire' as old men. Among the younger men their *yarafo* is distinguished by his playing a quasi-parental role towards the others, and he is trained as the first successor to lineage headship in his generation.

In dealing with kinship terminology within the clan, I have spoken as though kin terms are used for everyone in the group without exception. It is more common to use kinship terms only for members of one's lineage, and to refer to other members of one's clan by their proper name, by teknonymy, or as children of the clan of their mother. To use a kinship term in other circumstances means that one wants to put the person addressed into a particular relationship—addressing a clanmate as 'brother' may be a prelude to a request for the use of his shirt, while to call a woman of the village 'mother' prefaces a request for food. When talking to someone outside the clan, the speaker refers to other members of his own clan as 'brothers' to signify they are closer to him than is the person spoken to, and to stress clan solidarity. This principle has already been referred to in connection with the use of kin terms within the tribe.

Apart from those people of his own group with whom a Siane man comes in contact and whom he classifies, through his use of kinship terms, by generation, by sex, and by seniority, he also comes into contact with members of other villages who share no common membership in the same phratry. He can classify these people in three different ways, and by so doing he decides what form of behaviour to adopt.

First, it is always possible for a Siane man to trace some form of affinal relationship with a member of another clan and so to address him as '*nitofa*' (my affinal relative). It is enough for one sister of the other clan to have married a man of one's own clan in the distant past, or for a sister of one's own clan merely to be considering a future marriage into the other clan, to justify such a usage, although the specific individual through whom relationship is traced may be cited if the usage is questioned. In fact, the use of this term implies not that there is a personal relationship between individuals, or what Fortes (1949:281) terms a 'web of kinship', but that there is a relationship between the two corporate groups which results, under some circumstances, in the individual members of the two groups uniting for certain activities. Ties which form the foundation for common group activities, are termed 'clanship' by Fortes, to differentiate them from personal 'kinship'. In this sense the relations with distant affinal kin in Siane are 'clanship' ties, though the idiom the Siane use is one of affinity, and not of agnation as is the case in the groups studied by Fortes. One must be formally polite and hospitable to an 'affinal relative', and active hostility that would be the normal behaviour towards an unrelated stranger is forbidden. No affection is implied by the term, nor is any claim to friendship; merely a mutual suspension of hostility and an obligation to repay later any services one is given.

The second way a Siane man can classify individuals is in terms of a personal affinal relationship set up by his own marriage or by the marriage of his own daughter. He calls these people *'niamfa'* (my close relative-in-law), and uses the term to refer to the mother and the father of his wife, and to the husband of his daughter; they use the same term reciprocally to refer to him. The use of the term implies a relationship of great respect, with complete avoidance for the first years of the marriage, and effusive politeness thereafter. When a *niamfa* comes visiting he is hugged and praised ecstatically, given a clean board to sit upon, and he is anointed in oil. At his departure he is given a gift, but it is accounted for and must be reciprocated later. Underlying the formal politeness is often a deep hostility and rivalry between *niamfa*.

The third classification is in terms of a relationship which is traced through one's close female relatives—one's mother, one's clan sisters, and one's father's clan sisters. The last group of women one may call *meranefo* (father's sister), although in practice I heard the term used only for father's sisters of the same lineage. Their children and the children of one's own clan sisters are all *komonefo* (child of my clan). The brothers of one's true mother one calls *momonefo* (my mother's brother), and their children, *nofonefo* (my cross-cousin). It will be noted that these categories of people are complementary in a somewhat anomalous way. If I call someone else 'mother's brother', he calls me 'child of my clan'; but if I call my mother's brother's child 'cross-cousin', he has a choice of whether he calls me 'child of my clan', thereby making it seem that I am of a generation below his, or whether he calls me 'cross-cousin' which is a reciprocal term. This anomaly can be understood in terms of the behaviour patterns the different terms indicate. Thus to call a person 'child of my clan' implies that he is someone towards whom one feels a warm affection, over whom one has a certain claim, and in whose future one takes a close interest. One protects such a person, and is prepared to let him come and live with one, and at all times one can give gifts to him as tokens of affection and interest. To call a person 'my mother's brother' means that he is accepted as having a legitimate claim over one, and is treated as a protective, affectionate, gift-giving friend. To call a person 'my cross-cousin' implies that the two people are friends having a relationship of affectionate equality, neither being the superior protector of the other. Thus 'child of my clan' is frequently used when members of one clan wish to assert claims over members of another clan; 'mother's brother' is usually limited to the head of the lineage of the mother, thereby limiting the number of people who have or are acknowledged to have a claim over one; and the term 'my cross-cousin' is used when no overtones of claims or protection are implied.

Political Organization

The system of kinship terms, with the sharp distinctions it forces the individual to make between the friendly relations with members of his own clan (or of his own phratry) and the formal or hostile relations with all members of other clans (except for the few individuals with whom he can trace a personal tie), mirrors the political organization of Siane society. From the point of view of any one clan the world is divided into two parts: the friendly clans of the same phratry, and the vast number of hostile clans that surround this island of ostensible peace.[13] All the hostile clans are possible sources of brides and possible receivers in marriage of one's own sisters. At any moment it may be expedient for the clan to be allied with some clans and to exchange sisters with them while actively fighting with other clans. At any time the pattern of alliances may shift. As the Siane say, 'They are our affinal relatives; with them we fight', indicating that the erstwhile friends at the time of a marriage soon become hostile affines. In this situation no person can travel far, and ten miles from one's village is the normal limit. Few people have more than a sketchy knowledge of groups farther away. The Siane picture is of an entire world being composed of clan-villages, loosely linked into tribes, and each clan surrounded by latently hostile enemy clans.

Any dispute between clans can result in the latent hostility becoming open warfare. Such disputes usually concern the theft or seduction of a wife, the theft of a pig (either known, or presumed because a pig is missing), the death of a man, which has been shown by divination to be due to sorcery by another clan (usually the clan of the widow or of some other woman with whom he had sexual relations), or a homicide. The theft of a wife may be settled by discussion and by payments, as may, in some cases the

---

[13] The present tense is used throughout this section, although the coming of Australian control has almost stopped armed warfare. The other main change following the establishment of peace has been that the radius of travel and knowledge of other groups is now (1953) about 20 miles.

theft of a pig (especially if the guilty clan is the larger). The only other way in which disputes can be settled is by self-help in the form of a blood feud. Vengeance can be obtained either by the ambush and murder of a single victim belonging to the offending clan or by a form of ceremonial warfare on cleared battle-grounds. The renowned fighters of each side come to do battle, armed with spears and huge wooden shields, while their clan-mates line up at the ends of the cleared space, their bows and arrows at the ready. The 'champions' then 'joust' until one is caught off balance by his opponent, and is then at the mercy of the bowmen, who kill him with arrows. It is rare for a war to kill more than one or two men, and after a champion has been killed the defeated clan may flee, leaving its village to be razed by the victors while it seeks protection in temporary exile. Wars are not usually fought for territorial gain, however.

When an affront occurs, it is counted as one 'debt' to be avenged, and a knot is tied in a length of rope as a record of it. For each new affront a knot is added, while each time one member of the offending clan is killed one affront is wiped out and a knot is cut off. I have seen the ropes of one clan, recording the affronts of what was ostensibly a friendly clan. The relations between the clans had been 'frozen' by the coming of the Europeans, but the large number of knots suggested that it was common for grievances between allied clans to accumulate until, suddenly, violent warfare broke out. This was the signal for a complete realignment of the former pattern of alliances. After another period of ten years, the original pattern of alliances might be restored when the clans felt it was to their advantage to re-establish the original uneasy friendship and exchange of women in marriage. This is the background to the statement that the normal relationship between unrelated clans is hostile or openly warlike, while alliances and uneasy friendship provide an intermittent break to open warfare. Clans are sovereign units, and grievances against other clans can only be settled by resort to force or the threat of it.

There is, however, a mechanism by which two clans, without either one submitting to the other and without there being any externally applied force, can reach a settlement when they wish to cease hostilities. This mechanism depends on the fact that, if one clan of a phratry is engaged in fighting, then the other clans of the phratry remain neutral. In part this is an insurance against outright defeat, for it means that members of a defeated clan always have a friendly clan with whom they can take refuge. In part it means that whenever two clans are fighting, at least two other clans—one from each disputing phratry—sit on the side-lines watching. These neutral clans do not intervene in the fighting, but they shout advice on possible ways to settle the dispute. Gradually, as the desire to settle increases among the warring clans, the fighting degenerates into name-calling, and the name-calling into an impassioned but non-violent discussion. Both sides air their grievances, and eventually line up their wounded in two rows; assessors from the neutral clans walk along the rows, and estimate on which side the balance of damages lies. They then say how many pigs and valuables should be given to balance the damages that have been inflicted. I could not obtain an explicit statement of this, but the figures I was given for peacemaking payments suggest that the 'rate' for settlement used to be one pig for one man killed and a shell for each injury. The exchange of pigs is followed by a feast, and the two sides (literally) shake hands. Discussion about a stolen wife rarely reaches the stage of bloodshed, but the same sequence of violent abuse, mediation by neutral parties, eventual discussion of payments, and a final settlement where both sides 'give presents' to the other, is customary. Neither side admits having done wrong, nor does it acknowledge the other as right.

In the discussion of inter-clan relations I have treated each clan as though it were a corporate whole, in which individuals did not matter. This is, in fact, largely true. Thus, a wedding is described as being, for example, 'between Nematene (clan) and a sister of Winyo (clan)'. At such a ceremony all members of Winyo clan enter the village of Nematene clan in procession as one unit, and are met in the principal men's house clearing by a body of men from all sections of Nematene clan. Admittedly, the bride heads the Winyo procession, but she is closely followed by one 'big man' (*we namfa*),[14] who represents the whole clan. The receiving clan is also headed by a 'big man'. When the two clans are assembled facing one another, their representatives make speeches. After this the representative of the bride's clan gives her to his opposite number, together with the presents her clan has brought. When the visitors have been feasted, the groom's clan gives return presents, handed over by the single representative 'big man'. In theory the bride's clan know nothing about the groom as an individual except that he is a member of his clan, while the groom's clan is ignorant of the bride's individual parentage. Neither side is supposed to know about the negotiations conducted within the other clan to collect the pigs and valuables, which are given as wedding gifts. Neither side is concerned with the distribution of pigs and valuables

[14] See p. 28.

when once they have been presented. All the outsider learns is that 'Nematene gave presents to Winyo; Winyo returned the presents'. It is a relationship between corporate groups.

The widest level of political organization in Siane is thus one of the opposition of corporate clan groups, which appear to be internally undifferentiated. On a lower level, Siane political organization consists in the way in which authority is exercised within these clan groups and how this authority affects the relationships between the various segments of the clan. Since in the exercise of authority the 'big man' is of crucial importance, it is necessary to consider what this term implies.

Anyone may become a 'big man', for this title is not hereditary; it is based on ability and is open to anyone whose achievements can command sufficient respect from other people. Usually, skill in oratory, a mature age and the procreation of children, and a moderate degree of industry and wealth are essentials, as, in precontact times, was bravery in warfare. The way in which these achievements become recognized as worthy of 'big man' status will be described later. There are usually six or seven 'big men' in any men's house, and they discuss the performance of ceremonials, the making of new gardens, the contributions to and the disposal of any payments made or received. They pronounce prescriptive speeches. None of them has any right to command any other person or to force the acceptance of his suggestions when a discussion is in progress—they are all equals. One of their number, however, acts as the figure-head of the men's house; if there is a dispute with another men's house, he is the spokesman; if there is pork to be distributed in the men's house, he calls out the names of the recipients and holds up the meat for them to collect. In whatever he does, he normally receives the enthusiastic support of all members of the men's house, for his performance reflects to the credit of the group as a whole, and only when the group is behind him can he perform at his best. And he is sure he is doing what the group wishes, because his actions are the result of long discussions in the men's house, during which he has heard the opinions of all the 'big men'.

The figure-head tends to play a larger part in the discussions, but he does so by virtue of his ability and knowledge rather than because of any formal authority. The other 'big men' would be jealous, and would ostentatiously disregard any attempt by the figure-head to set himself up as a chief. To become a figure-head he must establish his position by skill in debate, by knowing when to put forward his suggestions with the greatest effect, and by making suggestions which prove effective when carried out. If he does these things, and has the requisite sense of theatre—if he can 'sell' himself to the men's house and the men's house to the world—he gains prestige and may become the figure-head. Once established, he can act on his own initiative in a crisis and be certain that his prestige and the solidarity of the group will gain support for his actions. The office of figure-head is not given formal recognition in a special native term, but the pidgin term *bosboi* is frequently used, following the example of missionaries and other Europeans. I propose to use that term here.

For a person to give good advice and to become a 'big man' and possibly a *bosboi* he must learn the correct ritual forms and the traditional agricultural and social customs. He must also learn the common prescriptive speeches, and if he also owns a hereditary right to make a particular speech, this will aid him in achieving status. In addition, if he is to join in the discussions of the ceremonial payments which form the largest part of social life in Siane, he must contribute to those payments himself. All these are within the power of any individual, yet a lineage *yarafo* can do them much more easily. He is explicitly taught the correct ritual and social forms by the previous lineage head, he inherits the title to all lineage-owned prescriptive speeches and to all the wealth of his predecessor. In short, most lineage heads become 'big men', but some do not; some lineages contain several 'big men', while a few contain none. Nor is the position of *bosboi* hereditary. When an existing *bosboi* is unable to perform his duties adequately, because of old age, physical disability, poverty, or over-assertiveness, his tasks are performed by other 'big men' as the situation demands. One of these eventually proves himself the best, and is considered the *bosboi*; his name is used to designate the men's house; the group become his men.

The *bosboi* does have one privilege—he can call on the man-power of the men's house to perform a task like building his wife a new house. Such a task gives his men's house a chance to out-shine the neighbouring men's house by building a better house for their *bosboi*'s wife, and by making a better food distribution after-wards. He has many duties, however. He must act as 'father of the house', looking after its members by sharing food, and giving an example by his work, his hospitality, and his energy. If there is a garden-clearing work bee, then the 'big men', and particularly the *bosboi,* work longer and more continuously than other men; if a visitor comes, then the *bosboi* gives him some of the food brought by the *bosboi*'s wife; if there is a communal entertain-

ment, the 'big men' and the *bosboi* provide large quantities of stored nuts, salt, and oil for the visitors; if work is flagging during the construction of a men's house, the *bosboi* leaves his seat, from where he has been directing operations, and throws himself into the task, working feverishly until the others follow his example.

Authority within the clan as a whole is exercised in the same way as it is exercised in each men's house. Just as in each men's house there are several 'big men', all equals and all jealous of the power of the others, and one *bosboi* who is only *primus inter pares* yet represents the whole group, so it is with the clan. There are three or four *bosboi*s who discuss matters affecting the whole clan and who are all present at ceremonies, representing their own men's houses, yet only one is spokesman for the whole clan. The *bosboi* representing the clan varies with the occasion. If the occasion is, as is the case with a wedding, a matter principally concerning one men's house (the men's house of the bride or bridegroom), then the *bosboi* of that men's house represents the whole clan. If the occasion is one where all members of the clan are equally concerned, as happens if peace is made after a long war, then the ablest of the *bosboi*s is chosen to represent his clan. While he represents the clan this *bosboi* may be a figure-head and spokesman, but other *bosboi*s will perform the same office on other occasions, and all members of the clan will frustrate any effort on his part to assume a more permanent status, asserting that he is merely the equal of every other adult male in the clan. This situation is changing as a result of the introduction of steel tools and the more recent imposition of Governmental control. Power is becoming more centralized, and the position of clan representative is becoming more permanent, but a fuller discussion of these changes and the process by which they have come about will be given in later chapters.

In the pre-contact situation (which still obtains in great part today), where no individual is recognized as having any authority to compel anyone to do anything against his will, disputes are settled only after long public discussion. The principal parties, backed by other members of their own group, either lineage or men's house, start by violently abusing one another, as happens in inter-clan fights; the verbal intervention of neutrals eventually causes them to calm down, and suggestions about means of settling are made; when the principals finally decide that they no longer wish to continue their mutual hostility, one of them makes a conciliatory gesture by offering large 'presents' to the other; a return 'present' is then offered 'to make the belly smooth'. The net result of the exchange is that one person pays an amount of compensation as suggested by the neutral intervenors, but by giving it as a 'present' he preserves the fiction of his autonomy in coming to a decision and gains a reputation for generosity.

The factors leading to settlement of disputes appear to be of three kinds.[15] First, the Siane set great store by maintaining good relations with other people. A man who is on good terms with others and whose 'belly is smooth, or calm' is respected, while the greatest respect attaches to a man who has friends in many other villages and 'can walk unharmed all over the valley'; a man whose 'belly is hot', though he may temporarily be feared, is not respected or liked. When his anger is over he gives gifts to anyone he may have offended by his anger, in order to re-establish good relations. Secondly, segments of a clan normally unite behind any member of the segment who is engaged in a dispute with a member of another segment. If the disputants are both in the same men's house, but in different lineages, the two lineages rally behind the principals, and dispute as units, while other lineages remain neutral, advising the principals to settle differences and not to split the men's house. If the disputants are in different men's houses, the two ward groups dispute as units. There may be no neutrals, but the threat to clan unity is so great that some individuals always counsel settlement. In fact, when a minor dispute—for example, over a stolen chicken—is magnified into something threatening the whole group, the ridiculousness of the situation becomes apparent and by then the initial anger has usually evaporated. In short, the way in which segments unite in opposition to one another either opposes groups of disparate size, when it becomes expedient for one side to settle, or it magnifies small disputes out of all proportion, allows hot tempers to evaporate in heated discussion, and then allows wiser counsel to prevail.

The third factor inducing settlement is that the group may decide not to support one of its members in a dispute. A man may normally count on his lineage for support, but his men's house may decide the matter is not their concern, or may offer to compound the affront against the offender's wishes. In such a case the man may try to carry on his dispute, but it is in face of a gradual loss of good relations and a loss of group support in other situations—notably economic help. Such diffuse sanctions do not offend against the Siane ideology that all individuals are their own masters, acting autonomously and subject to no man, yet they ensure that relation-

[15] The way in which these sanctions operate are discussed in greater detail in Salisbury (n.d.).

ships within the clan are predictable and are maintained with a minimum of friction.

The same ideology of individual autonomy persists even within the lineage, where the lineage head does exercise authority by making decisions, representing the lineage to outside groups, and rebuking young members of the lineage. But the lineage head (*yarafo*) does these things on behalf of other members of the lineage, acting as the personification of the lineage and not as a private person. Theoretically he does them after discussion with other lineage members, as his duty rather than as a privilege, and lineage members can say they do as he suggests from a free choice.

Religion

No extended discussion of Siane religion will be given here, although enough will be said to enable later descriptions to be understood. Basically, Siane religion is a form of ancestor worship. Each clan has a corpus of souls (*korova*), some of which at any one time are resident in the bodies of living persons, and in this state they are called *oinya*. *Oinya* are variously conceived as dream shapes or shadows (*amene*), and are localized in the hair, the head, the blood, and the sexual organs. *Korova*, or the spirits of the dead, are conceived as the obverse of living beings. They are white while the living Siane are black, they like quiet, cold, and damp while humans like warmth, noise, and dryness, and they are repelled by female reproductive powers, which are the essence of life. Many objects are used to symbolize the *korova*, and when they are so used they are referred to by the term *korova*. The sacred bamboo flutes, the masks used in fertility ceremonies during the First Fruits ceremonies, the various pantomimic acts that are part of this ceremony, certain species of flying fox, cold winds, and certain *gerua* boards—all these are *korova*.

It is the ancestral spirits of the clan that are responsible for the clan's welfare. They give fertility to the land, with which they are closely associated; they cause pigs to grow large, and they give good fortune in exchanges of pigs or shells, thereby making the clan wealthy; they cause children to grow to adult size, and so make the clan strong. They are continually being honoured and induced to return as *oinya* through children being given their names and so reincarnating the ancestors. However, the spirits are angry when the body they have been inhabiting dies. They hover near the house in which they have been living, capriciously attacking people in the bush and 'possessing' them so that they behave insanely.

To appease the dead spirit, all relatives, especially those of the dead person's lineage and those related through the dead person's mother, must observe mourning, and cover themselves with ashes and white clay till they look like *korova* themselves. To avoid attacks, the spirit must be exorcized, and his house abandoned while his body is buried in a cold, damp, low-lying place. Only at the next Pig Feast, when the dead person is specially honoured by having a piece of his clothing hung on his lineage *gerua,* does the spirit rejoin the corpus of benevolent ancestral *korova.*

The three main types of ceremonies in Siane are all in honour of the ancestral spirits, and are designed to persuade them to continue their blessings to the clan. These ceremonies are the First Fruits ceremonies—the most spectacular of which is called the *ka mafo* or Yam-Taro ceremony—which promote the fertility of the land, the Pig Feasts, which normally occur every three years and which promote the fertility of pigs, the flow of riches, and the prosperity and health of the clan; and the various rites of passage, which invoke ancestral interest in the growth of the individual.

The Yam-Taro ceremony is performed separately by each clan at roughly three-year intervals, in the intervals between Pig Feasts. Some time before the ceremony the sacred flutes are carried in procession round the clan lands, 'to show the *korova* the gardens'. When the crops from a large garden, planted specifically for the ceremony, are ripe, the young girls of another clan come *en masse* to visit the host clan for several days as 'temporary wives'. A ceremonial form of courtship dance and singing is performed every night by the girls and by the boys of the host clan, while during the daytime comic pantomimic acts depict the activities of men and women in raising crops. The ceremony concludes with a massive distribution of produce, taken from the prepared garden and given to the clan of the girls. At one ceremony I estimated that five tons were handed over.

The Pig Feast has two themes: the distribution of pigs, and the initiation of boys, but although both form part of the same cycle, I shall discuss the second as one of the rites of passage. The fact that a phratry is about to give a Pig Feast is announced ten months in advance by a distribution of pork and by the blowing of sacred flutes. This denotes that the *korova* are now present in the villages of that phratry, that peace must now be kept, that no pigs can be allowed to leave the villages, and that preparations such as the planting of large gardens and the rebuilding of the village must take place. At the end of the ten months large *gerua* boards are made, painted with designs representing lineage ancestors, and other clans are invited (by carrying the sacred flutes in procession through their villages) to come and dance at the feast, in return for gifts of pork. The climax of the ceremony occurs when hundreds of pigs are killed and one or two thousand 'foreigners' dance in their best finery before the ancestral *gerua* and are rewarded with pork, larger amounts being given to all the sisters of the phratry who have married into other clans. Some days later, clans within the phratry exchange pork with one another, and sometimes special presentations are made to outsiders who are treated as honorary members of the phratry in view of past services or special gifts. The *korova* receive their share of the pork; it is fed to them as pig-grease smeared on the mouthholes of the sacred flutes.

The rites of passage are all religiously connected through the belief that an individual at conception is composed of spirit material from his own clan, located in the semen of his father, and of spirit material from his mother's clan, located in her blood. The mother increases her contribution of spirit material by the milk and the cooked foods she provides for the child to eat. But if the child is to become a full member of its father's clan, with a soul composed of only its father's spirit material, the mother's contribution must be diminished. The first step occurs after a Pig Feast at the ceremonial weaning, which takes place when the child is between the ages of 3 and 6 and when its hair is first cut. The mother's clansmen (represented by her brother), whose spirit material is being driven out, attend this ceremony and are compensated for their loss (or thanked for their earlier help) by presentations of pork and shells. When a boy is between the ages of 7 and 10 a further drastic removal of his maternal spirit material takes place, and again his mother's brothers attend and receive presents. This is the ceremony of initiation, which occurs just before the Pig Feast. The boys are secluded from the women, must eat only food cooked by themselves or their fathers—mainly pork and yams, and are shown the hitherto secret representations of the ancestral spirits of their fathers—the sacred flutes. At the end of the Pig Feast they undergo an ordeal in which reeds are forced up their noses and down the backs of their throats. Out of their noses flows the blood their mothers provided at conception, and in this way they lose the maternal spirit material. During adolescence they continue letting blood voluntarily, to remove the last traces of maternal spirit material and so to make themselves acceptable to the paternal *korova* who alone can ensure that they grow up strong and healthy. At this time they must also avoid offending the spirits and must avoid having sexual relations with girls of other clans, and dissipating both their semen and their paternal spirit material. This taboo is ceremonially removed when, at the Pig Feast following the youth's having 'hair on his chest' after he has been married about three years, he is declared fully grown and able to cohabit with his wife. Again presents are made to the clan of his mother's brother.

A girl does not undergo the ritual of initiation. The spiritual danger for her is that she may lose spirit material which belongs to her father's clan by menstruating on 'foreign' soil (especially at her first menses) or at the time of her marriage. Her first menses is the occasion for an important ritual and for making presents to her mother's brother. Later, before her marriage and the loss of her physical body to her own clan, a form of *gerua* is made, representing her soul, and this is retained in the house of her lineage *yarafo*. Throughout her married life her brothers retain their interest in the clan soul, which still resides in her, feeding it with pork when pork is given to the descendants of the clan ancestors, guarding and protecting their sister's person, watching over the children who inherit part of the soul, and receiving compensation when any of the soul is driven out by the children's father.

Only when an individual dies are the last traces of foreign spirit material finally eliminated and the last compensation paid—the compensation for a married woman is paid by her husband's clan to the clan of her birth; for a man or a child it is paid by the father's clan to the clan of the mother's brother.

The Individual Life Cycle

The rites of passage described above can be interpreted as the symbolic representation of the social rights and obligations of the individual as these change during his lifetime. Thus at birth the child is solely the concern of his mother and other women, while his mother's clan has a strong claim to the child. This claim is denied when the father gives the child the name of one of his clan ancestors and gives presents to the mother's brother. The father, who can only give the child occasional fondling while it is young, gradually increases his claim to call the child his own and a member of his clan by the presents he makes to the child's mother's brother at the various rites of passage. Behaviourally, weaning marks the boy's entry into a peer group of other boys. With initiation the boy is admitted as a full member of his father's

clan, residing in the men's house, and henceforth the flow of payments to the mother's brother's clan becomes only token, until
death finally liquidates all claims.

Initiation also releases the boy from his mother's apron strings,
to which he has been closely tied since birth, and introduces him
into the male world of politics and work, centring round the men's
house. He retains, however, close ties of affection with his mother
and with her brothers, whom he has frequently visited in her
company.

During adolescence a boy makes contact with clans other than
his own and his mother's brothers', when he, in company with
other youths, visits the girls of other villages—a custom called
awoiro. He is taught all the dangers he is exposing himself to, in
visiting hostile villages and designing women (though actually
awoiro parties are given safe conduct if undertaken at night), but
he learns also the pleasures that come from defeating rival suitors
from other villages, from singing songs until late at night, from
sleeping close to (though never having intercourse with) the girl
who picks him out as her favourite, and from the triumphal march
home, singing songs, at first light.

In due course, according to the Siane ideal, a girl decides she
wishes to marry him, elopes to his village, and precipitates marriage,
usually when he is aged about 17. Now he is taught his responsi-
bilities towards his wife's clan, and becomes involved in the making
of payments or presentations to them. He becomes involved in the
political and economic decisions of the men's house, since he now
must make gardens for his wife (and later family), and must think
of his indebtedness to other members of his clan.

The way towards 'big man' status is open to him. Regardless of
his achievements, he can look forward to retirement at about the
age of 50, when he becomes 'an old man who sits idly in the sun'.

For a girl the pattern is different. She does not leave her mother's
house, or relinquish her dependence on her mother at the age of 7,
but remains at home learning women's skills until her first menses.
At this time she is made aware of her importance to her own clan
and her important role as the link between her clan and other
clans, for which she will bear children, children who must be taught
their ties with her natal village. From puberty till marriage, at
about the age of 16, the girl is given great freedom and licence,
entertaining suitors at night and doing no work during the day.
Girls of this age group often take over one of the women's houses
as a clubhouse, sleeping and entertaining in it without supervision.

At marriage the girl becomes a stranger in a foreign village, separated physically from her brothers, who nevertheless try to keep up their spiritual ties with her, but not accepted (as the kinship usages described on p. 20 show) as a member of her husband's village. Only when she begins to bear children does her position change. Now her husband's clan tries to assert she is a member of that clan, both by their use of kinship terms and by their payments to her brothers. In their turn her brothers try to keep up their relations with her through visiting, by wooing the friendship of her children with gifts, and by the symbolic gifts of pork at Pig Feasts. Her position is anomalous and the source of conflict, both for her and between her husband and her brother. Only when she becomes an old woman is her position in her husband's village fully established and her opinions respected. Such old women often become a dominant force in their adoptive village.

Summary

Three main themes run through the whole of Siane life, themes that will recur later.

The first is the discreteness of the village units and the self-contained nature of social relationships within them. These relationships, symbolized in the use of kinship terms and in the modes of religious expression, are close and friendly, and imply obligations of 'helping' or 'looking after' all members of the clan-village group. They find expression in common residence, common group activities, and a corporate unity and responsibility for the actions of all members towards other groups. To some extent the same pattern of relationships is extended to members of the same phratry and tribe, but in a very attenuated form.

The second is the way in which each clan (or phratry) exists as a sovereign unit within an environment of other clans, all of which are potentially hostile but with all of which a formal peace may temporarily be expedient. In kinship terms this is the relationship with affinal clans. The form of the relationship is symbolized in religious beliefs in the competition over the group from which a child's (or woman's) soul shall be inherited. Its main practical expression is in the presentations which determine the allegiance of wives, who must come from a foreign clan, and in the continual feuding and accounting for insults that occurs even between nominally allied clans.

The third theme is the way in which the individual has a network of personal kinship ties which cross-cut the clanship relations already described. The chief of these ties are those with the mother's brother, or with sister's children. These relationships are close and affectionate, and often involve the giving of mutual gifts and assistance. It need hardly be pointed out that any conflict between two clans involves many individuals of those clans in a conflict between their loyalty to their clan and their affection for friends in the enemy clan.

Underlying all the relationships is the Siane ideology of the autonomy and assumed equality of all people. Of their own volition individuals carry out the tasks they wish to perform, settle disputes when they wish to, argue about (and agree upon) every decision that a group makes. No one has authority over anyone else (except, perhaps, inside the lineage), unless those powers are delegated on an *ad hoc* basis through individual choice. Groups do combine in an hierarchical way, so that small groups like lineages oppose other lineages, larger groups like wards oppose wards, clans oppose clans. No group admits the superiority of any other, unless it be a group of a larger order. When groups come together they have temporary representatives. The system works through many intricate mechanisms, but chiefly because, coupled with their fierce individualism, people seek to remain on good terms with as many others as possible.

3

INDIGENOUS ECONOMIC LIFE

RECONSTRUCTING Siane economic activities as they were before the advent of steel tools is relatively simple. Much of the material given in this chapter is based directly on my own observations in 1952-3 and on statements that the same pattern of activity was current ten, fifteen, or twenty years previously. Unless I specifically indicate to the contrary, all descriptions are intended to apply both to 1952-3 and to 1933. In cases where changes have occurred, I have included a description of present-day activities; I have given informants' descriptions of past activities when available, and where informants gave only suggestive material I have described how the past can be reconstructed deductively from the information available.

An important problem is what to include under the heading of 'economic life'. In Chapter 1 I took as a definition of my field of study 'those activities in which people engage, and in which they appear to organize their behaviour in terms of a rational calculation of the quantities of goods or services produced, exchanged or consumed, in such a way as to allocate scarce means to meet competing ends'. In the descriptions that follow, this means that attention will first be drawn to activities in which goods are produced, exchanged, or consumed. Within these activities those aspects indicating calculation will be considered, while to completely justify calling the activities 'economic', it will be necessary to look at the ends that are served and the means available for serving them.

These steps, of proceeding from the empirical description of activities dealing in goods and services to an analysis of the calculations involved and later to a consideration of the ends striven for, closely follow the procedure of observation and analysis I used in the field. Like many observers of Highland New Guinea societies (cf. Gitlow 1947), I was immediately impressed by the fact that there were two main nexuses involved in the handling of goods and services. On an impressionistic basis these could be considered the activities concerned with the production of subsistence goods (an impressionistic term I shall leave for the moment and not define rigidly) and the complex arrangements for trade and ceremonial

39

exchange. These nexuses of activity were associated with distinct attitudes, were conducted in different locations, and involved different groupings of people.

The first took place, in the main, outside the villages. It seemed principally to involve individuals acting by themselves. There seemed to be no urgency, excitement, or enthusiasm about these activities, only a simple matter-of-factness. People performed them steadily and quietly, if no more exciting activities presented themselves, and generally did not talk about them in casual conversation. My inquiries about these activities were met by a failure to understand that I could be interested in such mundane matters. If I went out to observe what people were doing, they would desist, cut sugar cane, and sit beside me to talk, eat, and smoke my tobacco. If I asked people what they did, they would answer in pidgin *'Mi go long wok tasol'*, or in Siane *'Ronoma wone'*—'I just go to work'. In short, this was the nexus of routine daily tasks apparently performed to keep alive—the nexus of subsistence activities.

Contrasting with this there was the nexus of activities performed inside the villages, involving large groups of people (some resident and some visitors), and associated with an urgent excitement and concern. I did not have to inquire about such activities, but would be told in advance when they were to occur. My presence at them was accepted, and my questions about the quantities of commodities involved were met by eager recitations of exactly who had provided or received every article. To describe the calculating activities involved, such pidgin terms as *peim* (to buy), *bekim* (to reciprocate) or *skelim* (to distribute) were used. In the Siane language only one term—*gimaiye*—was used to denote the focal economic activity, that of the ceremonial handing over of goods. Impressionistically I called this nexus of activities one of 'ceremonial exchanges', but since this term prejudges the meaning of the activities, I shall refer to them here as *'gima* activities'. I shall translate *gimaiye* as 'to present' and refer to what is presented as 'presentations' throughout this work.

For a long time I did not differentiate these *gima* activities from certain activities also occurring within the villages and in an atmosphere of excitement and pleasure, but which involved only a few individuals. I was not told about these activities in advance, but would often learn about them when a man from the village would come to my house in the evening bringing two or three strangers, and say 'I have brought my cross-cousins to see you', and I would realize that the excitement and preparation of special food was for the entertainment of guests. Or I would be told, of a friend I had not seen for several days, *'Em i-go long niniburi'* ('He has gone visiting, or on holiday'). Several days later, when he returned, he would give me one of the several baskets of nuts he brought back with him. Or yet again a man would proudly ask me to come to his *marita* garden, and see the oil-bearing pandanus trees which I had not discovered in my tour of the village gardens, and he would be most excited over my reactions. But although these individual activities all involved the same attitudes and were clearly distinct from the subsistence and *gima* activities, the common focus for them all was not immediately apparent. Since they all seemed to concern the production or consumption of certain pleasant but inessential commodities, however, I tentatively designated them 'luxury activities', and the nexus as a luxury nexus.

During my fieldwork and in this summary I distinguished these three nexuses mainly by impressionistic criteria. I shall describe Siane economic activities in terms of each of these 'impressionistic' nexuses in turn, but in the course of the description it will become clear that these criteria do not rigidly distinguish between the three nexuses or permit a rigid separation of luxury from *gima* or subsistence activities. Subsistence commodities are occasionally handed over ceremonially (*gimaiye*) and are sometimes used as luxuries. This leads to a closer examination of the native concepts used in describing the transactions in each nexus, of the commodities transferred or consumed, of the circumstances under which transactions take place and under which apparently anomalous transactions occur. I try to isolate more analytic criteria to distinguish the types of economic activity in Siane. Till those principles have been isolated, it is hoped that the reader will bear with the approximation to them that is provided by the clear but impressionistic division of Siane economic activities into subsistence, luxury, and *gima* nexuses.

1. Subsistence Activities

Utilization of Resources

The staple crop in Siane is the sweet potato. If it is missing from any meal, natives will say 'Our throats are empty', as though they had not eaten. It is grown everywhere, even on 45° slopes, but is said to grow best on well-drained land with rocky outcrops of limestone and black soil. Some taro is cultivated as a delicacy, to vary the diet, on the wettest land available, in stream beds, or in the saucer-shaped depressions common in limestone country. A few yams are also grown as a delicacy.

Many green vegetables are used as relishes to accompany the sweet potatoes. Some appear to be varieties of coleus, called *namfa* in Siane (pidgin *kumu*), while others resemble Wandering Jew (*Tradescantio variegata*) and are called *ankuramfo* (pidgin *seiyor*). They are grown from seed, scattered among other garden crops, and single leaves are snipped off as required. The leaves of larger bushes and shrubs, such as the Greater Breadfruit and varieties of croton, are used to wrap food during cooking. They impart flavour to the food and are nibbled as savouries before a meal starts. A variety of wild sugar called *kumfa* (pidgin *pitpit*) is also grown in every garden, and provides soft shoots reminiscent of asparagus.

Maize and cucumbers are found in all gardens, and although they must presumably be recent introductions,[1] they are well integrated into the ritual complex, have native names, and so must be considered part of the 'indigenous economy'. No native could remember a time when they were not present. They are both eaten as light refreshment between meals—cucumbers as a 'drink', and maize roasted on the fire—although cobs of corn are also steamed for the evening meal.

Early Government patrols distributed seeds of European vegetables, and these are all grown to please 'the white man' and to have something to offer for sale to European visitors. Only cabbages (steamed whole when pork is cooked), Irish potatoes (to supplement sweet potatoes if supplies are short), and tomatoes ('drunk' like cucumbers, between meals) are eaten by natives.

Other cultivated plants include tobacco, celosia, and marigolds (used as red and yellow dyes), and many decorative flowers and exotic plants from distant areas (orchids or coconuts currently brought back from the coast by indentured labourers, for example). These are grown in the tiny plots of land surrounding each woman's house in the village.

More permanent plants which are grown and used include sugar cane and bananas. These yield over a period of eighteen months and remain standing in garden plots long after other crops have finished. *Tankets* (as *Taetsia fruticosa* is called in pidgin) are grown

---

[1] Maize, cucumbers, tobacco, and possibly sweet potatoes are generally considered to have been domesticated in the New World and to have been introduced later into South-east Asia (Carter 1950), the first three by Spaniards and the last by earlier Polynesian or other voyagers. The similarity in the native terms for the first three throughout New Guinea confirms this recent introduction, while there is some historical evidence that tobacco was not known in most of New Guinea before 1900 (Riesenfield 1951). The Siane also speak of having 'bought' their knowledge of smoking shortly before the coming of Europeans. A variety of sorghum or millet grows in gardens, but it is not utilized and I have no information on its introduction.

1   Antomona clan village

2   Three separate ward groups building a fence for a large clan garden

3   A garden fenced and divided for the women

as boundary marks and to provide the leaves with which males cover their buttocks. In the moss forest above 7,000 feet, nut-bearing pandanus palms (*ana*, pidgin *karuka*) are tended and owned by natives, who also plant pandanus palms bearing red, oily *roi* fruit (pidgin *marita*) in the swampy valley bottoms. Passion fruit was introduced as a cash crop by the Agricultural Department in 1952, but the fruit is not eaten. Coffee was also introduced in 1952, but no trees had borne berries by 1953.

Casuarina trees provide wood for fencing, fuel, and house building, and their growth as a secondary tree cover is facilitated by the weeding of garden sites. This prevents the growth of *kunai*-grass, which would crowd out young casuarina roots. If the casuarinas are given a chance to establish themselves, their shade then prevents the spread of the sun-loving *kunai*. The growth of casuarinas is deliberately encouraged, and gardens are often made when a boy is born, with the explicit explanation that this will provide a crop of timber for the boy at the time of his marriage, and so enable him to build a house and fence a garden for his wife. Occasionally, too, casuarina seedlings are deliberately planted in areas which no windblown seeds could reach. This happened, for example, in 1941 when Antomona clan of Emenyo tribe returned to their devastated village site, where all trees had been ring-barked following their rout and expulsion in a war. Thus casuarina trees may be considered 'cultivated' plants.

Many hardwoods grow wild in the moss forest. The properties of their timbers are well known, and for specific purposes and artifacts specific timbers are used. *Montu* wood is always used for house rafters, *ramfi* for making clubs, *otova* for carved arrow heads. The hardest wood, used for straight arrow heads, bows and spears is *ofia* (*Kentiopsis archontophoenix*, pidgin *limbom*) or black palm-wood. The *kafo*, or wild fig tree, provides bark-cloth when the bark is beaten out by men. When it is shredded and spun by the women, its fibres make the thread from which belts, bags, and clothing are made. Varieties of wild pandanus trees provide leaves for many purposes. Some are sewn together to form mats on which women sleep or in which they carry young babies; other varieties are used to insulate the walls of houses; yet others, noted for their water-proof and fireproof properties, are used as a layer under roof thatch.

Bamboo, both wild and tended, is the most useful plant growing on the lower slopes. Thick varieties, when their internodes are pierced, provide six-foot-long water containers holding about a gallon, and, when green, form useful cooking vessels for vegetables and chopped meat. When dry they provide tapers by night, and produce fire by friction by day. Suitably worked, the bamboo makes razor-sharp knives for carving meat, pipes for smoking, flutes for playing, flexible bowstrings, and passable bows. Rattan cane is woven to make decorative belts and arm-bands, often with yellow or brown orchid fibres as decoration. Wild *pitpit* reeds are beaten out flat and woven to produce a fabric suitable for a rough house-wall, or for a bed.

The lower hillsides also provide many decorations for the individual or for religious ceremonies. Small hibiscus blooms are worn in the hair, *kafo* nuts are strung into necklaces, earth is burnt to provide brick-red pigments, wintergreen bushes and citronella grass give scents to exorcize spirits. Some varieties of grass can also be burnt to give salt, which is notably scarce in Siane.

Against this picture of diverse vegetable resources must be set the scarcity of animals. Hunting is of little importance for the supply of food, though both birds and opossums are shot for sport, and incidentally for food. Opossum skins are worn for decoration, and their fur is spun with bark-thread to make softer belts. Smaller game, rats, grubs, and insects are often caught by youths, but they are eaten only by women and children. The most important form of hunting, although it is as rare as the birds themselves, is the shooting of birds of paradise for their plumes.

Pigs are all domesticated, but they roam the bush all day rooting for food. They return at night to the women's houses in the villages, or to the pig houses in the bush. Occasionally one does not return home, but runs wild, devastates gardens, and attacks humans. Such a 'wild pig' is then festively hunted by beaters, spearmen, and bowmen who rush headlong through the head-high grass, shouting wildly. It is an occasion for sport, not for adding to the food supply. The activities concerned with raising pigs will be further discussed in section 3 of this chapter; here only the existence of pigs as a source of food need be noted.

Chickens and dogs are also domesticated, but both species were extremely small before the arrival of Europeans. Little care is needed by either, except that a man will often carry a brood of young chicks in a basket for a week after they have hatched. Thereafter the chickens roost at night in the trees near the women's houses. Both dogs and chickens are occasionally eaten as delicacies, though eggs are not. A few domesticated cassowaries exist, kept in stout stockades for their plumes and for the shell of their eggs. Sulphur-crested cockatoos are fed like pets, and occasionally plucked of their crests. The list of animals kept or used has not been increased by European contact, except that occasionally a cat is found (and sometimes eaten). Horses, cows, sheep, and goats are known by sight but form no part of the native's way of life.

In short, the environment provides extensive resources to meet the needs for food, shelter, and clothing. Many of the resources I have called 'wild' are plentiful, are not systematically exploited, and their use is surrounded by a minimum of regulation. Others, such as meat and salt, nuts and *roi* fruit, are scarce, and their use is the subject of social arrangements to be discussed more fully later. Vegetable resources, though plentiful, require systematic exploitation to ensure a sufficiency. The nature of that exploitation is the subject of the next section.

The Agricultural Cycle

The even temperature and the constant rainfall mean that most crops can be grown continuously with little seasonal variation. True, the drier period from May to August may cause taro to wither, and it is recognized as a better time to burn the brush on newly cleared gardens, but some gardens are made at all times of the year, and most crops are grown in every garden. Only the tree crops show marked seasonal influences, the season for pandanus nuts being from November to May, with a peak in February, while *roi* produces its largest fruits in May. Of the newly-introduced crops, passion fruit bears in January and February and again in August, while coffee must be replanted and thinned out during the wetter months. Tuberous plants, on the other hand, when once they have reached maturity, sprout continuously and may be harvested at will. Seed-propagated plants resow themselves and produce several crops a year. Thus a garden, once cleared and planted, starts bearing its first crops in three to four months. It continues to bear until the fertility of the soil is exhausted—until the sweet potatoes are small and stringy and are 'food for pigs'— or until the upkeep of fences and the weeding prove prohibitive. The soil is not outstandingly rich, but the climate makes plant growth extremely rapid. On the other hand, this means that the natural reserves of fertility are soon exhausted. After at most three full croppings, the ground must be left fallow. Eighteen months after ground has been cleared and planted, the only crops still giving good yields are the bananas and sugar cane.

The cycle of gardening activities starts when a new area of ground is cleared of its trees and undergrowth. An area is chosen where the trees are said to be 'ripe' or 'dry', and have a diameter of about ten inches. Clearing the ground is men's work. They chop down bushes, clear thickets of *pitpit*-reed by a judicious mixture of chopping and burning, and fell some trees and pollard others till they stand bare except for a tuft of leaves on top. The felled timber is split and chopped to make sharp, five-foot-long fence posts, which are stacked nearby. Since the natives work only intermittently at clearing and chopping, even with the use of steel tools it may be a month before the ground is cleared and sufficient fence posts cut.

The next task is to build a strong fence to stop the inroads of the pigs that roam the bush. Fences are built in a spell of intensive, continuous work. The men drive two rows of posts obliquely into the earth, so that the posts cross, and their sharpened tops project fearsomely in both directions. The bases of the posts are separated by logs, while other logs are placed in the cradle formed on top. No gaps are left between posts, and the result is a formidable barricade.[2]

Before the gardens are ready for planting the men must chop down any standing undergrowth, and the women must grub out the roots of the *kunai*-grass with their digging sticks, pile up the refuse, and burn it in bonfires. While they do this, the men bring in long poles, called *mea,* and lay these across the cleared earth to divide the land into small plots. Each plot is about thirty feet wide by seventy feet long, and is 'given' to one woman to cultivate. Thenceforward she regards that plot of land as 'hers'.[3]

From a garden that is about to be abandoned the woman collects cuttings of sweet-potato vine or taro tops. Then she goes to the newly-cleared garden, where she scrapes the earth into little mounds about three feet apart and six inches high, and thrusts some sweet-potato vine into each. In low-lying ground she uses a simple digging-stick as a dibble to make holes, into which she thrusts taro tops. On areas where there has been a bonfire she scatters maize, cucumber, and green vegetable seeds, which she has brought from the village. Close to the *mea,* in what will be an accessible place, she plants shoots of wild sugar cane gathered from the derelict garden.

Men plant some crops—the so-called 'male' crops—in the gardens of their wives. They cut the suckers from banana trees in old gardens and plant these in the centre of the garden plots. Shoots from the top of harvested sugar cane and old yam tubers are planted near to the *mea* poles. These two crops require attention as they are growing—tying to long stakes—and the *mea* poles provide access to them.

---

[2] An avowedly inferior fence of single posts, bound top and bottom with creepers, is used for unimportant gardens or within the villages themselves.
[3] For a discussion of the rights implicit in such property concepts see pp. 61-76.

When a garden is newly planted it presents a neat pattern. The irregular fenced area is divided by the *mea* poles into rough rectangles. Within the rectangles the sweet-potato mounds, each crowned with a sprig of green, form an intricate pattern like the overlapping scales of a fish.[4] Scattered irregularly over the dark-brown earth are the yellowish-green leaves of young taro and banana plants. But the intersecting circles of the mounds are not merely decorative; they prevent erosion. On a steep slope the rain-water collects behind one mound before flowing across the slope to the depression of a nearby mound, and only gradually percolates downhill.

No native explicitly recognized the problems of erosion, when I inquired. This is probably because newly-cleared gardens remain bare earth for only a few weeks. Sweet-potato vines spread rapidly over the whole area, and within a month or two the yams, sugar cane, bananas, maize, and green vegetable provide a forest of vege-tation some six feet high. Weeding then becomes an activity taking a large portion of the women's time, while men must set about clearing the next garden site.

About three or four months after a garden is first planted the first maize is edible. Other crops begin bearing during the succeed-ing months until a full range of vegetables is available. There is no sudden glut, however, for many different varieties of the major crops are planted together, which mature in slightly different periods, so that they become harvestable over a period of months. Another method of spreading the time of first cropping is the practice of leaving the edges of a garden plot unplanted for some time after the rest of the plot is planted. These edges, termed *onawaruma,* are planted at intervals during the succeeding months and bear correspondingly later.

There is no systematic replanting after the first harvest, and few plants of maize, yams, or taro are found in the gardens thereafter. By the end of nine months only sweet potatoes, green vegetables, and half-grown bananas and sugar cane are left, together with eighteen-inch-high casuarina seedlings fostered by the weeding. Activities in the garden are limited to fence repairing by the men, while women gather crops, weed, and occasionally heap up the sweet-potato mounds.

[4] In other areas of the Highlands (notably the flat plains), deep drainage ditches separate large mounds about six feet square, on which the sweet potatoes grow to give a chessboard effect (cf. Leahy and Crain 1937:49, 150). Sweet potatoes thrive in well-drained soil, but drainage is no problem on the Siane hillsides. The Siane only dig drainage ditches in hollows or where some Eastern Siane groups have recently begun copying the plains-dwelling Gahuku.

After eighteen months the sugar and bananas are fully harvested, and the casuarinas are four to six feet high. The men tear down the fence posts and fell the remaining pollarded trees. Pigs root out the remaining crops and the area returns to bush. In about fifteen years the young timber is 'ripe' or 'dry', the pine needles, the tree roots' action, and the pigs' droppings have regenerated the soil, and the agricultural cycle can start again.

Native statements about when newly-cultivated gardens were cultivated previously indicate that in pre-contact times the cycle was adhered to fairly closely. The main interruption occurred during wars, when all the casuarinas near a defeated village would be ring-barked. If villages were situated on the lower slopes or on central ridges within the main valleys—both advantageous sites for ease of travel and obtaining water—they were particularly vulnerable to ringbarking. If their cultivated timber was destroyed, the villagers were forced to live and make their gardens high on the slopes near the moss forest. Except where villages inhabited by renowned fighters led a precarious existence, envied by less fortunate villagers, the lower slopes tended to become deforested and covered with kunai-grass, hot and uninhabitable.

Following European contact more gardens are being made on the convenient lower slopes, where the steel tools now make it possible to eradicate kunai and pitpit roots. On these garden sites casuarinas are now growing, while rocky and inconvenient gardens near the moss forest are reverting to bush. At the same time it is now possible to clear the moss forest, and some gardens are being made where before there was primary forest. I would say, after hearing native descriptions of pre-contact days, that in balance the Siane area is now more wooded than it used to be,[5] though more of the trees are casuarinas and less are hardwood eucalypts.

Since, with native techniques, there is no storing of subsistence crops, new gardens must be planted continuously if the food supply is to be maintained. In practice new gardens are cleared regularly at intervals of just less than three months. Since gardens are usually under cultivation for one and one half years and under timber for fifteen years, maintenance of soil fertility demands that ten times as much land must be lying fallow at any one moment as is under cultivation. This topic will be discussed again later.

[5] This interpretation differs from the picture of rapid deforestation described by observers both in New Guinea (e.g. Read 1952) and other areas (e.g. Freeman 1953) whose main experience has been in flatter, less wooded areas. There the scarcity of trees near the garden sites prevents reseeding through wind action, while the continued need for timber and the new tools cause greater inroads in the moss forests.

The Sexual Division of Labour

The rationale the Siane men give for the division of agricultural tasks, which has already been indicated in passing, is that men do any tasks requiring the use of an axe, while women do the others. Since the use of axes is considered the basic skill by the Siane, this means that men do the 'skilled' work, and women the 'unskilled' work. Men and boys gladly display their skill in splitting logs (to the delight of a European, for whom splitting firewood constitutes a chore), and spend hours polishing their axes to razor sharpness with wet sandstone.[6] Men without axes are said to be 'like women', while youths signify their approaching manhood by carrying an axe at their belts, eagerly seizing any opportunity to use their axes when they are permitted to do so as part of a work party. Tasks in the gardening cycle that require the use of the axe are the clearing of garden sites and the building of fences, the cutting of supporting poles for yams and sugar cane, which therefore become 'male' crops, and the chopping down of banana trees for replanting.

Women do the routine tasks of planting, weeding, and harvesting, and no man will do these, except under extreme pressure of hunger. The allocation of such jobs to women is explained by the way in which women are regarded by men in Siane. They are felt to be rather stupid, unable to learn the complex skills needed for axe-work, politics, making exchanges, or for fine craft-work. They are also felt to be irresponsible, fitted only for carrying out a routine under male supervision. Their irresponsibility is shrugged off by the Siane men with the remark *'Yaroma wena neta ne'* ('That is what women do')—rather as we say 'Women drivers!'—even when it extends to sexual peccadilloes. All promiscuity is phrased as the fault of irresponsible women.

This keynote of routine and repetition in female tasks extends to all spheres. Women must cook food daily, must be constantly ready to suckle infants and feed older children, must call home the pigs every evening, and spend hours patiently knitting net bags. It will be noted that skill is in fact needed by the women, although men despise their jobs as 'unskilled'.

The woman's main duty is to provide cooked food for her husband and children. Since sweet potatoes are not storable, she must repair to the gardens every day to bring home supplies. Typically, women wake early, feed their children with sweet potatoes baked on the fire in their houses, and leave for the gardens at about 8 a.m. After

---

[6] I had a coarse carborundum stone for whetting my own firewood axe. This was despised by natives except as a means of removing deep chips from axe blades.

an hour's walk to the gardens they work steadily, if unhurriedly and with frequent pauses, until about 2 p.m., when they must return home to prepare the evening meal. Half of their time at the gardens is taken up with harvesting food and collecting loose firewood which requires no cutting; half is taken up with grubbing out roots, planting new areas, or weeding old areas, as the state of the gardens determines. Between 2 and 3 p.m. women converge on the village, each carrying a bag of vegetables and a bundle of sticks—a load of some sixty pounds. They pause at the village spring to wash the vegetables and talk. Outside their houses in the village the individual women build large fires to heat stones which are piled on the fire. Using split sticks as tongs, the women lay these hot stones in the bottom of their ovens—hollowed tree-stumps— cover them with leaves and with the vegetables to be cooked, pour on quantities of water, and seal the oven with a thick cover of grass and leaves. As the water percolates through to the hot stones, steam is formed and the foods cook slowly.

During the hour and a half when the food is cooking, babies are nursed, young children are fed with titbits like corn-on-the-cob baked on the fire, and the women sit in groups and talk, while doing craft activities. These include teasing apart fig bark for its fibres, spinning the fibres by rolling them on the thigh with the flat of the hand,[7] knitting the fibre into net bags for carrying purposes or for men's front coverings, tying it to make sporran-like women's front coverings, or sewing together pandanus leaves to make mats. Net bags are the commonest article made, but though the tasks of passing the thread round the pandanus-leaf spacers and through the previous loops, knotting it, and rewinding the thread while holding the curved bone needle all require dexterity, women do the work with a steady rhythm, scarcely looking at their work, so that a skilful task appears a routine.

After the meal is cooked, children nibble at tasty leaves and sweet potatoes while the women carry the food to their husbands in the men's house, using wooden dishes or large leaves. Each woman walks up to the men's house fence, calls her husband's name, and he either tells her to bring the food to him or sends a small boy to collect it. Later the wife returns to collect any surplus food and the container. After she has eaten her own meal she often has to walk for an hour to her pig house in the bush. Wherever she spends the night, she must call the pigs home to

---

[7] My own experiments at spinning thread in this way soon showed me how male hirsuteness makes this a painful, if not impossible, task for men to perform.

sleep. The 'br-r-r-r' noise, used to call pigs, and produced by flapping the lips, is the familiar sound of the end of the working day in Siane.

Even on days when there is a village festivity, the women must go early to the gardens to fetch food, though on such days they return by midday. The main breaks in a woman's routine occur when she remains at home sick, or when she visits or is visited by her brother. At these times friends provide her with the cooked food for entertaining or for her husband.

By contrast, the men's work varies from day to day. On days when they are working on a new garden or building houses, they work strenuously and for long hours. At other times they are more leisurely. When they work hard they wake with the dawn and sit huddled round the fires in the men's house on which they warm their breakfasts of sweet potatoes. They leave for the gardens about half an hour after the women, and the delays for sharpening axes and discussing the day's work mean they are not at work till about 10 a.m. Half of the men work at any one time, relieving each other at intervals. At about 2 o'clock a short rest is often taken, with a 'drink' of sugar cane or cucumber, but otherwise work continues until 5 p.m., when the long trek home begins. By six o'clock the men are sitting in the men's house clearing eating their evening meal. After dark the older men sit in the men's house talking, while the youths may depart on *awoiro*. Their work is over.

When men are building houses they have a similar daily timetable, some departing early to collect materials, others working at clearing and levelling the site. The morning is occupied by the strenuous work of erecting and insulating the low walls. A break comes in the work as a few men measure and drive in the house posts and secure the main rafters in position. Then all men return to strenuous work, fastening the remaining rafters, until the house frame is complete. If it is a woman's house that is being built, the future occupant then provides a meal for the men who have built it and for her female friends who have meanwhile collected grass for use as thatch. If the house is a men's house, all the wives will have brought thatch, and some of the men will have spent the afternoon preparing a meal of nuts, yams, and other 'male' foods, to feed the workers.

Mere maintenance work—fence repairing, for example—is done at a more leisurely pace, and men return home by 4 p.m. carrying the logs they have cut for firewood. On Sundays and Mondays, the days which missionaries and Government have pre-empted for church or for work on Government Rest Houses or patrol roads, the day's tasks are over by noon. The leisure hours are used for chopping firewood for the men's house, for sharpening axes, for craft activities, and for the playing of football by the younger men.

The craft activities include the smoothing of new axe-handles; removing the brown outer covering of gold-lip shells by rubbing with sandstone, and then cutting a circular piece out of them to leave a crescent of mother-of-pearl; sewing small cowrie shells on to bark to make headdresses; weaving cane armbands and belts; plaiting ropes of grass for tethering pigs; carving jews' harps out of bamboo and decorating them with poker-work designs burnt with glowing sticks; and beating out *kafo* bark to make bark-cloth. Parenthetically it must be said that leisure and craft activities were much less common in 1933.

The men may vary their activities even more. Not merely may they remain home sick, but sometimes they may spend a day leisurely at home, beating out bark-cloth or stencilling coloured designs in ochre, soot, or dye on it. Men also visit, occasionally hunt, and frequently spend the entire day in ceremonials or in discussing political or legal questions.

The Organization of Work Groups

Although tasks can be classified as 'men's work' or 'women's work', this does not mean that all the men or all the women of a village work co-operatively. The whole male population of the village does co-operate when a large garden is cleared to provide food for a First Fruits ceremony, or when the men's houses are being rebuilt before a Pig Feast, but the groups which work together *at the same spot* and within which further division of labour occurs are usually men's house groups.[8] At the clan-village level there is merely close co-ordination of work.

Such co-operative work is initiated by informal evening discussions in the men's houses, in which all men present take part, although the more active 'big men' naturally have more to say. Since men's houses are rebuilt at three-yearly intervals, there is little debate over whether one should be built or not; rather, discussion centres around the details of size and location within the compound. Since the sequence in which areas were last used for gardens is also generally known, there is little discussion of where to make gardens, unless the trees are 'unripe' for cutting or the area too small for the ceremony planned for when the garden is bearing. Major issues are such matters as which clan to invite to the eventual ceremony. After unanimity has been reached in informal discussion within

[8] Cf. the organization of ceremonial and religious activities (p. 15).

the various men's houses, there is further informal consultation between the 'big men' of different men's houses. Final agreement is announced by the appropriate set speech, made in each men's house, by the *yarafo* of the lineage owning that speech. In form such speeches merely describe the sequence of actions supposed to occur—in a Pig Feast ceremony,[9] for example—but their effect is that on the next day everyone carries out those actions.

Decisions are not announced outside the men's house, although all details are common knowledge within the group, even for newly-initiated boys. An advantage of this lack of publicity was demonstrated when I was told informally that a certain clan would be entertained at the First Fruits ceremony of one garden. A dry spell intervened, and despite the efforts of rain magicians the all-important taro withered, so that clearly no ceremony could take place. When I later inquired about the ceremony I was met with blankness. There would be one next year for a different garden, they said; at the moment it was too soon after the last Pig Feast. Privately I was told how the drought had caused the plans to be cancelled, but since no other clan knew of any plans, no face was lost.

When work starts, the 'big men' take the lead and commence clearing land owned by their particular men's house.[10] They do not force other men of the ward group to accompany them, but within a few days all men are helping. Youths are often intractable, but if they fail to work, physical force may be used to compel them. Once work is proceeding in earnest, all members of the men's house are expected to assist as part of their obligations. If for some reason they cannot attend in person, they obtain substitutes, such as wife's brothers, or mother's-brother's-sons, who come from other villages and work in their stead. I never saw more than five such substitutes at any one time, and they do not contribute much to the actual hard work. They are well entertained, and their presence is symbolic of friendship and respect rather than materially productive.

[9] The speech used the evening before the climax of the Pig Feast is given in Salisbury 1956c:475. The relation between the ownership of such speeches and the authority structure of the clan is dealt with more fully in Salisbury (n.d.). Here the relevant points are that owning the right to make the speech predisposes a lineage head to participate in the preceding discussion but gives him no authority over the decision. If he is not present, any other man may make the speech, though if he is present and makes the speech prematurely he does cut off discussion. Speech-making is a ritual marking of agreement, not a factor in arriving at a decision.

[10] Land tenure is discussed later (see pp. 61-76). The land cleared by 'big men' is land to which their lineages have special rights, but what is important here is they act as members of a ward group on land over which the ward has other rights.

From their point of view they are visiting and assisting the clan
of their affines; from the point of view of the workers they are
ensuring that the whole complement of the men's house (or substitutes) is present at a task defined as being performed 'by the
men's house'.

While clearing is in progress, individuals (or lineages) tend to
work separately on strips within the garden which are owned by
that individual (or lineage). The smaller groupings synchronize
their work, however. No land within the garden area may remain
uncleared, so that if a strip of land belonging to a lineage of a
different men's house is included, it may be cleared either by a
member of the owning lineage or by a member of the working men's
house group if the owners do not clear it. Joint work groups are
rare, however, since the holdings of most ward groups are con-
solidated; the main occasion on which they occur is when youths
assist age-mates in other men's houses. If a lineage is unable to
clear its own land on schedule, because of sickness, for example,
it is assisted by other lineages of the same men's house.

After the land is cleared, all men of a ward group combine to
erect the surrounding fence. If the garden areas of the several ward
groups are contiguous, rather than merely near to one another,
one fence may be a joint construction by all men of the village.
Even so, each ward group works as a discrete unit on its own
section of the fence.

In the building of men's houses the same pattern of organization
appears. Each ward group makes its own decision to rebuild, but
the plans are co-ordinated on a clan basis. The 'big men' take the
lead in collecting timbers and insulating material, and each ward
group, in a rough synchronization, tears down its own house before
levelling the site for the new one. When the site is level and the
walls are to be erected, some men from all men's houses of the
clan come to assist the nucleus of workers from the ward group.
When the next men's house site is ready, assistance is then given
by the occupants of the first house in their turn. On such occasions
affines and mother's-brothers come 'to help', but, as with their help
in gardening, their presence is symbolic rather than productive.
They are visitors only.

Thus in these work groups, the largest in Siane, about a hundred
men and youths may be seen working at one time. Rarely, though,
do as many as sixty combine in one group within which there is
any delegation of tasks; normally the largest organized group is
one of thirty workers from one men's house. Whenever there is
less need for a division of labour by skills (see pp. 56-7), the work

group splits up into numbers of individuals or lineages working independently on similar tasks. It is noticeable, however, that the fastest and most concentrated work is performed when the largest and most differentiated group combines.

During the loosely co-ordinated garden clearing, work is performed, on the average, about every other day and at a fairly leisurely pace. Ceremonials or other activities usually cause the ten to fifteen days of work to be spread over a whole month. When fences or house walls are built the tempo of work increases, no day is lost, and work continues as long as the light lasts. The intensive work is enjoyed and parties come back from the gardens singing. The women cook extra amounts of food, and, with the entertainment of 'helpful' visitors, food consumption is about doubled. The larger the work group the greater the festivity.

When the men work in large groups the women tend to do likewise, collecting thatch for the new houses or planting and weeding the new gardens. All the wives leave the village together, and work near one another, although each woman plants her own garden plot or collects her own bundle of *kunai*-grass. When the wives return with their thatch they are entertained collectively by the men of the house for which the thatch is destined; when they return from planting large gardens each men's house gives 'male' food to its own women-folk. The women sit in rows in the men's house clearing and are ceremonially presented with food by the assembled men, organized as a men's house. Nevertheless, each woman has worked as an independent individual, synchronizing her activity with other women.

More common work groups than either the clan or ward group are those of lineage size. Such groups build women's houses and pig houses. They also clear gardens which individuals wish to make for their wives and lineage dependants to supplement the plots received in the partition of the larger gardens. Any individual may initiate such activity, younger brothers as well as lineage heads. He merely states that he intends to do such work and he is sure of the co-operation of other members of his lineage. His close friends, especially his age-mates, probably accompany him also to the work site, and any member of the clan who passes the work site stops for a short time to talk and help.

This size of work group thus usually has a nucleus of about four adult members of the lineage together with two youths. Other individuals attach themselves to the group and at any one time about seven adults and five youths are normally present, half of them being non-lineage members. They work at the instance of the work-initiator, who may be the lineage head but who may equally be a married youth who has just attained adulthood and is building a house in which to start cohabiting with his wife.

When the day's work is over, the wife of the initiator brings food for the workers, the work-initiator himself providing them with sugar cane to drink throughout the work. Food is provided in larger amounts than is usual for an evening meal, but this is not considered a 'payment', except, perhaps, by youths who are given food personally on such occasions, while normally they only receive food passed to them by older men. Thus, although sharing of food is the normal rule, I once saw a youth refuse to give any sweet potato to a small boy who asked for some. He gave as his reason that he had worked for the food, and did not wish to give any to someone who had not worked. For the older men the only 'reward' is to eat earlier than usual and to have a long evening for talk and laughter.

Tasks such as repairing garden fences, planting banana trees, cutting yam poles, and clearing undergrowth round *roi* and pandanus trees are performed by adult men acting alone. When they leave the village on such tasks their sons have the choice of following them or remaining with their age mates. My observation is that boys below the age of 10 tend more to go with their fathers and those between 10 and 16 tend to remain with their peers. Boys of 17 and 18 work with their fathers as willing helpers. In general, though, these tasks are for individuals working alone, and the sons are present as learners rather than as co-workers.

As well as the differential participation by individuals of different statuses in the process of *initiating* work groups, there is also a division of the work of production in terms of skill and status. 'Big men', who are acknowledged as men of good judgment, set the standard for work and supervise its execution. They do this exclusively by example and free comment, rather than by exercising authority. They are the first to start work, but once their example has been followed they stop work and sit near the work site, smoking and commenting on what is being done. If the tempo of work flags, they seize their axes and feverishly attack the work until others follow their example. Otherwise, they intervene only at crucial points in the work—when, for example, a decision must be made to mark out the line of a fence or to place house posts in the right position. They make these *ad hoc* decisions, not by argument but by one of their number actively doing what he thinks is correct. Only if his lead is not followed by the ordinary workers does another 'big man' come forward and do what he thinks is correct, and so on until an effective solution is found.

'Big men' perform these tasks even in lineage work groups when they are not the work-initiators. The initiator's task on such occasions is to facilitate the work rather than to direct it—a task requiring skill and judgment he may not possess. The initiator must previously ensure that the required materials are available, and he indicates the general site of the proposed house or garden fence, but during the work he merely provides refreshment for the workers, brings materials to them, and directs any youths present to do the same.

The majority of men at any work site are unskilled workers (Siane *faivya we* or 'nothing men'). They perform routine tasks like levelling a house site, dragging in undergrowth for burning, or driving in fence posts, but even within this group there is some differentiation of tasks on the basis of assumed skill. Older men take over tasks in which they can use their axes, younger men do the hand labour, youths and boys are left to fetch materials and to bring lights for the older men's cigarettes. Yet whenever an older man rests, a younger man jumps into his place; when a younger man stops driving in fence posts, a youth will try his skill at it. To be skilful is to be important.

There are some skills in the performance of craft activities or of esoteric rituals which are possessed by single individuals, irrespective of their status or age. All men have some abilities in these directions, but those who are more proficient are called *hori we* (men who hear, or understand). When an unskilled man wishes to make a cowrie-shell headband, for example, he collects the shells and a strip of bark and may even sew a few shells to the bark before he takes the work to a 'man who understands'. Usually he goes to a skilled man of his own lineage, but if there is no such person he may call on any classificatory clan brother for help. The skilled man does the more intricate parts of the work, such as designing the diamond motif in the centre of the headband, but then calls upon other less-skilled men to do the routine tasks (in this case the sewing on of a thousand shells to fill out the design). These unskilled men include the age-mates and lineage-mates of the man who commissioned the work, but may be from any part of the clan. No specific reward is given for the work of the skilled man and his assistants. When I asked skilled men about rewards, the answer was always, 'No, we are his brothers; we are helping him'.

On the other hand, rewards are given for the practice of esoteric rituals. Men who treat 'sorcery sickness' in humans or pigs, and men who work rain magic in times of drought, receive payment in pork. If the ceremony is performed for a member of the specialist's own men's house or clan the pig is killed as part of the ceremony and is then distributed by the specialist to all members of the clan, and he receives one portion himself. If magic is worked for members of other clans, the pig must be killed and handed over before the specialist starts work, and it is then his to use at will. If the magic is ineffective the 'clients' may try to reclaim their 'fee', but they have no way of enforcing their claim, especially since magic appears to be commissioned only from distant clans.

The work of women is organized on slightly different bases from the work of the men. Synchronization of individually-performed activities, such as that of women in collecting thatch or planting sections of a large garden, described above, is the result of individual men telling their wives what to do and when to do it. The groups of women who travel to the gardens together and who talk as they work are formed on the basis of the distribution of garden plots by the lineage head who owns the entire strip. Since he allocates the plots primarily to lineage wives, but also to other dependent women, widows, etc., this produces an association between the women, although each woman works her own plot by herself and jealously guards her own produce.

Sometimes the same group of women co-operate for cooking purposes; at other times women who were born in the same village co-operate in cooking. When there is such co-operation, three or four women all assist with the work but use one fire and oven, using different fires and ovens in turn. They pool their stocks of vegetables as they put them in the oven, but each woman takes a separate portion of the food to her own husband in the men's house. At a ceremonial, one hundred women may bring food to a men's house simultaneously, but only about twenty ovens will have been used for the cooking. In theory each woman individually cooks food and brings it to her husband; in practice the women combine in small groups to share the work and to make provision for the times when one of the group is sick or visiting.

It may at this point be asked, 'What are the incentives to work, or the punishments for failure to work, which the society provides to maintain the labour supply?' The answer one receives to a direct question of 'Why do people work?' is 'Within the clan all men are brothers and all brothers have an obligation to help one another', while extra food given at working bees is ignored. The rationale

4   A woman dyeing a bridal gift

5 A woman clearing
kunai and planting
sweet potatoes

6 Akome's wife pre-
paring her family's
evening meal

of 'helping brothers' also explains the sequence by which a work group is started. A man may publicize his need for help in many ways—by announcing his intentions in the men's house, by starting to lay the line of a new fence by himself in front of many other men if he is a 'big man', or by building his pig house near a path on which men walk. All indicate a desire for assistance that cannot be ignored unless the ignorer can show good reason or is prepared to disclaim his obligations publicly and so obtain a reputation for laziness or unsociability. No strict account is kept of who helps whom, but if an individual frequently refuses to help others, other men will eventually refuse to help him.[11] In this context the obtaining of substitutes (who do little work), when one cannot attend a large work group in person, can be seen as a symbolic statement of good intentions rather than as a means of maintaining the labour supply.

But if such work is an obligation, why is food given at the end of a day's work? The gift of food does not absolve the giver from his obligation to return any assistance he has received, whenever the occasion arises. In fact, giving food is also one of the obligations of clan membership. The special gift of food after assistance has been received could well be interpreted, therefore, as a special recognition of the existence of clan obligations. To the recipient of the food, what is received is not merely food but an assurance of friendship, of obligations to him, and of common membership in the group of 'brothers'. This, rather than a more general 'pleasure obtained from festivity' adduced by some authors, may be the incentive to work in a group which is feasted when the work is finished. Such an incentive also explains the gaiety surrounding the feasting of women who bring thatch to the building of a men's house. At marriage the women are incompletely included into the clan of their husbands, and retain links with their clans of birth. By their work they show their wish to fulfil the obligations of full members of their husband's clan; the men, by giving them food and allowing them inside the men's house compound, assert that they are members and assure them of protection and help.

The same incentive, that of appearing to fulfil clan obligations, can be adduced to explain the different types of work done by 'big men', by unimportant men with dependants, and by young men

---

[11] In my own village there were four men who regularly lived with their wives and children in pig houses outside the village, which they entered only for important ceremonies. They were not harmed in any way, and seemed quite hard-working individualists who preferred not to rely on other people, and to do all their own work. They did have reputations of being strange and spirit-possessed.

without dependants.[12] Thus the greater concern of the 'big men' with appearing socially responsible is reflected in their readiness to perform tasks which give them little direct return in material goods—work on communal gardens, and often, since they are 'men who hear', craft work for others. For unimportant men with dependants the incentive to participate in clan activities is less effective, but the incentive to obtain direct returns of material goods is more effective. They most frequently initiate lineage work groups for gardens for their own wives. Young men who are still dependent on the clan for support in making bride-price and other payments are found working assiduously on all occasions, presumably both because they wish to appear socially responsible and because they are most vulnerable to the withdrawal of support by others.

The frequency with which help is given obviously varies, as does the closeness of the relation of 'brotherhood'. Help for lineage brothers is given most frequently, although help to age mates is about as frequent; help to members of one's men's house is common; help to men whose only relationship is that of clan brothers is least frequent.

Wife's brothers and matrilateral cross-cousins might also be considered as giving their labour as 'help due to kinsmen'. The same word *umaiye* is used for 'to help' and for 'to substitute for' (as is the pidgin word *alivim*), and it describes the behaviour both of clan brothers and of these outsiders. But there are differences. I have stressed the small amount of productive work done by outsiders; it would be as true to say that they are not *allowed* to work since they are held in conversation, offered cigarettes, and fed with delicacies. Their hosts treat the visitors with the same effusive politeness as they use to affines, rather than expecting from them the reciprocal help and feeding expected between kinsmen. If the outsiders' visit is their attempt to maintain a close and lasting relationship with the individual for whom they are substituting, the unrelated hosts by *their* behaviour attempt to make the relationship formal, limited, and unconnected with labour.

The most formal relationship in which work is done for another person is the contract for services to a distant clan. A tangible object is presented and services given in return, and then the relationship is at an end.

Between unrelated clans, in short, labour and services are com-

---

[12] These activities have been indicated earlier. A more detailed quantitative treatment of the types of work done by different individuals is contained in Appendix B, 'Time Budgets'. Since this material is analysed in other contexts it will not be further discussed here.

modities with an exchange value in terms of pigs. Within the clan, labour for others is one aspect of mutual social obligations: work for one's self gives the prospect of an eventual material return; work for others strengthens ties and obligations. Between kinsmen of different clans labour can be a means of strengthening lasting ties, but in such a situation other members of the clan always attempt to deny any such ties.

Property Ownership and Land Tenure

In the foregoing discussions I have often used such terms as 'owners', 'clan land', and 'women's garden plots'. By these property concepts I am referring, in the first instance, to the replies I received when I asked 'Whose is that?'—I received replies such as 'It is mine', 'It is Waifo clan's', or 'It is Tene's wife's'. To understand such statements fully, at least two further questions are necessary: 'What rights or privileges with respect to that object did the respondent imply by associating a person or group with it?'; and 'What in the conversation made the respondent associate that particular person or group with the object, out of the many other groups and individuals who are associated with it?'

In Siane terms a person can mean two types of right when he says an object is 'mine': either that he is a *merafo* of the object, or that he is its *amfonka*. *Merafo* is the ordinary word for 'father', and the *merafo* of property looks after it (*hentaiye*) just as a father looks after his son, acting in his best interests, and being responsible for his wellbeing to the community, to the ancestors, and to posterity. The property an individual *merafo* looks after is thus comparable with an entailed estate, while his position is that of a trustee. Estates usually consist of land, sacred flutes, and incorporeal property such as pigs' souls, *gerua* designs, ritual knowledge, and rights to make speeches. The term *amfonka* was derived for me by Siane informants from the word *amene* or 'shadow'. As a shadow is attached to the person who casts it, so are objects attached to their *amfonka*, and just as the shadow is identified with the soul, so are objects 'identified' with their *amfonka*. A suitable term to describe the relationship of objects to their *amfonka* would be the legal term 'personalty'. It has both the association with 'personality' and the opposition to the term 'estate'.

A man's personalty consists of his pigs, his ornaments of all kinds, his axe and other tools, his clothing, his wife's house, trees which he has planted on land of which he is *merafo,* and numbers of *tanket* shrubs scattered over the clan land. A woman's personalty consists of the necklace of pigs' teeth her husband's father gave her at marriage, other trinkets, her bone needle for making net-bags, her supplies of bark-cloth, fibres, opossums' wool and cloth-ing, her mats, her cooking utensils, her house, and the crops she has planted in her garden.

These objects most often become personalty by virtue of the work done in creating them. A man plants trees and builds his wife's house; a woman sews her mats and plants her crops. But the relationship can also be established by transfer from an individual whose personalty they were previously. Thus a man commonly receives an axe in exchange for a shell, and he makes bark-cloth and gives it to his wife, who gives him net-bag aprons; a woman is given her house by her husband. The transfer need not involve any 'consideration' in return, for men commonly transfer their *tanket*s to younger brothers, or to their sons, and receive nothing in return.

Even if work in connection with an object does not automatically make the object one's personalty, it renders possible a claim to such a relationship. Thus pigs become part of a man's personalty by virtue of his work in bringing back to his wife's house litters of newly farrowed piglets from the bush where they are born (a task that involves courage in braving the anger of the mother sow). He indicates his ownership by cutting the pigs' ears or by other mark-ings. But it is his wife who calls the pigs home at evening time to sleep in the front section of her house, who fondles them, scratches their bellies, and cleans their skins. When a man wishes to kill his pigs, his wife will commonly wail and weep, saying the pigs are her personalty, until her husband gives her a small gift to prevent further argument. Similarly, when I was trying to obtain ornamental items of men's clothing, husbands were willing to sell, but invariably they returned later to say that their wives had worked so hard on the aprons they did not like to see them sold. In some cases a small gift to the wife was all that was needed, in others I had to return the articles.

If there is any dispute as to who is the *amfonka* of an article, the most important issue is to decide who actually made the object. Thus in the case of *tanket*s or trees, whose ownership is most often in dispute, no case can be decided without a discussion of which ancestor, in the distant past, planted the trees. Thereafter the dis-cussion traces the transfers of the property into the hands of the rival claimants.

On the other hand, if the work is performed on objects over which the worker has no claim to be a *merafo* or trustee, he cannot claim *amfonka* ownership. Thus one clan of Komunku tribe drove another Komunku clan into exile after a war in the 1930s, and planted pandanus palms on the estate of the exiled clan. In 1953 the returned trustees of the land collected the nuts. The tree-planters fought them, but in the native peace-making discussions they admitted they had no real claim to the trees. They told me they thought that Europeans might have supported them if they had been able to take the matter to a Government court. The final exchange of peace-making presents did not involve any great imbalance that might be construed as an indemnity for the work they had put in.

It is only where there is already a trustee relationship that work performed can set up a claim of rights to personalty. If a man makes a garden on land, of which another lineage is *merafo,* he may cause trees to grow. He has a weak claim to those trees if he is a member of the same clan as the lineage *merafo,* since he is then a trustee of clan property. The claim may be recognized by the lineage head's transferring to the cultivator the personalty rights over the *tanket*s on that strip of land, although the cultivator is powerless if no transfer is made. Such transfers occur fairly frequently, largely, I believe, because, as will be shown later, there is no shortage of land.

The personalty rights involved in an *amfonka* relationship regard the object as part of one's own person. Any assault against personalty is an assault on the person. Theft (*inkere*) is therefore abhorred within the phratry where physical assault is prohibited; theft from members of enemy clans is praiseworthy. In either case an outraged *amfonka* is publicly supported if he resorts to physical retaliation against a thief, just as he would be if he defended himself against assault. Thus if a man enters a garden on which there are growing crops, the personalty of a woman, he must first obtain the permission of that woman, even though she be his wife.[13] Otherwise he is assumed to be stealing crops, and the woman may punish him by beating him with a digging stick or scratching him with her nails. Other men do not intervene as they normally do in male-female quarrels, but laugh at his discomfiture.

When a person is not at home he puts a plank across the door-

---

[13] This rule is ceremonially broken before the Yam Taro ceremony, when the men 'steal' the new corn from the women's growing crops as they carry the sacred flutes in procession round the gardens. This is, in fact, an assertion that the crops belong to the ancestors (personified by the flutes), since they have made them grow, and they are entitled to eat them. This is the story that is told to the women.

way. To enter the house without permission, even though the rain is pouring down outside, is to risk a physical assault in return for the assault on personalty.

The corollary of the statement that theft is an assault against the personalty is the fact that use of goods over which one has trusteeship rights is not theft. One cannot 'steal' cooked food or land from a clan-mate. If one wishes to prevent such use of land or food, one must attach an item of personalty to the goods. Food can be tied in a package, or a *tanket* may be used. If a person finds a useful but wild tree which he wishes to claim as personalty, he ties a leaf of one of his *tanket*s to it. If he wishes to prevent his clan-mates from walking across his land, as they have a perfect right to do when he is not cultivating it, he thrusts a branch of his *tanket* into the pathway. This implies also that he has buried a magic arrow in the ground to protect his personalty, and that anyone who passes the *tanket* will be 'shot' in the foot by the arrow. Unless the trespasser confesses and makes amends he is likely to die. In other words, *tanket*s are used as 'Keep off' signs to turn estate objects into personalty, and as a warning that supernatural and indiscriminate means of protection are being used.

The close association between a person and his personalty is shown in many other ways. Thus sorcery, which is supposed to cause the owner's personalty to enter into the possession of the sorcerer, is described as 'stealing his soul'. For this reason the box in which returned labourers keep their ornaments is kept firmly padlocked. Such boxes, and their pre-European counterparts of tied mats, are never opened when strangers are present.

The presence of a woman's personalty in a village is taken as a sure sign that she will later return in person. A wife may visit her brothers for several months without this disturbing her husband, provided that she has left her trinkets and supplies of bark-cloth behind. On the other hand, if a wife tries to take these goods with her on what is ostensibly only a short visit, her husband will immediately act as though she has deserted him.

When a man dies, his personalty is said to 'die' also. This means that his clothing and some of his ornaments go with the corpse to burial. His clothing is hung upon a tree near the grave and some ornaments are buried, though others are divided among those who perform the interment. Natives speak as though *all* his ornaments are buried, but in fact most of them are presented to mourners at the funeral, as are the dead man's pigs, after they have been killed. His house is left derelict, or occupied only by the widow until the next Pig Feast. His *tanket*s go to the person to whom he has previously 'shown' them—usually his son—during his walks round the clan land.

Pigs cannot be eaten by their *amfonka*, and such an act is treated with the same distaste and horror as is expressed at the idea of cannibalism. A distinction must be made, however, between the meat of a pig and its soul. Though the *amfonka* of a pig may kill it at will, he is responsible to the clan for transferring the soul of the dead pig into its progeny, since he is merely the trustee of the soul. He must placate his pigs' souls before the Pig Feast, in ceremonies involving special *gerua* boards. If he transfers the pig's body to another person, he must either kill the pig first so that the soul is not lost, or he must ensure that the pig is eventually returned. This aspect of a man's relationship to his pigs will be dealt with more fully in later sections.

But the pig's being personalty implies that the owner is responsible for his pig's actions. Thus if his pig breaks through a garden fence and eats the crops, he is liable for the damage. If his pig is killed by the gardener, he must accept this without complaining. In such a case, however, the gardener has no rights to the body of the pig; he has revenged the assault on his fence and his wife's garden, and the pig's owner may come and collect his personalty.

Personalty may usually be transferred or alienated at the whim of the *amfonka*. The *amfonka* may (subject to argument with his wife, perhaps) transfer ornaments, tools, pork, or *tanket*s to whomever he wishes. But there are many occasions on which individuals transfer personalty when they do not particularly desire to.

The commonest of such transfers are temporary—mere borrowing. If an object of personalty is not being used by its owner, any other member of the owner's clan may indicate his desire to use it, and the owner may not normally refuse him. New articles of clothing are worn by the owner for a few days, but within a day of his ceasing to wear them, several other members of the clan wear them in turn. A new tool, owned by one man, will be used by all his clansmen and quickly worn out. To some extent the owner is recompensed if breakages occur, for he is given a gift 'to prevent bad feelings', but such gifts rarely equal the value of the damage. They do not prevent the private grumbles of individuals whose property is worn out by borrowers.

More permanent transfers occur when the clan must make a ceremonial payment, or kill a pig. There is often only one pig in a village of a suitable size for a ceremonial killing, and it is being kept by its *amfonka* for a forthcoming rite of passage. Nevertheless, if, during the discussion of the payment, a suggestion is made that he should kill his pig, he will not usually refuse. So, too, with ornaments provided for ceremonial payments: many of them are provided unwillingly by their owners, as a result of suggestions by fellow clansmen.

Do these instances imply that an *amfonka* does not have absolute control over his personalty? My interpretation would be that he does have absolute control, but since the individual and his personalty are treated as one indivisible whole, all clan obligations incumbent on the individual apply equally to his personalty. But the clan has no rights over the personalty that it does not have over the individual. An *amfonka*'s title to his personalty is an absolute title, impaired only by more general restrictions on his conduct, and these do not directly relate to the personalty itself.

By contrast, the rights of a *merafo* are those of a trustee momentarily exercising control over goods the absolute title to which is vested in a corporation which exists perpetually. The ancestors made these goods at the beginning of time when they emerged from holes in the ground, and their descendants (or reincarnations) must be handed these goods in unimpaired condition in the future. The trustee justifies his position in terms of his descent from the ancestors,[14] and validates the privileges he obtains from his trusteeship by the performance of rituals in honour of the ancestors. I have already described (pp. 21-2) the rights and duties of a lineage head or *yarafo* concerning the incorporeal estate of his lineage, and also the way in which clan ceremonials are a corporate obligation to care for the clan's most important incorporeal estate—the souls of the ancestors and their symbolic representations. These constitute the major forms of trusteeship over incorporeal estate objects. The remainder of this section will deal with trusteeship over real objects, chiefly land.

In the first place it will be remembered that the term *merafo*, in its kinship meaning of 'father', is a classificatory term, and within the class of 'fathers' there are different degrees of closeness. So it is with the term *merafo* in its meaning of 'trustee'. Trustees, and the rights and obligations of those trustees, are differentiated in terms of whether they are of the same lineage as the estate, of the same clan, or of the same tribe.

[14] This descent is usually patrilineal, but long genealogies are not kept and adoption is easy though infrequent. The short genealogies facilitate the creation of descent fictions. Of more importance than descent in determining one's relation to the ancestors is one's residence in the village and one's performance of the right ceremonies. See Salisbury 1956a for a longer discussion of adoption and genealogies.

In regard to lineage trusteeship rights over land, it will also be recalled that individuals within lineages own absolutely numerous *tanket*s scattered over the area in which the clan lives. These *tanket*s were not present when the original ancestors emerged to occupy the land but were planted by specific individuals, many of whose names have now been forgotten but who are remembered, for example, as 'Grandfather of Famti'. They constitute personalty and can be transferred or alienated by the individual. However, when these *tanket*s were planted, they marked the boundaries of land which had been brought under cultivation from the virgin forest by the planters. This is the native theory, adduced to explain the fact that the *tanket*s now form the boundaries of strips of land which men of the *tanket*-owner's lineage may cultivate as they wish without consulting other members of the clan. They may enclose the land with fences and prevent other people from walking over it. They may build pig houses on the land without consulting outsiders. They may allocate a plot from the strip, when it has been fenced and cleared of undergrowth, to any female they wish, whether she is resident in the clan village or not. The female then has the right to crops grown on that land, as an *amfonka*.

Typically, each strip of lineage land measures about thirty yards by sixty yards, and the members of a lineage are trustees, with these 'exclusive rights', over between 100 and 200 such strips. These strips are located in all the cultivated areas within the three square miles inhabited by the clan. Five or six of the plots are covered by pandanus or *roi* palms; at any one time six or seven plots are being cultivated as part of the large communal gardens, and another three or four form small gardens cultivated by individual members of the lineage; the remainder are fallow and covered by bush. This is the typical picture, but it varies little between lineages or over time.

There is an anomaly in the foregoing statement. The *tanket*s marking a strip of land may be the personalty of individual A; the strip may have been cleared and divided by individual B of the same lineage, while other lineage members, including individual C, the lineage head, are also trustees over the land. To the question 'Who is the *mika merafo* (father of the ground)?' all lineage members may with equal correctness say 'I am', although if one asks a non-member 'Who is the trustee?' he is likely to reply that C is. Only if one asks 'Who is the *firinka amfonka* (owner of the marks, or boundaries)?' will everyone reply that A is. To discover that it is B's garden one must inquire 'Whose is the *rono*?'. *Rono* means 'work', but like the pidgin term *wok* it is often best translated as 'garden', although its denotation is clearly that of 'the increment to the untilled soil caused by labour'.

The reason that C is most often cited as *mika merafo* is that he represents the lineage to non-members of that lineage. In addition, he is the person who usually executes the joint trusteeship rights. He decides whether land will be cultivated or not, and organizes the work group if a garden is being made on any of the lineage land. He also ensures that enough gardens are made for each lineage member's wife to receive a plot to cultivate. He himself owns the largest number of *tanket*s, but when a small individual garden is made for a junior lineage member on a strip bounded by the lineage head's *tanket*s, it is common for the head to transfer his ownership of the *tanket*s to the cultivator. If an individual clears his own small garden, without calling on the assistance of the lineage head, he may use any of the lineage land, but most commonly he uses a strip whose boundaries he owns personally.

In most cases there is no conflict between the rights of *firinka amfonka* and *mika merafo*. Usually they are rights owned by the same person, and where they are not, they are owned by members of the same lineage, who work together and have the same set of potential heirs. Only if an individual alienates his personalty rights to *tanket*s to someone outside the lineage (as he may freely do), is there conflict. In such a case the lineage head may, with the consent of lineage members, alienate the trusteeship rights to the owner of the *tanket*s. This had been the sequence in the two histories of alienation of *tanket*s which occurred in all my investigations of land transfer. In both cases the land and its boundaries had been given to individuals whose genealogies were fragmentary, not connecting them with other clansmen. It was my impression, based on nearness of residence and linkage in the village census book, that these men were in the process of being adopted into the lineages that originally owned the land.

On the remainder of the clan territory the members of the illustrative lineage have other rights by virtue of being classificatory clan *merafo*s of the land. On unclaimed land, where no *tanket*s are planted, they may clear and cultivate it, and plant *tanket*s, which thenceforth are the planter's personalty. The planter's lineage then acquires trusteeship rights. On such land they may gather wild produce, cut down timber, or hunt wild game; without asking anyone's permission they may build pig houses and their pigs may forage freely.

On land that has been claimed by having *tanket*s planted on it but is not currently being cultivated they may do all these things, except establishing further rights, subject to their asking permission from the trustee lineage before cultivating the land, cutting timber, or building a house. The lineage trustees, if they do withhold permission, must then show sufficient reason why the land should *not* be so used. 'Sufficient reason' would be that they themselves were soon to make gardens there or that the trees were 'unripe'. The most common use of land that is the estate of another lineage is to build pig houses on it. If a man clears an individual garden for his wife, he utilizes an entire strip of his own lineage's land; if he then wishes to build a pig house nearby, he is forced to ask permission to build on another lineage's land. In such case, the user (who now has *rono* rights: cf. pp. 67-8) cannot be forced to vacate the land until he himself terminates his use, either by leaving the house derelict or by abandoning a garden if he has cultivated another lineage's land. At no time are the lineage trusteeship rights extinguished, and at the end of the period of use the user reverts to having only clan trusteeship rights.

If an individual dies with no heir to take over his *tanket*s (i.e. his lineage becomes extinct), or if no one can remember to whom the personalty in certain *tanket*s on infrequently cultivated land belongs, then the enclosed land is treated as unclaimed clan land, to be cleared and claimed by any member of the clan who wishes. The total land unclaimed, either because it has never been claimed or because claims have been forgotten, comprises, typically, almost one-half of the three square miles of clan territory. It is composed mainly of moss forest, but includes some of the lower *kunai*-covered slopes and marshy areas.

The boundaries of the land over which the clan has trusteeship rights are of two kinds. Natural landmarks such as streams or mountain ridges are used where appropriate—usually in areas of 'unclaimed' land. Where land is cultivated, the boundaries of clan land are the *tanket*s marking the boundaries of lineage strips. These *tanket*s do not form continuous straight lines, and pockets of land belonging to one clan may be found within the boundaries of another. Exaggerated claims are made to any outsider about the extent of clan territory, but closer inquiry establishes generally agreed answers. The natural boundaries have either been present 'since the ancestors emerged from the ground', and the myths are widely known, or they were demarcated by specific culture heroes whose relative priority in time is ignored by natives when making claims, but this can usually be established by the outsider. Thus Feramana clan of Emenyo tribe had very general boundaries established when its ancestors emerged from the ground itself. Later a legendary hero from Komunku tribe assisted Feramana clan when they were fighting their southern neighbours, and he was given land to the north of Feramana. He himself planted the *tanket*s now forming the boundary between the immigrant Rofafogu clan of Komunku tribe and Feramana clan. Feramana clansmen will say with a wide sweep of their arms, 'All of the valley is ours'; Rofafogu clansmen will say, 'When Wire was alive we were the guardians of all this valley'. Both have some truth on their side.

The boundaries are spoken of as being immutable. In 1953, however, under Government pressure a few small exchanges of land were made to straighten out clan boundaries. These followed discussion with both assembled clans, and show that, even if boundaries were not, in fact, immutable in pre-contact times, alienation of clan land could only take place with the consent of the whole clan. The natives do not consider the areas of land the Government has taken over for Rest Houses to be alienated. *Tanket*s on the land are still maintained as individual personalty, and, in my own experience, Europeans living there are considered as visitors to the clan (if the visit is short) or as adopted members of the clan on whose land their house is built. Thus, early in my stay I was once given 'compensation' after I cut my own finger. I was told that as a visitor my blood had been spilt on clan land, so the clan was responsible. Later, I became *Emenyo we rafa* (Emenyo red man)—a member of Antomona clan—or *Fira merafo* (father of the land called Pira). In other words, land is not usually alienated from the clan; new occupants are absorbed into the clan in terms of the land they are living upon.

The only case of outright alienation known to me occurred in 1953. The Government made a payment to the appointed headman of one clan of Namfayufa tribe and took over some land for clearing and levelling as an emergency landing ground. I left the area before the work of levelling was completed, but at that time the headman had distributed half of the payment to the lineages with trustee rights to strips of the land, and had retained half for himself. This excited no criticism, which I take as showing that natives considered the division equitable and that the lineage trusteeship rights constitute one-half of the total rights, and the clan trusteeship rights the other half. The appointed headman, as the representative of the clan, would appear to be trusted to use for the benefit of the whole clan the money received by the clan in exchange for its rights. A further insight into native property concepts is given by this same case. The Government paid a separate sum for the trees on the land, which had to be cut down. This sum was included in the distribution with the amount for the land itself, indicating, perhaps, that individuals' personalty rights to trees become null if they lose all trusteeship rights to the land on which the trees are growing (cf. p. 63).

That there is a balance between clan and lineage rights is also illustrated when a clan decides to move its village to a new site on its own territory. The strips of land on the new site may be owned by a small number of lineages, but these lineages cannot refuse to permit their land to be built upon by members of lineages not owning land. No benefits accrue to the lineage trustees, or to the men owning *tankets* on the land, although the *tankets* must not be removed, and the lineage rights persist when the village site is next moved. So, too, when a ward group decides to make a large garden on a particular area, no lineage with land in that area can refuse to let its land be used. In short, lineage trusteeship rights enable the lineage to over-ride individuals who wish to exercise their clan trusteeship rights to usufruct; they do not permit a lineage to over-ride a larger group wishing to exercise its clan rights.

An individual may also have some trusteeship rights by virtue of his membership of the tribe whose name is used to describe the land. He may ask permission to hunt, to gather wild produce, or to settle on such land, and may expect to receive permission unless sufficient cause can be shown why he should not. The right to hunt is the one most commonly exercised. On one occasion a wild pig had broken into some gardens of Emenyo tribe, and was hunted on to land belonging to Waifo clan of Komunku. When the pig entered Komunku land, some Komunku men who had been watching took up the hunt while the Emenyo men retired. When the pig was killed it was divided among the Komunku men of Waifo clan together with a man from a distant Komunku clan who had been visiting his Emenyo affines. The Emenyo men were excluded as not belonging to the same tribe.

The right to settle on tribal land is infrequently exercised, since clans have their own territories and individuals rarely wish to leave their own clans. Once, apparently about fifty years ago, two southern clans of Komunku tribe decided to move to land nearer the ancestral Komunku home in the north. They moved to unclaimed land, the estate of a third Komunku clan, which not only permitted the move but also helped in building new villages.

The importance of these 'tribal' rights is mainly seen in the reaction to attempts by members of other tribes to hunt or gather produce on tribal land. When some Emenyo men passing through

Yankariti (a Dene tribe) picked up some brushwood to make a fire they were attacked and forced to pay compensation. When men of the Dene tribe of Mami cut timber and shot two birds of paradise in the Komunku moss forest, an ambush was laid to kill the offenders if they returned.

Outside his tribal area a man has no property rights, and his use of 'foreign' land is by consent and not by right. A man may ask his mother's brother for permission to build a pig house on his land, if his own tribal land is worm infested or infected with anthrax. Such permission is commonly granted as a favour, but only to a single individual. In one case I witnessed, a second 'sister's' son from the same foreign clan asked for permission to build and was refused. The owning clan said, 'Our land is better than theirs; soon they will all be coming and taking our land'. On the other hand, similar hospitality is commonly given to whole clans driven out of their own territory in warfare, but when the exiles return to their own land after making peace, they give their hosts pigs as a mark of their thanks.

The term *merafo*, or 'trustee', can thus be seen to refer to several sets of rights all concerned with the same piece of land yet all vested in groupings of different size. Since the same term is used for all types of right, one must understand the context of a conversation in order to know which ones are referred to in any one instance. Thus to say to a member of a different tribe, 'The land is mine' need imply only that one has tribal rights to hunt and gather wild produce (although one may have other rights in addition). To say the same to a member of another clan of one's own tribe need imply only that one has clan rights to usufruct. If speaking to a member of a different ward group of one's own clan, one implies merely that a lineage of one's own ward group has lineage rights of exclusion. To say the same to a member of a different lineage of the same ward group implies that one's own lineage has the rights of exclusion, in addition to all the other clan and tribal rights which both speaker and hearer have in common. To designate further rights, one must say, 'It is my *rono*', 'They are my *firinka*', or 'These are my wife's *minkuri* (growing crops)'. In short, 'The land is mine' implies that the speaker has more trusteeship rights to it than the listener, because, although they both may belong to a group which has some trusteeship rights to the land, the speaker belongs to a sub-group different from the listener's, and his sub-group has additional trusteeship rights.

Which trusteeship rights are referred to when two people, who have equal (or no) rights to a strip of land, are talking about the ownership of it, are similarly determined. The men will refer to those rights which neither of them possess, but which are vested in the largest sub-grouping to which neither of them belong. Thus if I (considered either as an outsider, or as a member of Emenyo tribe) was talking with an Emenyo man about land within the Komunku tribal boundaries, he would only tell me that the land was Komunku's. We were alike in having no tribal rights, so he referred to the largest group (i.e. the tribe) having rights which neither of us had. If two men of Feramana clan of Emenyo tribe talk about Emenyo tribal land not within their own clan boundaries, they will refer to it as belonging to Antomona clan, or possibly nowadays as belonging to the Government-appointed head-man of Antomona village. If I, as a member of Antomona clan, Emenyo tribe, asked a fellow clan-mate about land within the clan boundaries, I would be told the name of the head of the lineage which had the rights of exclusion, or possibly the name of his men's house.

In short, the system of land tenure is of the kind common in segmentary societies. An individual has different rights by virtue of his membership in various groupings, hierarchically arranged in order of increasing size. The totality of rights is of the kind called 'overlapping stewardship' (Sahlins 1958: 148). Which level of grouping, and thus which set of rights, is being referred to at any one moment changes in accordance with the relations between speaker and listener—a source of confusion for the outsider, but perfectly clear to anyone who has mastered the principles on which the groupings are arranged.

Inheritance of rights has already been described incidentally. *Amfonka* rights to personalty either lapse at the death of the owner when property is destroyed, or they are transferred absolutely, usually to the eldest son. An old man may transfer his rights before his death, and then retire to 'sit idly in the sun'. A father may tacitly transfer rights when he 'shows his son the marks (*firinka*)' when they clear land together, and the son publicly assumes the rights when he makes presentations to the mourners at his father's funeral. *Merafo* or trusteeship rights to an estate are not, strictly speaking, inherited. Rather, whoever takes over the 'social personality' (cf. Nadel 1951:97) of the dead man succeeds to them. Thus if a lineage head dies the trusteeship rights vested in the lineage remain in the lineage, and they will now be referred to as belonging not to the dead man but to his successor.

One deliberate omission in the catalogue of objects which are owned should be noted. No mention has been made of the ownership of cooked food. Growing crops (*minkuri*) are the personalty of the individual woman (or man in the case of 'male crops') who planted them. But when the crops are harvested the concepts of ownership no longer seem to apply. When I inquired about the *merafo* or *amfonka* of cooked food I was met with puzzlement and was told 'They are things of no account' (*Faivya neta ne*). The only answer I received connecting individuals with harvested vegetables occurred when I asked about small piles of uncooked produce, brought by individual women and proudly displayed at a small First Fruits ceremony. 'They are hers. She looked after them' was the reply. 'Looking after' (*hentaiye*) is exactly what a *merafo* does to land. I interpret this as meaning that it is only while crops are growing that they constitute true personalty. Once harvested, they are part of an estate over which all members of the clan or tribe have some rights, but an individual can claim special rights little different from personalty rights while using them as evidence of his industry as a gardener. The importance of the clan trusteeship rights in the distribution of food will be discussed in the next section.

The expression, 'things of no account' (*faivya neta*) requires closer consideration, however. *Faivya* (like the pidgin term *nating*) can mean 'nothing, of no importance, useless'; *neta* means 'thing, something', and the whole expression can be used as a deprecatory remark, 'Think nothing of it'. In the context of property concepts, however, the expression can be contrasted with two other terms, *neta* 'things' and *kevora neta* 'small things'. *Neta* refers to shell ornaments, plumes, etc., axes and pigs; *kevora neta* to baskets of nuts, gourds of oil, cakes of salt, tobacco, and small articles of clothing. All these articles are owned by individuals as personalty and will be discussed more fully later. On the other hand, crops other than nuts and oil do not constitute personalty, are not owned by individuals, and are classified as 'nothing things'. Like land they are far from useless; rather, they are so essential that good reason must be shown before any clan-mate can be deprived of them. The important thing is that the giving of them is not a matter for accounting. In this sense they are 'things of no account'. The giving of them is termed *umaiye*—'to help'—as is the giving of labour. Like the giving of help with work, giving food constitutes part of the obligations of any clansman, and sets up no new obligations for making a return. No accounts are kept of the amount of food given, and only persistent refusal to share food and persistent acceptance of food from others without making any return can put a person beyond the limits of obligation.

Now it is possible to consider the importance of the Siane property concepts in organizing and maintaining the system of production. At first sight, the system of individual, lineage, clan, and tribal rights to food and land might seem needlessly complex, since any individual at any one time may obtain the food and land he needs by using someone else's. So, too, with personalty: a man can always borrow tools, ornaments, or pigs from a clan-mate. In short, to be the *merafo* or the *amfonka* of property adds little to the use one can make of the property, over and above what *any* member of the clan can make. This appears to be associated with the fact that there is no shortage of land or food, so that all people can be ensured free access to whatever they need of these commodities. Yet the existence of more specific rights does allow the individual to obtain two kinds of reward from his activities—by his labour he can create for himself *amfonka* rights to personalty, and so can demonstrate to others the effectiveness of his labour by the display of his personalty, or he can use his personalty to satisfy whatever whim he wishes to; by the diligent use of his *merafo* rights, he can put himself in a position to 'help' other people by feeding them or giving them plots of land for cultivation, and so he can obtain a reputation for fulfilling clan obligations and for being a responsible member of the community. The recognition of his property rights by others ensures that his labour will not be wasted to him (he cannot be driven off a plot of land until his use is terminated), and that his 'help' will be publicly known (for example, his permission must be asked before his land is used).

For the society at large the property rights do more. In the first place, the involvement of a large group of persons—a clan or tribe—in the control of property ensures that the property will not be dissipated through the actions of any single individual—no land can be alienated without group consent, and no food is wasted if many people are present to eat it. (This aspect of property rights, considered in reference to the preservation of capital accumulations, will be discussed again later.) In the second place, the rights also apportion to a smaller number of individuals the responsibility for maintaining the usefulness of the property. It is up to the individual lineage, for example, in the person either of the lineage head or of the individual *firinka amfonka,* to see that land is not returned to cultivation before it is fully regenerated, by refusing permission for others to use the land. In the third place, the trusteeship concept justifies an individual calling upon others, who are also trustees, to help him work, and it also designates which individuals shall routinely initiate new work. In brief, property rights in Siane are not an allocation of objects to persons so that the persons gain power or importance through possessing objects, but are rules allocating people to objects so that those objects are not wasted or dispersed, are used to the maximum extent compatible with the labour supply, are conserved carefully, and have their periods of use organized in a regular manner.

The Distribution of Food

The distribution of food has been described in outline in previous sections. Women harvest crops, cook the food, and take it to their husbands in the evening. The men share the food with their sons and return the surplus to the women. Some of the complexities of the process of distribution have been indicated in the discussion of women's cooking groups, which share the labour and enable women to provide for their husbands when they are unable to cook themselves.

Further complexity occurs after husbands have received food from their wives. Each husband places the food he has received in a heap in front of him and is soon surrounded by his sons and lineage mates. Before they eat, however, he gives some food to all other men who are present in the men's house clearing. If more men come in while eating is in progress they receive food too. Only then do the husband's lineage mates receive portions or take sweet potatoes from the general heap. Since men of only one ward group are normally present, food is primarily distributed within the ward group, but no distinction is made and men of other wards or clans are given food if they are present. As the Siane say, 'If they saw us eating and did not eat, they would feel badly'. Food is given with the invitation, '*Umutoko no*!' (eat what is given as 'help', which sets up no new obligation), and to be known as 'a man who says *Umutoko no*!' is to have a reputation for generosity.

The distribution ensures that food supplies are evenly distributed and that no man of the clan need ever be without food, even if he has no wife to bring him any. Despite this, the one permanent widower in my own village resented any dependence on 'handouts', and avoided the men's house during meal times, cooking and eating his own food elsewhere. The material significance of the food given to outsiders is negligible, since the quantities are small and normally the pattern of visiting is random.[15] As much food is given to visitors as is received by clansmen when visiting others.

More materially significant is the feeding of guests at ceremonials,

---

[15] Some effects of a non-random pattern of visiting are discussed in ch. 6, in connection with the effects of wage-labour for Europeans.

since these number up to two hundred individuals and always come from other villages. Although the random pattern of ceremonial visiting means that each clan visits as often as it is visited, the amount of food needed is large. Yet, as has been described, ceremonials are always corporate affairs at which one *group* entertains another *group*. In other words, if a clan-village entertains another clan-village, all fifty wives of the host clan together collect enough to feed four hundred people instead of the normal two hundred. Since people eat about twice as much at a feast as they do on a normal day, this means that four times the daily amount of food is eaten, and each woman has to bring back from the gardens four times what she normally does. She does not do other garden work on such a day, but returns home at noon and cooks the food. At about 3 p.m. all women carry food to the men's house, where it is distributed freely to all guests. The regular system of production and distribution can cope with a temporary fourfold increase in consumption without undue strain.

At Pig Feasts the ceremonies last a week or more, and the village population is at least doubled for this period. Food supplies are made more accessible by the planting of communal seven-acre gardens close to the village during the preceding six months, so that women do not have to walk far to obtain food. Food is cooked at an early hour and is either retained at the women's houses and the women proffer it to anyone who cares to take it as they pass by, or is ceremonially presented to dancers and other guests. There are intervals of a day between the major dances, which give women a chance to obtain food from more distant gardens if need be, but in general there is little concern with vegetable foods at such a time. The existing distributive system comes near to chaos, but the superfluity of pork (the distribution of which will be discussed later) more than makes up for this.

An entirely different form of distributing vegetable crops occurs in First Fruits ceremonies, in the ceremonies when large gardens revert to bush, and in the presentation of food to the clan of the groom a week after a bride has gone in marriage. On such occasions vegetables are given away to other clans in an uncooked state, and the bulk of them are the relatively storable crops of yams, taro, bananas, and sugar cane. The quantities involved amount to about three thousand pounds for each ward group in the first two ceremonies (or about five tons for each village), and about fifteen hundred pounds for the presentation 'to the bride'.

For the first two ceremonies the food is collected for several days before its final distribution, and is stored near the women's houses.

Women appreciate comments about the crops they have raised, but men appear to ignore the preparations. On the day of the ceremonies the women carry the crops into the men's house clearing, where everything is piled on the ground, or, in the case of a ceremony at the abandonment of a garden, piled by the men on to a thirty-foot structure of poles. The mass of food is then handed over amidst speeches by the *bosboi* of the host men's house to the *bosboi* of the guest men's house. The presentation is greeted with cheers of '*Mika mika e-e-e-e* (Land, land)'. When food is presented 'to a bride', although the quantities are less and do not need to be collected over a period, the vegetables are carried in procession, uncooked, and are handed over amidst formal speeches.

It is clear that these forms of distribution do not compare with the normal pattern of distribution of subsistence commodities. Some of these anomalies will be discussed more fully later. While the rest of the system of food production and distribution is geared to providing a sufficiency for all members of a clan, plus a margin for entertainment, these are occasions on which there is a planned surplus. The surplus is disposed of, as far as the producers are concerned, by giving it away uncooked. In terms of the previous discussion of property rights to food, what is being given away is not unaccountable cooked food, but objects of personalty which serve mainly to demonstrate the productivity of the clan's land and labour. It is fitting that the receiving clans compliment the land with their shouts and their hosts with their speeches.

After the food has been received by the guests, they themselves distribute it further, but they now use it to express clan obligations to 'help'. Food brought 'to a bride' is distributed by the *bosboi* who received it to the wives of men who 'helped' the groom in making his bride-price payment. Like food given to a work group, it does not discharge obligations, but serves as an acknowledgment of their existence. Food received at a First Fruits ceremony is not so easily disposed of, in view of its quantity, but is taken by men of the receiving clan, accompanied by their wives, to their married sisters in other villages. In this way as many as ten villages may share in consuming the food, and ten thousand pounds of food is soon eaten by 2,000 people. The ultimate source of the food is known, so that the original producers gain renown, while the receiving clans affirm their clan ties with their sisters.

Consumption

Food seems to be consumed in Siane at all times. Men eat in the early morning, while walking to the gardens, during work when they eat snacks or 'drinks', in the afternoon when their wives bring food to the men's houses, and in the evening until the last man home has received food. To determine the quantities consumed is difficult. Direct observation of how much is eaten by individuals throughout a day is impracticable; direct calculation of the crop yield from a single garden is impossible, since crops are gathered daily in small amounts and are not stored. The largest amounts of food are collected together while they are being cooked every evening, and these can be directly estimated. To these figures can be added approximate amounts for quantities of food eaten at other times to give an estimate of total daily consumption by a village.

I made my estimates of food cooked in the village on five evenings during one month, fairly soon after a new garden had begun yielding. My impression was that the timing did not affect the figures considerably, except that at a later stage in garden growth the composition of the 'green vegetables' would have varied. There would have been more *kumu* or green vegetables, and less *pitpit* and beans. My figures were based on considerable experience of estimating (and checking my estimates with a spring balance), since I bought large quantities of vegetables every day for my own household use. If anything, my figures are low since they are based only on what I saw. The average amount cooked each evening was:

    270 lb. sweet potatoes
     30 lb. maize
     20 lb. taro and yams
     90 lb. green vegetables (45 lb. *pitpit,* 35 lb. *kumu*
               and 10 lb. beans)
     10 lb. cucumbers
    small amounts of pandanus nuts

This represents what is consumed on a typical evening by people resident in the village, about eighty-five adults and fifty-six children. If children are assumed to eat half what an adult eats, this represents 113 'average adults', each of whom on an unfestive evening consumes:

    2·50 lb. sweet potatoes
     ·26 lb. maize
     ·17 lb. taro or yams
     ·80 lb. green vegetables
     ·09 lb. cucumbers and a few nuts

In addition, an adult eats during the day about another pound and a half of sweet potatoes for breakfast, and about half a pound of cucumbers and two pounds of sugar cane as 'drinks'. On festive occasions he eats twice as much, and since individuals are guests or hosts at a rite of passage about once every three weeks, and attend Pig Feasts for about three weeks every three years, the 'un-festive' figures should be increased by one-twentieth to give overall figures. Consumption of yams, taro and sugar cane is increased by the amounts received at First Fruits or garden abandonment ceremonies. These amounts equal the amounts given away, or about 10,000 pounds per village of sugar cane and of yam-taro—that is, about ·16 pounds per average adult per day. On festive occasions meat is eaten also—the amount obtained from hunting or killing chickens on other occasions is insignificant. Pork is distributed by a complex system which will be described later; suffice to say here that all clan members share equally in what the clan receives corporately. In one year I counted that a single clan-village re-ceived 15 pigs from three weddings, 10 pigs from five funerals, 5 pigs from other rites of passage, 3 pigs at peacemakings, and 4 in sickness-curing ceremonies—a total of 37 pigs. No Pig Feasts occurred nearby during the year, but between 150 and 200 pigs were killed at feasts I witnessed. Presumably each clan receives during a three-year period about the number of pigs it kills, or an average of about 60 pigs a year. From the figures given it will be seen that pork is eaten in large quantities at some periods and not at all at others, with orgiastic eating at Pig Feasts. Converted to a daily figure, however, about 100 pigs per annum, each giving a hundred-weight of meat, means that the average adult eats about ·17 pounds of meat daily.

My best estimate of food consumption per adult per day, after totalling these figures, would then be:

4·20 lb. sweet potato	1,890	calories
·25 lb. maize	105	„
·33 lb. yams or taro	135	„
·87 lb. green vegetable	90	„
·66 lb. cucumber	31	„
2·20 lb. sugar cane (say 2·2 oz. sugar)	305	„
·17 lb. pork ⎫ a few nuts ⎭	371	„
Total	2,927	„

The calorie estimates are based on Chatfield (1947). The total of almost 3,000 calories is more than sufficient to maintain health in men weighing ten stones, which is about the average for Siane men. Siane women weigh less. In terms of protein (estimated at 1·77 ounces per day) and fats the diet is possibly somewhat deficient. Since the general method of food distribution ensures that all individuals obtain equal shares, and since periods of great physical activity generally coincide with times of high food consumption, the problem of food-getting must be considered solved in Siane.

Productivity

Harvesting methods in Siane make it impossible to obtain any direct estimate of the yield obtained from any particular piece of land, but an indirect estimate can be made on the basis of the consumption figures. Over a period of eighteen months a village of 200 (men, women, and children) consumes about the following quantities of food:

		Rate of Production (tons per acre)
166	tons of sweet potatoes	4·2
12	tons of maize	·3
14	tons of taro or yams	·4
35	tons of green vegetables	·9
25	tons of cucumbers	·6
90	tons of sugar cane	2·25

The figures for production per acre are obtained by dividing the total production by 40. At any one time a clan-village has under cultivation four large gardens, each about 7 acres, and about fifty small lineage gardens, each about a quarter of an acre, a total of about 40 acres. Each garden produces over a period of eighteen months, hence the taking of this period in calculating total production. I have no figures for other New Guinea native agriculturalists, but these figures may be compared with the yields obtained by Schindler (1952 : 306) at the Government Agricultural Experimental Station, Aiyura. Using the best techniques (but no additional fertilizer), he obtained eight tons of sweet potatoes and one ton of maize per acre. In comparing these figures it must be borne in mind that *all* the above crops are grown from the same acre in Siane, while the experimental yields appear to be based on single-crop agriculture. The Siane use of land might also be compared with the use made of rice land in South-East Asia, where it is rare to find an acre of cultivated land providing all the food for as many as five people—corresponding to a population density of 3,200 per square mile where all land is cultivated. In short, Siane agriculture is not only effective, it is efficient.

Summary

Siane subsistence activities consist of exploiting a difficult terrain in an agricultural cycle that involves eighteen months of cultivation of cleared plots of land, followed by fifteen years of fallow under casuarina trees. There is a sexual division of labour, men doing work requiring the use of axes, while women do other routine tasks. The clan is the largest unit working together for subsistence tasks, but smaller groups of thirty or ten men are the most common groups within which there is specialization of tasks. Except for some small token help from outside, the clan is a self-sufficient productive unit.

Labour is made available to all clan members by the existence of clan obligations to help. The system of land tenure ensures that all clan members have free access to it, that specific people are designated for the entrepreneurial tasks, and that a worker is guaranteed the right to reap the product of his labour. The food that is produced is then distributed freely throughout the clan as part of the same system of clan obligations; it is *'faivya neta'*, 'a thing of which no account is kept'. The other factors of production, tools and houses, are owned absolutely by individuals as *neta* or 'things'. The part they play in the total economic system will be dealt with separately.

The total subsistence system in Siane could generally be described as a number of self-sufficient clans, each one working independently, and each one organized to provide its members with equal access to both the factors and the products of production.

The exceptions to this general picture must be noted. They include the absolute individual ownership, not only of tools, but of ornaments and some articles of food such as nuts, *roi*, salt, and tobacco, of *neta* and *kevora neta*. They also include the occasional presentation of large quantities of uncooked food to persons who are not members of the clan. Pigs, which might be regarded as subsistence commodities, have not been discussed except to indicate the activities performed in their raising, the concepts of ownership applicable to them, and the way in which their meat, when it is received from other clans, forms part of the diet. The reason why these exceptions constitute anomalies will appear later.

It remains to consider to what extent these activities are 'economic', or based on a rational calculation of quantities so that scarce resources are allocated between competing ends. The choice of how to meet certain ends appears to be made on 'technological' grounds (cf. Weber 1947:160). Clothing is not felt to be necessary for warmth during the day, but is worn for modesty or decoration; little time is spent in its manufacture. Men choose not to venture out in the rain, while women put their pandanus sleeping mats over their heads. At night when it is cold few people go out. Houses, built with easily available resources, have low roofs and thickly insulated walls to solve the problems of warmth at night and serve as shelter generally, but need only easily available resources. The indoor fires keep down the nuisance of flies and (non-malarial) mosquitoes, while ventilation is adequate for people sleeping only on mats. Sanitation is minimal, but the bush is large and requires fertilizing.

Certain competition between ends is illustrated in these choices, however. More lasting and healthier houses could be built, but to do so would then necessitate the making of warmer clothing or the provision of vast supplies of firewood, and this would mean diverting labour from satisfying other ends. To grow more storable vegetables would add to the women's comfort by obviating frequent trips to the gardens, but would increase the men's work in the cutting of numbers of yam poles, and the new crops might not prevent erosion, as sweet potatoes do. To use warmer clothing might save time now lost from work by colds, but the frequent rains would also present drying problems. The building of larger communal houses in the villages might reduce the labour of building numbers of small houses, but concentrating larger numbers of people together would mean a greater separation between villages and longer journeys to gardens at the edge of clan territories. However, the choice between competing ends in these cases seems to be most frequently made, not on the basis of calculation, but on traditional grounds (cf. Weber 1947:117). These are the ways the Siane have always done things, and the individual has little freedom.

More obvious examples of rational calculation are evident in the way in which production is planned to provide over a long period both a fixed quantity of food plus a margin for entertainment and occasionally a huge surplus for distribution. Gardens of specific size are made for specific purposes, and the competing ends of convenience in cultivating nearby gardens and maintaining the fertility of the soil are explicitly weighed against one another. It might even be argued that the balance between population and available resources is the result of conscious planning. I have shown how forty cultivated acres support 200 people. Perhaps another twenty acres are under fruit trees. To maintain the fertility of forty acres,

400 must lie fallow. Even if a clan area of three square miles is half covered by unworkable moss forest, rocks, swamps and precipices (as appears likely from my own surveys), it contains more than twice the minimum agricultural acreage needed. The tribe of Aranko, however, has only some sixteen square miles of exceptionally precipitous land to support seven clans. In 1953 there were signs that the Aranko men recognized this as about the maximum population density possible; some were migrating to other tribes, saying that lineage strips at home were too small and not numerous enough.

In short, there is some competition between the various obvious ends served by the subsistence activities, and there is also some rational calculation in terms of quantities, which, as I have tried to show, leads to scarce resources being allocated to give satisfaction of some competing ends. There is an 'economic' aspect to these activities, although many decisions are made on traditional or technological grounds. Most competition between ends, however, occurs not between those subserved only by subsistence activities, but between those subserved by subsistence activities and those subserved by other activities. The discussion of this competition must await the description of the other activities.

2. Luxury Activities

Luxury activities were tentatively defined at the beginning of the chapter as the production, distribution, and consumption of certain luxury commodities. They involve excitement and pleasure, but are not usually public events involving whole clans. The commodities are owned as personalty by individual *amfonka,* and are referred to as *kevora neta.*

The most common luxury commodities are tobacco, *roi* palm-oil, pandanus nuts, and salt. Other articles such as snake-skins for drums, fine stone for axe blades, palm wood for spears, and nowadays some European articles, are treated in the same fashion. Tobacco grows best in western Siane, and in Chimbu beyond the Erimbari ridge, but some is grown everywhere. *Roi* is grown principally in the marshy valleys to the south of Siane; pandanus nuts grow best in the higher northern mountains, but small amounts of both are grown in most villages. Native salt is extracted from salt springs outside the Siane area, to the south and west,[16] although small quantities can be produced everywhere by a process, known

---

[16] There were no salt springs within Siane territory, and I shall not describe the process of purification here. For a description which tallies closely with that given by Siane informants, see Vial (1938:16).

to a few specialists, of burning grasses and leaching out salt from the ash. Axe stone comes from the north-east, near Korefa tribe; snake-skins and black palm-wood come from the far south. The commodities are thus not uniformly distributed over the Siane area, and to some extent their distributions are complementary.

Tobacco is grown inside villages, in the areas around each woman's house. Men snip out side shoots from the plants as they pass along the street, and the plants, when fully grown, are cut and hung up inside the men's house beside the men's beds. As soon as the leaves turn brown they are used for cigarettes, except sometimes in western Siane, where the leaves are stripped off singly and packaged in bundles. Here men will commonly give a bundle of tobacco to a sister's son when he departs after a visit.

When *roi* fruits are ripe they are composed of hundreds of small red fruitlets, adhering to a central core. The fruits are cut from the trees, wrapped and carried to the village, and the fruitlets are scraped off on to banana leaves. Carefully folded in the leaves, the bundles are steamed until they form a pulpy mess. This mess is squeezed in bark-cloth to extract a bright red oil, which is stored in gourds or bamboo containers. The residual pulp is eaten as a delicacy.

The small pandanus nuts, each about three inches long and a half-inch in diameter, grow bunched in large spheres which resemble coconuts in appearance. They are harvested in two forms: as large fruits cut from the trees when almost ripe, and as individual nuts gathered after they have dropped ripe to the ground. The large fruits are delicacies which do not keep. They are split in half with an axe, the inside core is roasted over an open fire, and the outside cover is singed off to expose the nuts. Natives carry split fruits with them, cracking off individual nuts and drawing out the kernels, like Europeans eating sweets from a bag. Fully-ripe nuts are collected and dried in the sun for several days (they need to be watched against the rapacity of birds), wrapped in quantities of *kunai*-straw, and tied into bundles with strips of bark and cane. The resulting basket-like containers vary in size and shape. The largest are shaped like cheeses, two feet six inches in radius and eighteen inches high, and hold about forty pounds of nuts. Together with oil gourds, such baskets hang from the rafters of the men's houses, over the owners' beds, out of reach of the mice, which can soon devour forty pounds of nuts.

At the seasonal harvesting of *roi* and nuts the owners of the trees are assisted by their mothers' brothers or sisters' sons, who come for prolonged visits at such times. Their help is reciprocated when the visitor's crop is due. Helpers going to a *roi* harvest take with them quantities of bark-cloth and gourds, but no tools are needed at a nut harvest. Helpers are entertained warmly by their kinsman during their stay, and when each harvest is completed, the owner of the trees gives them presents of large quantities of the crop—two or three gourds of oil, or the same number of bundles of nuts. Since owners of *roi* trees tend to visit kinsmen who own nut trees, from whom they receive nuts, and since the nut-owners later visit the *roi*-owners and receive oil, a system resembling barter can be seen to arise. When natives talk about such harvests, however, they stress the 'help' that is given (*umaiye*), and minimize the exchange of goods.

Although mothers' brothers and sisters' sons form the bulk of the harvest help, many men go to help people whom they call '*emona we*'. Literally, this term means 'my male sister', and it is often translated into pidgin as *pren* ('friend'). It can be applied to a sister's husband, a wife's brother, a daughter's husband's father, a son's wife's father, or to more distantly related persons whom one wishes to acknowledge as kin. Such a relationship can be set up by a betrothal of children, when the fathers call each other *emona we* since they are potentially son's-wife's-father and daughter's-husband's-father to each other. Generally it is a nebulous relationship whose importance consists chiefly in the exchange of goods and services it facilitates. A man often has one *emona we* in each area where an out-of-the-way commodity like python skins is obtainable.

One other form of luxury-harvest help must be noted. Some clans maintain tenuous kin relationships with other clans, based on legends of the migration of those clans to distant areas. Once a year, when the luxury crop of one clan is ready, the other clan comes to help 'their brothers'. Parties of about thirty men, fifteen women and fifteen children walk for about two days to the village of their 'kinsmen', where each individual is entertained by a 'friend' in the host village. After a week's work harvesting, the helpers are given presents of the crop before their return home. Each individual host makes a present to his particular guest, but all the presents are pooled. One of the host *bosboi*s takes up each present from the pile and calls the name of its recipient, who comes to collect the present before the assembled hosts and guests. This form of 'presentation' is termed *gimaiye*; the differences between it and 'giving' (*umaiye*) will be discussed later. When the presentations are over, the helpers depart. Their help is reciprocated when their own luxury crops are ripe and when they can reciprocate with presents of a different crop.

Such clan 'trade-partnerships' connected, for example, one southern Komunku clan and an Asaro clan from which the Komunku clan was reputedly a migrant offshoot. In 1953 the Komunku clan gave nuts and *roi* oil, and received European trade goods, but in earlier times they had received stone for axes. An Emenyo clan had relatives who, legend said, had split off and migrated south of the Wahgi, into what was in 1953 uncontrolled territory. Emenyo received *roi* oil and black palm-wood, and gave nuts and, in 1953, steel axes and coloured handkerchiefs to the uncontacted southerners.

Salt is not produced in Siane and I saw no expeditions to obtain any. Informants described the way a few 'big men' of a clan wishing to obtain salt have 'friend' relationships with 'big men' in distant salt-producing villages. They collect parties of about ten men, and, carrying several pigs strapped to poles, walk to the producers' village, where the pigs are killed and there is great festivity and much entertaining. The guests do no work (the site of the spring is a closely guarded secret), but on their departure are presented with cakes of salt. Each producing village makes cakes of a distinctive shape, but generally these are circular, about ten inches in diameter and three inches thick, with a depression in the middle. They are wrapped in pandanus leaves, and are stored and carried in loose, basket-like containers, eighteen inches in diameter and six inches thick. Return visits by salt producers were reported to occur occasionally, but were never as frequent as the visits of salt consumers.

Several things appear to the observer to indicate that a simple buying and selling relationship exists here. There appears to be a relatively fixed equivalence of one salt cake given for each pig killed;[17] only widely separated clans are involved, and they only relate to one another when a transaction takes place; the return visits of salt producers are rare. Yet Siane informants insist on the permanence of the relationship, the festivity of the visitors being entertained by killing pigs (omitting until challenged to mention that the guests provide the pigs), and the generosity of the hosts in giving salt to their friends. It takes close questioning to estab-

[17] The present tense is used to indicate that such exchanges still take place, despite the introduction of European salt. Native salt is said to 'bite' more than European salt (it is quite impure), and is needed to make meat 'hot' in certain religious ceremonies when it is chewed with ginger roots and spat over the meat.

lish the approximate equivalence of the presentations made and the fact that the relationship is relatively impermanent. In native theory the exchange fits the normal pattern of 'exchanges between friends'.

Distribution of tobacco, nuts, oil and, in theory, salt is thus normally conducted by individuals making presentations to other individuals who have come to visit and help them at their work. Even visitors who do not come to help with work are always given small presents on their departure—a woven cane armband, a small shell trinket, or some tobacco, for example. Such presents indicate the donor's sorrow at the departure of his friends and are given freely as *umaiye,* thereby implying that they are tokens of the lasting and diffuse obligations between friends, and need not be strictly accounted for. There is, however, more formality between 'friends' than there is between fellow clansmen, and a donor will often give a short speech before giving by *umaiye* to a friend. If more than two individuals are involved, the formality is increased still further until it culminates in the ceremonial presentation made by a *bosboi* to a village 'trade' expedition, where it is no longer termed *umaiye* but *gimaiye.*

Within the village, the reciprocal obligations of helping implied by *umaiye* are maintained by diffuse social sanctions and an ulti- mate threat of ostracism. In the less closely-knit, extra-village 'friend' relationship, reciprocity is maintained more by direct self- interest. Only if visitors return home satisfied will they be generous with their gifts at the host's next visit. Once, after an Emenyo clan had made presentations to a visiting group from the uncontacted south before their departure for home, silence followed the presen- tation instead of a speech of thanks. The awkward silence was broken when one of the hosts gave a length of red cloth to the visiting *bosboi,* who then made his speech. Without speaking the guests made it evident they were dissatisfied with what they had received. The hosts then added to what had been given, rather than risk the loss of their supplies of *roi* oil. In a sense 'bargaining' does occur, but it is not haggling about the exact equivalence of in- dividual items that are exchanged. It is discussion of a more diffuse satisfaction given by a continuing relationship. But the relationship can always be broken, and a new supplier found, if one is really dissatisfied.

Luxury commodities are mainly consumed in the entertainment of visitors. When a visitor arrives he is offered foods such as sugar cane or cucumbers, but he is also offered luxuries like tobacco. He is seated on a clean log and given nuts, and for his evening meal his sweet potatoes are salted, although his host's lineage eats theirs unsalted. On arrival, and again before departure, he is washed with *roi* oil. On special occasions—when parents-in-law visit their daughter's husband, or when mourners arrive coated in clay for a funeral—luxuries are provided in excess of these quantities. Salt is applied 'till their throats bite', and oil is poured over their heads till it drips to the ground.

When a clan is entertaining as a corporate group—at a funeral, for example—there is no previous discussion to bring social pressure on men to contribute to the entertainment. No disapproval attaches to the man who possesses nuts but does not use them at such a time. Even so, many men provide large quantities, although they may belong to a ward group other than the dead man's. They receive no direct return for their contribution to the entertainment, only the satisfaction of increasing the clan's reputation for generosity and of demonstrating their public spirit and concern with the clan's welfare.[18] Every man has some stocks of these commodities, but while some use them to entertain private guests, to gain a reputation for generosity, and to increase the size and frequency of the gifts of luxuries they receive when they visit, others use them for the benefit of the clan.

It is my impression, of which some statistical confirmation will be given later, that the largest stocks of luxuries and the largest contributions of them to entertainments were not those of 'big men', but those of men aged between 30 and 45 who had not achieved success through the normal channels (see Ch. 2).

Not all luxuries are used in entertaining guests. Small amounts are regularly consumed in the course of everyday life. Everyone smokes whenever there is a break in work. When nuts are in season, the roads are littered with shells, thrown away as people nibble their own nuts on their journeys. On special occasions—when youths return from a therapeutic blood-letting, when women complete a menstrual flow, or men successfully settle a legal case—people wash themselves in *roi* oil. Children are frequently washed in oil 'to make their hair grow black', and are often given lumps of salt to eat as titbits. In short, just as one indulges visitors, so can one indulge one's children or, if the occasion warrants, one's self.

In terms of property concepts this is understandable, since these luxuries all constitute personalty to be employed according to the

[18] I found that the easiest way to participate in any ceremony was to make a contribution of the luxury, salt. I became a 'host', took part in discussions, and could move about freely, but I received no direct return for my contribution.

personal choice of their owner. They are also described by the term *kevora neta*—things that *could* be accounted for and are thus not 'things of no account', but that at the same time are not important things for which accounting would be imperative. It will be noted that 'friends' never (with the exception of the salt trade) exchange 'small things' for anything but other 'small things'.

Summary

Luxury activities primarily concern the production, distribution, and consumption of commodities by individuals, and not by groups of people. These commodities are not evenly distributed throughout Siane, and no individual is self-sufficient in them. Instead, kinship or fictive kinship ties are used to obtain what is wanted from other individuals. The system of distribution works, not by a strict accounting system but through self-interest, since individuals wish to keep their friends satisfied and so preserve their relationship. The possibility of changing suppliers makes it almost a system of free market exchanges.

When large groups of men combine to obtain luxuries there is an anomaly in the fact that objects are given, not as informal 'help', but as formal presentations. When the luxury is as scarce as salt, there are two anomalies: pigs are given in exchange for a luxury, when they themselves are not luxuries; and a stricter accounting system is in evidence. The reason for these anomalies will be discussed later.

3. *Gima Activities*

The tentative definition of *gima* activities is that they are public events, involving the handing over in a ritual way of commodities termed '*neta*' or 'things' that are owned as personalty by individuals. I shall call these objects 'valuables'.

Production

Before 1933 valuables consisted in pieces of various types of shell (mainly gold-lip but also some small cowrie, nassa, and other shells), ornamental stone axes, chips of cassowary egg shell sewn on to bark or threaded like beads, necklaces of dogs' teeth, bird-of-paradise plumes, and headdresses of cassowary feathers.

Natives pointed to the north-east as the source of shell, but, until labourers went to the coast, knew nothing of the sea or sea creatures. The ornamental stone axes apparently resembled the so-called Mount Hagen axes, of delicately-ground green stone (cf. Gitlow 1947). I was never shown one, but was told they were extremely

7   Young men do the hard work in housebuilding

8   Older men discuss the size of house posts

9   A bride's mother gives *kevora neta* to the groom's 'mothers'
and sisters

rare in Siane, were not mounted with decorative bindings, but came from the far north-west (cf. Leahy and Crain 1937:148). When I obtained a Mount Hagen axe I was told it was 'just like the good old days' (*'pesin bilong bipo'*). Cassowaries were few in number, being difficult and dangerous to keep, and in 1953 there were three in an area whose human population was 3,000. The supply of their egg shells and plumes was limited accordingly. Entire villages, even in 1953, had only three or four dogs, and since only canine teeth were used for necklaces, each one of which required about 200 teeth, the quantity of necklaces produced was minute. They were, in fact, worth more than other valuables and were treated as heirlooms. Every year three or four birds of paradise might be shot locally, but the plumes, unlike shell or stone, decay from mould, are destroyed by mice, and are damaged by wetness. In short, the production of all these valuables was extremely small, and probably did little more than replace the amounts destroyed through decay, loss, or burial with dead owners.

Pigs are the one valuable that can be produced in any quantities. The male owner first secures the piglets and claims them as personality; and then his wife constantly tends the animals (see p. 62). To start raising pigs a man borrows a young sow either from his father or from another clansman. The young pig is tended by the man's wife (or mother if he has no wife), mates with some boar in the bush, and eventually produces a litter. One piglet is given to the original lender of the pig, and any increment is the property of the man who fetched the litter from the bush. One sow loaned is fully repaid by one sow of any size returned, although the borrower may return more if he chooses. This is normal for loans of pigs both to fellow clansmen and to outsiders.

Thus one unmarried youth, who had obtained a pig when his father died, left the pig with his classificatory father while he went away for indentured labour. During his absence the sow had three litters, each of six piglets. When the youth returned he was told that two of the piglets were his, although they remained in the care of the 'father's' wife. When the classificatory father later killed the original sow for the wedding feast of his own daughter, the youth could do nothing about it, though he did grumble.

Often a man lends a pig to his wife's brother or to his mother's brother, in what might be better regarded as a form of 'farming out'. Anthrax may break out in a pig-owner's village, and if he does not choose to move his entire household to another village until the epidemic is over, he may send some pigs to be looked after in each of several other villages. This obliges his affines or maternal kin to return exactly that number of pigs later on, so that even if all the pigs in his afflicted village are wiped out, he is assured of a certain number of animals from which to breed. Naturally, a man can insure against pig disease by lending pigs before any sickness occurs.

Another reason for 'farming out' is to disguise the number of pigs one owns. If a man keeps many pigs in his own village, he is frequently called upon to contribute pigs to ceremonial payments. Although to do so is prestigeful, many unimportant men in a village prefer to have pigs of their own, available if some urgent need arises. This they can do only by maintaining secrecy about the numbers they own.

Some pigs are farmed out as an almost permanent loan, where both lender and recipient acknowledge the debt, but neither takes any steps towards effecting repayment. Such loans are common between a man and his wife's brother. Then the wife's brother has a pledge that the husband will make the appropriate payments at the birth of children, and will not harm his wife. The husband has an acknowledged claim over the brother's pigs,[19] and, if the wife deserts her husband, her brother may prefer to make her return rather than surrender his pigs. In this way the lending of pigs and the indebtedness involved serve to maintain the existing relationship between the husband, his wife, and her brothers.[20]

It might seem from this description that large numbers of pigs are kept by everyone, some owned personally and others being looked after for other people. In fact, few individuals, except those with new litters of piglets, have more than three pigs in their possession at any one time. A survey of the village in which I lived gave the following numbers of pigs owned by each household head:

5 households had no pigs
14 households had 1 pig
14 households had 2 pigs
10 households had 3 pigs
5 households had 4 pigs
2 had 10 pigs, and one had 11 pigs from recent litters.

[19] This claim is acknowledged because both lender and borrower believe the pig has a soul which, barring accidents, is permanently part of the lender's clan and lineage estates. This soul might cause other pigs to run wild, die, or run to the lender if it, in the body of whatever pig it had been transferred to, were not returned on demand. The parallel with the Maori case discussed by Mauss (1951:8) is striking, but this is a very different form of transaction from that discussed by Mauss.
[20] Compare this with the relationship between farmer and town store in Western Ireland (Arensberg 1937:170), where debts are never fully settled, since this would disrupt the lasting relationship.

Although this number would probably double in the two years before the next Pig Feast, the figures are small. Discreet inquiry among men with one or two pigs elicited the fact that they claimed to have lent ten or more pigs to other groups. They were silent about how many pigs they owed, but it is reasonable to assume that men of other villages had lent as many as they had, and that they owed as many as they had borrowed. In short, the number of *real* pigs in circulation is nowhere near as large as the number of publicly avowed *claims* to pigs (since debts are not publicly acknowledged). The system of lending pigs has thus some similarities with the western banking system, in creating more 'credit' than there is 'currency' in existence; the credit is then used to 'finance' undertakings like ceremonials on a larger scale than would be possible if an individual or group was dependent on its own real resources.

The largest ceremonial, and the ultimate aim of all 'financial' manipulation of pigs, is the Pig Feast, which each group holds every three years. Piglets that are too small to kill at one feast are kept to form a basis for future pig raising and to be in their prime for the next feast. Large pigs are jealously hoarded by using piglets from later litters to repay debts, to provide for unexpected rites of passage, or to create new indebtedness. The announcement ceremony, performed about ten months before a Pig Feast, in effect creates a moratorium on pig dealing. If another group asks for the repayment of a pig, the claim can then be refused by saying 'The pig belongs to the ancestors' and cannot leave the village. A feast-giver tries to obtain more pigs by claiming repayments from other clans, but may be frustrated if another clan announces it is giving a feast. Thus there is much competition about announcing future Pig Feasts. Sometimes it is advantageous to be the first to celebrate in an area and to forestall other clans; it may be best to be last, for then no other clan can refuse to repay debts; sometimes a year's delay may put a clan in the position of being the only celebrants.[21] But although the production and accumulation of pigs is directed towards having the maximum number at one moment in time, the ultimate aim is not to eat them but to distribute all, except a nucleus for future production, to other clans.

[21] This economic, calculating aspect of the deliberations about the timing of Pig Feasts is outweighed in importance for the Siane by the need to initiate a new group of boys and to obtain ancestral blessings. A significant contrast might be made with the somewhat similar Pig Feasts of the Mae and Mount Hagen peoples to the west described by Goodenough (1953) and Vicedom and Tischner (1945), where economic considerations appear to be primary. The Siane ceremonies are primarily affairs involving corporate clans; to the west, the accumulation and distribution of property is on an individual basis.

Inter-clan Distribution

This distribution of pigs is by means of the *gimaiye* ritual already described in connection with village 'trade' visits. The same method is used for ceremonial payments of valuables of all kinds at marriages, at ceremonies for the birth of children, at initiations and other rites of passage, at deaths, at peacemakings and when deaths or thefts are compounded by payments, or at ritual distributions such as those of the Yam Taro ceremonies. One difference from the presentation at trade visits must be noted. At the ceremonial presentation of a valuable, the *bosboi* calls out the name, not of the individual to whom he is presenting it, as in the 'trade' presentation, but of a clan. The *bosboi* of the receiving clan then comes forward to accept the presentation. It is a presentation from one corporate clan, represented by its *bosboi,* to another corporate group, similarly represented (cf. p. 27). Members of the receiving clan claim to know nothing of the individual who provided the presentation (the groom's father at a wedding, the next-of-kin at a funeral); members of the presenting clan claim to know nothing of the individual to whom the valuables are going.

Though the final presentation is corporate, the preceding negotiations within the corporate group are complex. For example, when a marriage is contemplated, the father of the prospective groom opens his pandanus-leaf containers (now often wooden boxes) of valuables inside the men's house, and lays out on display the valuables he wishes to present to the bride's clan. His lineage brothers watch and add many valuables of their own to the bride-price. They discuss what is to be given, and are joined by the *bosboi* of the men's house and other 'big men', who also make contributions before entering the discussion. The display is rearranged after each contribution, and some items may be removed if it is agreed that the payment is too large or that there are too many valuables of one type. In 1953 it was common for 'big men' of other men's houses to contribute and join in the discussion, but in pre-contact times this was extremely rare.

By contributing, people are said to 'help the groom' because he is their 'brother'. 'Help' is given freely, with no formal obligation to return an equivalent. Members of the groom's lineage appeared shocked whenever I suggested that their 'help' might later be repaid, and stressed that no father expected a return from his son, and that brothers were 'one man'. In response to the same suggestion, more distant clan-brothers often said that the groom might later help them, or that he had previously helped them and they were now reciprocating. Reciprocity in helping is in fact usual outside the lineage group, but it is not enforced by direct sanctions, nor is it good taste to mention its existence. Within the lineage, help is given without question, and is mainly from fathers to sons, without reciprocation. All that the fathers receive are the valuables presented by other groups as return payments and part of the presentations given to the clan when daughters marry. They retain control over a son, however, until the son's wife has raised sufficient pigs to repay his obligations to other clansmen and to make contributions to the payments of others.

All men of the men's house see who contributes which article, and remember it for several days. No formal record is kept, however, and the knowledge is soon forgotten except by the contributor and the recipient. But when the total payment is ritually presented (*gimaiye*) to the other clan, a formal record is made by cutting small chips of bamboo as tallies. These tallies are about an inch long, and are called *uma* or 'shoots'. Each tally represents one valuable or pig presented. They are carefully wrapped in a dry leaf, and kept with the private possessions of the man on whose behalf the payment was made. If there is any dispute over the presentation, the tallies are brought out, and the exact content of the presentation is enumerated. With the help of the crowd that gathers on such occasions the contributors to payments of many years ago can be traced.

When a total payment is referred to, it is spoken as being composed of, say, ten *'neta'*. In calculating the total, pigs, shells, and plumes are added together, each one being equivalent to one *neta*. Small luxuries, which are sometimes given at the same time as a presentation, are not included in the total and constitute 'small things' (*kevora neta*), of which no formal account is kept (cf. pp. 89-90).

When a clan has publicly received a presentation, it behooves them to give value for what they have received and to return an equivalent (*uto gimaiye*). Each time one *neta* is returned, one *uma* is removed from the collection of tallies and is put in a separate bundle. When payments are enumerated both bundles are laid out and the occasions of repayment mentioned as the 'returned' tallies are gone through. The bundle of unrequited tallies is called the *mona* ('trunk', or 'root'), and the idiom for repayment is that shoots are cut off, as from a tree, reducing the trunk until at last the root is fully removed. In another sense *mona* can mean 'cause', or the reason for making a payment (as in the transfer of a woman at a wedding), so that to say the *mona* of a bride-price has been repaid means both that there is a balance in the payments of valuables, and that the transfer of the woman has been equitably repaid. Specifically, the bride-price is repaid and the *mona* returned when two children have resulted from the marriage; if the wife then deserts her husband no more *uma* are returnable. The valuables a bride wears at her wedding, which are distributed among her husband's age-mates, are repaid by the care and shelter she receives during married life; the few valuables given to the bride's mother at the end of a wedding are 'to stop the mother's tears', and are repaid by the bride's household services.

If the *mona* is not repaid (if a newly-wedded wife deserts, for example), the valuables originally presented should be returned. This is usually impossible, since payments are normally immediately distributed and used for other payments. In one case I saw, a bride's *yarafo* did not immediately distribute the bride-price, and this was taken as a sign of bad faith, indicating he was intent on wrecking the marriage. Where the identical articles cannot be returned, *neta* to the same number and of equivalent size should be substituted. The 'equivalent size' provision leads to endless discussion. If a small gold-lip shell is offered in place of a large one, it is refused and either a large shell or pig must be substituted or no agreement is reached. An *atana* shell (green-snail or *taribun* in pidgin) can be substituted for a small gold-lip, while various types of feather head-dress equate with a medium-sized pig or a headband of cowrie shells sewn on bark. The variations in size and relative merit form a subject for infinite discussion, but it is possible to equate any valuable with a certain size of pig or gold-lip shell. These commodities form the standard of value, and the generic term for ceremonial payments is *ruruafo*—a combination of *ruru* (a shell) and *yafo* (a pig).[22]

Presentations are made on many occasions (see Chapter 2). At the birth of a child one is made to the brother of the mother, and new *uma* are cut and added to the *uma* of the marriage payment, for accounting purposes. At this time the child's mother's brother hands over valuables as 'gifts' to the child. Though he gives them by *umaiye* 'to the child', they must be reciprocated by the child's father; otherwise, the mother's clan can demand the return of the child to their village. Payments are made only at the birth of the first two children.

At the ceremony at the end of weaning, when a child's hair is cut for the first time, and again when a boy is initiated, another

[22] The term *ruruafo* was first translated to me as 'bride-price', and it is most commonly used in this specific sense. However, it is also used in speech for other payments for which there are specific terms, e.g. *aigavo* for a birth payment. From this I infer that *ruruafo* is a generic term, most commonly used for bride-prices.

exchange of presents takes place, with a balance again going to the clan of the child's mother's brother. At any time during a girl's life, but most commonly when she emerges from seclusion after her first menses, a payment may be made by a non-relative to her father's clan. Such a payment is said to be *homaiye,* or 'given in advance', as part of an eventual marriage payment. When a marriage payment is received by the girl's father's clan, some portion is presented to the clan of her mother.

At funerals the chief mourners are the brother's clan of a woman, and the mother's clan of a man. They arrive bringing 'gifts' to their dead relative, and these 'gifts' must be repaid by presentations from the clan with which the dead person was living. Any mourners, whether related or not, must be compensated for the grief they have displayed, so that, for example, a finger chopped off by a mourner must be repaid by one *neta* presented.

At peace-making ceremonies (see pp. 26-7) a pig is presented for each man killed, while one valuable expiates one affront, or 'loosens one knot'. In addition, a number of voluntary presentations are made and pigs killed. These must be immediately returned in kind if there is to be goodwill after the ceremony.

At the Pig Feasts, the major distribution of pork (according to the set speeches) is to clan sisters who have married into other clans. As is the case with intra-phratry distributions, this pork is said to be *umuto* 'given freely' to the sisters; in practice it is formally presented (*gimito*) to the sisters' husbands as representatives of their clans. Some presentations of pork are made as immediate payment for services rendered in dancing for the ancestors; yet others are the direct return of specific payments. These payments occur when, as the flutes are carried through other clans' villages to invite them to dance at the Feast, individuals in those villages 'give' (*umaiye*) valuables to the ancestors, personified by the flutes. These valuables decorate the *gerua* boards used in the dances, and the givers of the valuables become *emona we* ('friends' or 'male sisters') of the feast-givers. As 'male sisters' they receive pork when female sisters do. Informants clearly recognized their motives and said 'They are hungry for meat; they are buying pigs'. Here it will be noted that the transaction approaches a buyer/seller relationship in its speed, exactness of reciprocity, and lack of permanence, but the form it takes is the usual one of ceremonial presentation.

Less formally, mother's brothers can give valuables to their sister's child whenever they visit him, but the clan of the recipient must make a presentation in return, on pain of being shamed as unable to provide for the child.

Intra-clan Distribution

When a presentation is received by a clan representative, it must then be further distributed among the members of the receiving clan. The presenting clan takes no part in this distribution and pretends to ignore its existence. At a wedding, for example, cooked pigs are received by the *bosboi* of the bride's father's ward group. He sits with the head of the bride's lineage and together they divide the meat into portions; one for each lineage of that ward group, one to each of the other ward groups of the clan, and several for sisters of the clan married into other villages.[23] A few small portions are specifically allotted to individuals who helped with contributions during the ceremony, but the largest portions are given to lineage heads or *bosbois*, who then give pork to individual members of their groups. The distribution is described as 'help' (*umaiye*) and is principally a recognition of clan obligations and only secondarily a recognition of specific obligations incurred when 'help' was received in the past.

When a payment of valuables is received the distribution is conducted similarly, but more is retained by the lineage head, more is given to specific individuals, and less is given in recognition of clan obligations. Thus of one bride-price received in 1953 for a girl of a lineage of Kunturo men's house, Antomona clan, and consisting of fourteen gold-lip shells, four headdresses, one cloth *laplap*, and one pound note, the bride's *yarafo* (lineage 'eldest brother') retained five shells and two headdresses. To four youths, from various men's houses, he gave three shells and one headdress, to the village headman he gave one *laplap* cloth, two lineage heads of Kunturo men's house received two shells, the bride's 'second father' received two shells, one headdress, and one pound, and an 'other father' of the bride, two shells. The shells retained went into the *yarafo*'s father's box of valuables, and were later used for the *yarafo*'s bride-price. The gifts to the headman and to the marriageable youths represent recognition of clan obligations. The gifts to lineage heads were spoken of as 'help', but close questioning elicited the fact that both men had previously 'helped' the bride's father in some way. Both contributed to the *yarafo*'s wedding a month later. Parenthetically it must be remarked that this bride-price is much larger than pre-1933 bride-prices. This inflation will be described later, but there is no reason for believing that the *channels*

---

[23] When I was given pork at distributions it would be given to my 'ward group' and the name of the land on which my house was built would be called out, along with the name of the land on which other men's houses were built.

of distribution have been altered. The proportions of about one-third of a bride-price retained, one-third given away as clan obligations, and one-third to repay specific obligations appear to be typical.

Also typical is the reluctance to admit that gifts, supposedly given as voluntary 'help', are in fact the repayment of specific obligations incurred by receiving 'help' on previous occasions. In theory, 'help' in making ceremonial payments is a clan obligation, as is help with work or food. In practice, members of the same lineage do help one another indiscriminately; members of different lineages may ignore their obligations, but if one person recognizes them and helps, his help will be reciprocated; everybody recognizes them symbolically by giving some help to people (like marriageable youths) who are in no position to reciprocate.

Consumption

At first sight, the only objects 'consumed' after these complex distributions are pigs. Looked at from the donors' point of view, however, what is important is merely that they rid themselves of the pig's body and that they obtain no further use from the pig, either by eating or breeding. For a donor to be able to give away more meat than recipients can eat, so that 'the meat stinks', is something to be proud of. At many ceremonies pork is put on one side as 'spirit food' (*korova wera neta*) to be used in greasing sacred flutes or for exposure. For the donor, in the context of *gima* activities, mere disposal (or diminution of the utility) of the pig is equal to consumption.

Consumption, so defined, occurs constantly with the more storable valuables, although physical destruction is rare except as wear-and-tear and in the form of amounts buried with dead bodies. I shall accordingly limit my treatment of the consumption of valuables to this sense. Lest this should be thought atypical, a comparison with consumption in our own society might be made. In our society he who consumes valuable objects, through eating, using, or wearing them, is considered of high status; in Siane the man who consumes large quantities of valuables is also considered to have high status, though his consumption is confined to the disposal of objects. Similar phenomena have been noted in many pre-literate societies (e.g., Malinowski 1922; Barnett 1938).

Even the display of valuables as ornamental clothing is not an advertisement of large stocks, which the wearer could consume in use if he wished. Rather, valuables are worn to indicate that men of other villages have given them to him, as they have been sure he will faithfully return an equivalent. In more familiar terms, they are worn to display one's high credit rating among other people, and they imply little about the total stocks owned.[24] This can be seen most clearly in the shells worn by a nubile girl, which are supposed to be those given as an advance marriage payment when she emerged from her first menses ceremony. Implied is a confidence in her father's providing a large present, when she is married, to ensure her good treatment in the village of her husband. A girl changes her display frequently, implying that new offers are continually being made for her, and so, hopefully, improving her marriage prospects. Needless to say, many of these attempts to establish a credit rating are actually deceitful, but the same logic also lies behind the frequent changes the adult men make in the shells they wear. The more new payments you say you receive, the more payments you have made yourself.

Before 1933 the number of valuables presented in payments was always small. Informants say a bride-price was normally two or three pieces of gold-lip shell (not whole ones), a cowrie shell headband, some plumes, and at least one pig. It might be inferred that the one pig and one shell implied by the term *ruruafo* was often the total payment. Payments at other rites of passage were even smaller. Since it was rare for more than two or three men to be killed in a war, only one or two pigs were killed by each side in the peacemaking. The number of valuables owned at this time was also small. Even 'big men' rarely owned enough to pay a bride-price entirely from their own stocks, while some men owned no shells at all.

At present, even though the number of valuables in circulation has greatly increased, few men possess enough to pay a complete bride-price themselves, though many lineage heads have three-quarters of a bride-price. Changes in valuables worn do represent a high rate of disposal of valuables. I estimate that a similar ratio prevailed between the sizes of stocks of valuables and of bride-prices when both were at a lower level.

To be a man with a reputation for frequent disposal of valuables does not mean that one must own large stocks, for the man who contributes most often to the payments of his clan-mates is also the man who receives most in the distribution of payments received. The critical factors in gaining such a reputation are the

---

[24] A similar means of establishing a 'credit rating' has been reported for the Mount Hagen area of the New Guinea Highlands (Vicedom and Tischner 1945). Men wear four-inch-long tallies of bamboo called *aumak* suspended from their necks like venetian blinds, to record the number of ceremonial exchanges they have participated in. They do not record the amount of wealth actually owned.

possession of one or two valuables as a basis for contributing, and the seeking out of occasions on which to use them. This can be done by contributing whenever a clan-mate has a payment to make, and by taking the initiative in making payments to other clans in the form of child betrothals or by 'giving' valuables to a sister's son. To have such a reputation implies that one has numerous extra-clan relationships, which in turn means one can 'walk unharmed all over the valley'—the ideal in Siane eyes (cf. p. 31), and that at one's death non-relatives will come to mourn. In short, consumption by disposal of valuables is the means of individual social mobility in Siane and is only possible if one actively seeks opportunities for participating in public affairs. Putting this another way, a person's consumption of valuables provides an index of his standing in public esteem.

The Total Gima System

So far, *gima* activities have been considered as single transactions, seen from the individual's point of view. These activities can also be considered as a total system, and it can be related to other activities of the society.

Ceremonial presentations occur in a situation where two corporate, independent groups are present. Whereas permanent diffuse obligations to give 'help' exist *within* a clan, no such permanent obligations exist *between* clans. Each payment of valuables creates a specific obligation, which is publicly recognized in the *gimaiye* ceremonial. There is actually a *continuum* between 'help' and 'payment', the obligation created by the presentation of valuables being made more ceremonially as the pre-existing obligations between the two parties to the transaction decrease in number—in Evans-Pritchard's terms (1940: 108), as the structural distance between them increases. The *gima* presentation of luxuries to a departing village trade expedition fits in this *continuum*: the obligations incumbent on a trade-friend are not so well established that a public re-stressing of them is superfluous.

But if *gimaiye* and the public transfer of valuables stress links between two clans, they also serve to mark opposition between clans. This is clearly expressed in the spatial relationships between donors and recipients as they stand at opposite sides of the men's house clearing during a presentation. *Gimaiye* marks the limits of clan co-operation, for where it occurs, *umaiye* cannot. Thus men whose mothers came from Roanti clan refused to accompany me to a wedding in a Roanti village between their clan sister and a Roanti boy. They said, 'We would be giving payments (*neta gimaiye*) to our mother's brothers, and we would be ashamed.' A formal opposition between clans was incompatible with their 'help' relationship with their maternal kin. Only where *gimaiye* and corporate opposition occur can there be marriage. In one case a bride-price was given directly to a girl's parents in an informal negotiation. When the rest of the girl's clan refused to accept shares in the distributed bride-price, the payment was returned and the wedding called off. The bride's clan declined to become involved as a corporate whole, and the marriage was impossible (cf. the similar case on p. 96). The marriageability of people who come to receive presentations is pointed out to children.

The correlate—that where help is given no *gimaiye* can occur—is also true. Thus, when a sick man gives pork for distribution to all his clan in a curing ceremony, or a father distributes pork and 'small things' to fellow clansmen in his child's weaning ceremony, it is given by *umaiye*. This form of distribution does not oppose the donor to the recipients, nor create new obligations. The cooked pork is taken round the assembled clan without being cut into portions, and each individual tears off a piece of the carcass with his or her teeth. Everyone must eat, taking bites in turn until the meat is all consumed. Valuables are distributed by *umaiye* by piling them in a heap and then giving a signal for everyone to grab at will. In both distributions the recipients remain anonymous, and everyone has had the same opportunity to receive something.

In yet another way the *gimaiye* ritual serves to maintain inter-group boundaries. The commodities needed for making presentations, with a few exceptions to be discussed later, can only be obtained by receiving them in presentations. They can never be exchanged for luxuries or for food, and the people with whom one exchanges luxuries and food cannot be people with whom one exchanges valuables. A man who gave away a shell to obtain food or pandanus nuts would be regarded as mad or as the victim of sorcery. He would be considered either as unaware of the implications of his act or as having had his soul stolen by the food-giver's clan so that his valuables followed his soul.

To obtain valuables from a person it is necessary to maintain some social distance from him. In these terms, the reason why pigs (valuables) can be exchanged for salt (a luxury) is that social distance is adequately maintained by the physical distance and infrequent visits of the salt producers. The fiction that the exchange is only a transaction between trade-friends, involving luxury commodities only, can be preserved. Another anomaly—the giving of huge quantities of uncooked vegetables by *gimaiye*—is explicable in similar terms. Vegetables given by *umaiye* are cooked and immediately usable by the individual to whom they are given. In a *gimaiye* presentation the food is uncooked and the quantity so great that clearly it cannot be used immediately by any single individual, and so cannot be interpreted as 'help'. It is therefore a corporate transaction, a presentation of goods to be stored and allocated as the receiving clan wishes.

These exceptions to the rule—that types of commodity are used in only one nexus of activity—in fact strengthen the rule by showing its more general form. The more general rule is that commodities are used only in situations where the nexus of activity is clearly one of intra-clan help, inter-clan presentation, or exchange between trade-friends; no commodity can be used in an ambiguous situation. Either the situation must be clarified by external means (e.g. the distance of salt-producers) or the commodities must be distinctive of a particular situation (e.g. uncooked vegetables).

The outside observer, looking at all *gima* activities, sees little total production: the many transactions produce little change in the numbers of goods owned by each clan and little increase in the amount of pork eaten by each clan, over and above the quantity they themselves produce. There is a flow of pork and valuables from group to group, but it results in no tangible production. This ignores the fact that each group also produces women, and when they move out of their own village at marriage a flow of payments starts to come in. The valuables constituting the payments flow *out* of a village as wives come *in* from other groups. In short, if the *gima* activities appear as a constant circulation of a limited stock of non-utilitarian valuables, each movement of valuables is matched by a movement of women (and their children) in the opposite direction. Lévi-Strauss (1951) calls such a situation *'échange généralisé'*.

The Siane rule of preferential (but not obligatory) patrilateral cross-cousin marriage means that no group gives wives continually to any single other group, nor does the 'flow' of women go permanently in any one direction. At one time about the same number of women should go from clan A to clan B as come from clan B to clan A. If this is not so, relations between A and B become strained. Thus, when a distant Yamofwe clan had not reciprocated a wife they had received from an Emenyo clan, the girls of Emenyo refused to have even *awoiro* relationships with other Yamofwe boys, saying, 'They do not give their vulvas to our penises; we will not sleep with them'.

As long as the number of wives given and received is balanced, the flow of payments must be balanced. If the relationship were unbalanced, one group would give more sisters in marriage and receive more valuables; the other group would receive wives, but disperse its stock of valuables. When all its valuables were gone it would be forced to let more of its women go, in order to recoup valuables, while other groups could dispose of their valuables and obtain wives. In this way limitation of the total supply of valuables ensures balanced circulation of women within the society—a topic which will be returned to later. Alternatively, the possibility of exchanging valuables for rights over women can be seen as a sanction ensuring the balanced distribution of valuables throughout the society and reciprocity in ceremonial presentations.

These theoretical considerations, which are implicit in the Siane ideology of reciprocity, can be supported by statistical evidence.[25] Even before 1933 the north-eastern areas were slightly richer in valuables, since they were nearer the seacoast from which shells ultimately came. There was a statistically significant but materially unimportant drift of women from south-western groups towards the wealthier groups, as would be expected if *equal* distribution of valuables ensured *equal* distribution of women. Since 1933 the discrepancy in wealth has increased (as will be described later) and the drift of women towards the north-east has increased considerably.

Summary

The *gima* nexus of activities is concerned with the relations between corporate, inter-marrying groups. It involves the formal transfer of non-utilitarian goods in a ceremonial that publicizes the obligations created and stresses the distinctness of the two groups concerned. Strict accounting for the goods transferred and the obligations incurred is the rule. The *gimaiye* ceremonial thus expresses, using material symbols, the more general relationship between clans of opposition or hostility, alternating with calculating politeness and alliance.

Valuables can be used to express intra-clan obligations of 'help', in much the same way as food or assistance with work are used, but the use of valuables as contributions to the payments of others tends to set up additional, relatively specific, obligations. It is by virtue of setting up such obligations that men gain power within their community, a reputation for public spiritedness, and, indirectly, more relations outside their own clan.

[25] The statistics on which these statements are based are given in Salisbury (1956b), where there is a fuller treatment of the discrepancy between Siane ideology and practice in contracting marriages, and where the implications of the 'flow' of women for the structure of nearby societies is discussed.

Pigs are used in *gimaiye,* and intricate mechanisms analogous with credit and insurance are employed to make sure they are available when needed. But pigs are useful in *gimaiye* only in so far as the owner can destroy their utility for himself. In this sense they, too, constitute non-utilitarian goods when transferred.

The element of calculation in the *gima* nexus has been illustrated throughout the foregoing description, and, in pig production, for example, it is in terms of units which, although not subdivisible, are universally and explicitly recognized in much the same way money is.

Yet a difficulty has arisen in talking about the 'ends' to which *gima* activities contribute, for they produce nothing material and they result in little change in the aggregate stocks of any group. The one clear aim of many of the activities is to obtain women from other groups. In this, *gima* activities can be seen as involving the circulation of a set of tokens and regulating the distribution of women between groups. This apparent aim will be re-considered in Chapter 8.

4. *The Total Economic Activity*

By the three nexuses of economic activity already described (their characteristics are tabulated in Fig. 2), the resources of Siane society—its labour, its land and the products thereof—are converted into goods through which certain ends can be mediated. This division into three nexuses was based on impressionistic criteria, and it may now be refined by using more analytical criteria.

The subsistence nexus is concerned with the use of goods to fulfil obligations incumbent on members of the same clan. These obligations are summed up in the term *umaiye,* which can mean variously 'to help', 'to give freely', and 'to substitute for'. They apply directly to the use made of commodities over which an individual has only *merafo* rights, that is, trusteeship rights over an estate the ultimate title of which is vested in the clan. The obligations also limit an individual's use of property he owns as *amfonka,* his personalty. The articles of property to which clan obligations apply are classed as *faivya neta* or 'things of no account'; personalty consists of *neta* or *kevora neta.*

The *gima* nexus is concerned with the use of goods in situations where there are no pre-existing obligations—the relationships between corporate clan groups. The ceremonial act of *gimaiye* sets up specific, publicly-recognized obligations, which are discharged either by tangible performances, such as producing offspring, or by reciprocal acts of *gimaiye*, termed *uto gimaiye*. In making a presentation, the practical utility of the objects given to the recipient is immaterial; what is important is that the donor destroy any utility the goods might have for him. The goods so used are mainly tokens, owned as personalty, and called *neta*.

The luxury nexus of activities involves the use of goods to set up diffuse personal relations between individuals in situations where no clan obligations exist. Both parties obtain practical utility from the exchange of personal property of the kind called *kevora neta*. The transactions are variously described in terms of *umaiye* or of *gimaiye*. But where *umaiye* is used to describe the handing over of goods, the strict reciprocity appropriate to *gimaiye* is the rule; where *gimaiye* describes the handing over of goods, the diffuse friendliness more characteristic of *umaiye* is also evident.

The three nexuses exist relatively independent of each other. Different goods are used in each nexus, and the goods used in one cannot be substituted for the goods used in another, except in a few anomalous cases whose exceptional nature is clear. A few cases will be described in the following chapters where *neta* are given to trade-friends, who give *kevora neta* in return, but these involve European goods, the categorization of which is not fully established. Before European contact these anomalies did not occur, since goods were unequivocally categorized. Different situations also unambiguously demand behaviour of one specific type. If the nature of the situation is not perfectly clear, it is clarified by the nature of the commodities involved (e.g. trade visits involving salt).

Within each of the activities some economic decision must always be made in choosing how best to use the limited range of resources appropriate to that activity. Thus there may be a choice between giving shells or plumes in a bride-price—a choice decided in terms of the likelihood of repayment and the payer's future needs for plumes or shells; in such a situation there is no choice of whether to obtain valuables from outside the clan or whether to give food to outsiders instead of valuables. But if each nexus is so self-contained that only particular resources can be used to obtain the ends towards which each particular nexus is directed, wherein lies the 'competition between ends' implicit in the use of the term economic?

The one resource used in all activities is the *time* of the participants. At all moments an individual has to choose whether or not he will enter a situation where a specific activity would be appropriate. At all moments the cost of doing one activity is the activities of other kinds which must be forgone.

10   Yofantena opening his valuables box

11 Making a presen-
tation at a Pig Feast

12 Ritual killing of
a pig. Note *gerua*
board to the left of
the group

Before discussing the bases for choosing how to use time, it is first necessary to consider what are the choices actually made. The description of 1953 is based on my own observations, that of 1933 on reconstructions. Women regularly perform the same sort of tasks, day after day, so a consideration of the typical daily schedule and of the occurrence of exceptional days is all that is needed to establish the pattern of allocation of their time. The exceptional days are those when individual women visit other villages, or when all the women of a village go as a body to a ceremonial in another village, and the days spent at home incapacitated from normal work through sickness or from the 'uncleanness' associated with the menstrual flow. Since about three female visitors can be seen in a village of sixty women on a typical afternoon, an estimated one-twentieth of the village women's time is spent in individual visiting. Ceremonials in other villages take up about one day in thirty, while sickness and ritual disability is probably no less frequent than male sickness (which will be documented later) and takes up at least one day in ten. One-fifth of a woman's time is thus spent 'exceptionally'. Of the 'normal' days, one-quarter of the time is spent travelling to and from gardens or to call in the pigs, another quarter is spent in productive garden work, such as planting or weeding, another quarter in collecting produce and firewood, and the remaining quarter in cooking and serving the food and knitting while the food is in the oven.

There are more ceremonials now than in 1933, so the time spent in ceremonial visiting may be slightly more now than then, but the only other likely change in the pattern of time utilization following the introduction of steel axes (since women do not use steel tools or wear European clothing) would be if larger gardens were now cultivated. Informants deny that the size of gardens has increased greatly, so that the 1953 figures constitute the best estimate possible for time allocation in 1933. They are summarized in Table 1.

To establish how men spend their time I observed and recorded the activities of a representative stratified sample of individuals from one village during a period of three months. The procedures used and the individual allocations of time are treated in detail in Appendix B. The activities observed in 1953 can be simply divided into the same categories as the women's activities—sickness, visiting, ceremonials, and subsistence work (some of which can be further subdivided)—together with introduced activities such as Government work (clearing roads or digging latrines close to the village), playing football, and attending mission services. The average amounts of time spent are summarized in Table 2.

TABLE 1

Estimated Distribution of a Woman's Time in
both Stone and Steel Technologies
(%)

Activity	Time Spent	
At home sick, etc.		10
Visiting individually		5
Ceremonials		3
Subsistence work		
Travelling and pigs	20·5	
Garden work	20·5	
Collecting crops	20·5	
Cooking and crafts	20·5	82
		100

TABLE 2

Allocation of a Man's Time in Siane
(%)

Activity	Time Spent			
	Stone technology*		Steel technology†	
At home sick	10		10	
Visiting individually	3		6	
Ceremonial				
Religious	?		14	
Courts	?		4	
Fighting	?		–	
		7		18
Subsistence work				
Clan work	55		22	
Lineage work	24		16	
Home crafts	1		12	
		80		50
Introduced activities				
Government work	–		10	
Mission	–		3	
Football	–		4	
		0		17

Note: Because of rounding, figures may not add to 100.
* Estimates for the stone technology derived as explained in the text.
† Figures for the steel technology summarize Appendix B.

On the basis of these figures one can estimate the allocation of time when stone tools were used. The major effect of steel tools has been to shorten the time needed to clear and fence gardens. Informants say it took three or four times as long to do these jobs with stone axes, and that instead of going to garden sites every second or third day for one month and working ten to fifteen days, they then went every other day for about two months and worked between thirty and forty-five days preparing each garden. Gardens were of approximately the same size at both times, and since new gardens must be prepared every two and a half months to ensure the supply of food, no sooner was one garden prepared than it was necessary to start a new one. Repairs and planting, which did not involve axes, took as long then as now, while housebuilding must have taken a little longer. Clan work, being mainly axe work, can be estimated as taking two and a half times as long in 1933 as in 1953; lineage work, involving more repairs, as taking one and a half times as long.[26]

These forms of work would have been essential for the maintenance of the food supply. Also a 'given' would be the amount of time spent in sickness, which cannot have been less prevalent before the introduction of European medical techniques, while the time spent in 'Introduced activities' must have been nil in 1933. Individual visiting by men has probably increased somewhat since peace has been imposed; I estimate it has doubled. Craft work at home probably took a negligible amount of time in 1933, when many of the materials now used were lacking and stocks of personalty were much smaller; I arbitrarily estimate one per cent. Ceremonial and warfare I treat as residual categories and obtain percentages for them by subtraction. The estimates thus obtained are given in Table 2.

In stone-using times the distribution of the men's and women's time was similar, each spending about 80 per cent in subsistence activities. The difference, that men spent twice as much time in ceremonials as in individual visiting, while the pattern of the women's activities is the opposite, is easily explicable. Ceremonials and fighting are the male activities *par excellence,* while women have more important ties with their natal villages. Apart from this there is little evidence that men had easy lives largely spent in social activities and aggressive theatrical oratory, while women were hard-working drudges, as is undoubtedly true in many New Guinea societies today. It is an interesting speculation that much of the contrast between the stereotypes of what men and women are like

[26] See Appendix B, pp. 216-20, for the calculation of these figures.

in New Guinea, which has been described by Margaret Mead and others, may be due largely to the differential effect of the introduction of steel tools on the activities of the two sexes. Here merely the decrease in the strenuous productive activity of men and the lack of change in the activities of the women in Siane must be noted.

What do these figures imply about the choice that individuals make concerning how they will allocate time? Figures for time allocation at any one period might be considered the result of individual choices determined wholly on traditional grounds—'Siane men have always done thus and so, and that is why now I should do this particular activity'. But such traditional canons clearly could not apply in a situation of change. The new technology reduced the 'cost' of producing subsistence goods from 80 per cent of a man's time to 50 per cent, so that he had a disposable amount the utilization of which was not governed by established patterns but could be allocated to competing ends. In so far as the choice was made in terms of quantities of goods or services produced it was economic, as I am using the term—one that involved comparison of the different satisfactions afforded by the different nexuses of activity. How the changes in choice patterns occurred historically is the subject of the next two chapters; why they occurred in the form they did is the question the final chapters try to answer.

An indication of the different ways in which the different standards for evaluating the attractiveness of different nexuses of activity affect people, thereby indicating that 'traditional' patterns are not completely normative at any one time, can be seen from the figures on the different patterns of time allocation among different groups, given in Appendix B.

The clearest consistent difference in the figures is that the higher a person's social status, the more time he spends in corporate clan work, ranging from village officials who spend 40 per cent of their time in this way to youths and men without children who spend 9 and 10 per cent respectively. On the other hand, men without children and unimportant men with children spend 31 and 26 per cent of their time, respectively, working on their own private gardens and houses, while 'big men' spend only 5 per cent. Men without children do not visit individually, as would be expected from the in-law avoidance rule, but there is a clear difference between the 11 per cent of time spent in visiting by unimportant men and the 2 per cent spent by village officials. Everyone spends about the same amount of time attending ceremonials, except that officials attend many more court cases. The amount of time spent in Government work is also roughly equal for all categories, except that officials attend more often, while 'big men' choose to ignore the officials' decrees (and can get away with doing so), while less important men do not. 'Big men' spend the most time in craft activities. Youths have taken up the new activities and spend much time at home, often asleep after staying awake all night during an *awoiro* visit.

These differences in allocating time can be interpreted in at least two ways. One is by stressing the way in which the division of labour leads to a greater aggregate productivity for the whole society—thus, for example officials, by doing Government work and settling court cases, free 'big men' for craft activities. Division of labour produces an efficient combination of land trustees, work initiators, and unskilled labourers, as has already been indicated. The observed patterns of time allocation, then, are the working out in practice of the socially prescribed division of labour. An alternative interpretation would stress individual motivation arising from different aims: important men work for the benefit of the clan as a whole, while unimportant men work for their own material advantage—by working on their own gardens, for example, or by seeking personal relationships with individuals of other clans. Both of these types of interpretation—in terms of the contribution of particular nexuses of activity to the aggregate product of the society, and in terms of the standards of value used by individuals in making their economic choices—will be carried further in later chapters, after the changes in Siane economic behaviour have been described.

4

INDIRECT CONTACT WITH EUROPEANS

In MAY 1930 the Highlands were first entered by M. J. Leahy and M. Dwyer in a search for gold. They entered from the east and prospected on the Benabena River, east of Goroka, before continuing along the south-east bank of the Lower Asaro River, just to the south of Siane territory. Eventually they found their way down the Purari to the south coast of New Guinea. At this time (Leahy & Crain 1937:49) 'the only tools in evidence were crude stone working axes and sharpened sticks'. They saw no metal of any kind, but at one Pig Feast they 'bought a pig for a tomahawk' (p. 57). Food generally was abundant and cheap (p. 60). They noticed that 'the farther [they] penetrated from the coast, the fewer became the shells worn by the natives, the shell ornaments being in most cases old and broken, suggesting that they had passed through many hands' (p. 64). As they passed near Siane territory, they offered one man a steel axe for a pig, but were met with refusal until they 'tried him with a strip of small *tambu* [cowrie] shells sewn on bark, and he accepted eagerly' (p. 65). The reconstruction of Siane society already given can be seen to compare with the impressions of the first European visitors to the Highlands.

It was not until 11 February 1933 that the first reconnaissance party set out from the Benabena area to explore the country farther west (Leahy 1936:245). The explorers left the airstrip they had levelled, crossed the Lower Asaro River and entered the south-east of Siane territory, camping for the first night in Yaviyufa tribal land.[1] The second day was spent climbing the eastern mountain wall and circling round the tribes of Nivi and Wanto. From the second camp-site the rugged mountains to the south-west were seen. On the third day the party turned north-west up the valley of the river which drains the central part of Siane (called Urami in Leahy 1936:287 map). As the explorers walked up the grass ridge separat-

---

[1] The account given here depends on Leahy (1936) for dates but on native accounts for the exact locations described. The two accounts are consistent, though Leahy and Crain (1937) occasionally are confused, while Simpson (1954), in a popularized version of Leahy and Crain, confuses matters further. Thus in his narrative (p. 12) he says that Dene terms for greeting and for cowrie shells were heard before the party reached Dene territory, and does not mention any Siane words till later.

ing Aranko from Fowe tribe, they were followed 'by hundreds of natives, many leading pigs along, tied by the foot asking us to buy them' (1936:245). From the summit of the ridge, in the territory of Waifo clan, Komunku tribe, the party obtained the first glimpse of the distant Wahgi Valley—even when expected, a breathtaking view as the morning sun clears the mist from the intervening hills. They descended from the ridge and passed through the village of Roanti clan, Komunku tribe. They were greeted with shouts of '*We turi(mo)*': 'Men possessed by spirits'.[2] After crossing the pass through the Erimbari ridge, they camped among the Dene-speaking tribe of Duma. Here they saw the first examples of the Mount Hagen axe, and met the custom of *awoiro* which is less restrained among the Chimbu and Dene peoples than it is among the Siane. Next day the party descended to the Mai River but could not cross (February being the month when rivers are fullest). They turned north-east through the northern Siane tribes of Raya, Ono, Komunku, and Yamofwe, who continued the shout of 'spirit men'. The party climbed out of the Mai Valley through the villages of Yamofwe tribe, continued along the mountain ridge, and descended to the Goroka plain through Yauna territory.

One month later a large expedition accompanied by a Government Officer, Mr J. L. Taylor, retraced the returning route of the reconnaissance, through Yauna and Yamofwe and north of Komunku, before passing on westwards. Several parties travelled along this route from the Benabena area to the Wahgi Valley at intervals during the next twelve years, but the main part of Siane to the south was not entered again by Europeans till 1945. It was considered beyond the reach of 'centres of influence', such as were established nearer government posts and manned by native police. In 1940 the area was scheduled for exploration and the extension of control, but the 1939-40 report of the Chimbu District called even the Mai River Komunku 'generally uncontrolled and uncooperative'. World War II ended further exploration, although several parties travelled from Goroka to Chimbu and surveyed a more northerly route with an easier gradient.

The war also meant great activity at Goroka, including the building of police barracks, a hospital, several airstrips, and the passing through of large numbers of troops, Australian and American, both negro and white. Much native labour was used at Goroka and was recruited either locally or from villages along the route to Chimbu.

---

[2] The same expression is used generally for 'mad men'. It has been variously transcribed as *wendulee* and *wenduli* by Leahy (1936), Leahy and Crain (1937), and Simpson (1954).

Occasionally, visitors from uncontacted groups dared to go and watch the happenings. Experiences vividly recalled by Siane men include gifts of 'tailor-made' American cigarettes from negro troops, and being machine-gunned by Japanese planes. But the majority of Siane people had no direct contact with Europeans and were left alone to their private inter-tribal wars and ceremonial exchanging. Finally in 1944-5 a dysentery epidemic forced the natives to call for help from the Europeans, who came in immediately.

The native reaction to the 1933 visit was that the spirits had returned from the land of the dead, *Makana*. Old men still call Europeans *Makana we*, or 'Makana men'. Europeans were white-faced, like the spirits, and were assumed to have an intimate relationship with valuables and the welfare of pigs. Anything they touched would turn into a valuable, while if they accepted an offering of a pig, its progeny would grow and flourish. This is why the party was followed by natives dragging pigs, and why natives collected 'whatever empty tins or bits of paper [were] left behind' (Leahy and Crain 1937: 153)—not merely to collect souvenirs. The native beliefs were strengthened by the incomprehensible behaviour of the newcomers and by their lavishness in giving valuables in exchange for 'things of no account', like food. The 'spirits' had seemingly inexhaustible stores of valuables, for (Leahy and Crain 1937: 152) they took no food with them but only 'shell money'. Confirmation that the newcomers were kinsmen of nearby natives was provided by the frequency with which they used the greeting of the next linguistic group, *'Dene'*[3]—as they shouted to Danny, Mick Leahy's younger brother.

Only a few warriors and 'big men' dared to come near the 'spirits' and collect pieces of waste-paper, lids of tin cans, and portions of food. They took these objects back to the villages as 'ancestral relics', and hid them in the men's houses. Ceremonies were performed, sacred flutes blown, and pigs killed in anticipation of the relics turning into shells. But after some weeks nothing had happened. The natives now realized that the visitors were men and not spirits, but they could not use this knowledge to exploit a new source of valuables, since the explorers did not return. But when the expedition returned to Benabena in August 1933 the northern tribes saw nothing to prevent them taking valuables by force. The patrol was forced to shoot in the more westerly Sinesine area, and in Siane

---

[3] This greeting, like the greeting *'Siane'*, means 'There are buttocks'. An alternative greeting is 'That is your penis' (Dene *mone*, Siane *moka ne*). Both are praise of a person's masculinity. Simpson (1954: 12) is incorrect in his translation of these terms.

'just at the junction of the Kormigi [Komunku] a line of warriors came to meet us, shouting and yelling. Battle was in the air. . . . [We fired] over the heads of the approaching warriors. They turned and retired' (Simpson 1954:59, quoting J. L. Taylor's patrol diary).

In the brush with Komunku peace was kept largely through the use of a native guide, named Heruku, from Yamofwe tribe. When the returning party passed through Yamofwe villages 'Heruku [was] left behind. He was covered with glory, a hero among his people.' In the same way the first reconnaissance party had taken 'a husky young warrior' named Lobonoguie back to Benabena, probably from Yamofwe also. He had acted as guide, interpreter, and sponsor, taking 'a leading part in persuading other natives to bring food', and introducing the party 'to the people of each new village' (Leahy and Crain 1937:148) as they went along. When he returned to his people he was rewarded with knives, beads, and some dog's hairs.

The help of these guides had been in accordance with the native pattern for luxury activities. The guides gained prestige by making contacts outside their own villages, and returned home, after giving help, laden with gifts. But the gifts the Europeans gave away were not merely luxuries as would have been expected, but also valuables such as shells, fine axes, or knives. I shall discuss this discrepancy of using valuables in a context of luxury activities later. Here the point I wish to make is that the goods were given to 'big men' who represented their villages and who made the first contacts. The new goods they received resembled the valuables already known to the natives—finely-shaped axes, and many types of shell—and were immediately accepted as such. Naturally, few goods were acquired in this way, for few visits were made, but even so the goods acquired through luxury activities went into the hands of men who would use them in *gima* activities.

Some new-style valuables were also obtained through *gimaiye*. When travelling Europeans wished to eat pork they 'bought' pigs, as early reports phrase it. As the natives saw it, pigs were killed in honour of the visitors, who later made presentations of valuables in return.[4] The men who killed the pigs and received the valuables were 'big men' and the valuables presented to the northern tribes were fed into the *gima* nexus of activities, through the men who were most active in it.

[4] Even in 1953, whenever a Patrol Officer wished to 'buy a pig' the natives insisted on going through the forms of *gimaiye*. The officer had to hand over the gold-lip shell in person, although native policemen did the buying of vegetables. He was prepared to do this since he would not trust such valuable articles (worth £3) to helpers. If he attempted to take the pig away alive, as would be impossible in *gimaiye*, natives would try to call the whole exchange off.

An airstrip and Government post were soon established at Bena-bena, and in 1935 a Lutheran mission station was founded at Asaroka to the east of Siane, while several other European estab-lishments were set up in the Wahgi Valley far to the west. Although these posts did not affect the Siane directly, they did so indirectly. Considerable quantities of shells and steel axes were given away at these posts in return for labour and food, provided mainly by natives living nearby. These natives, though they are not Siane, used the new goods in bride-prices and in exchanges for pigs. As has been mentioned, the new sources of wealth threw out of balance the old system of giving and receiving wives: the newly-rich groups took more women in marriage. This can be seen in the pattern of marriages in Siane, where more women tended to marry into north-easterly groups than into south-westerly ones (cf. Salisbury 1956b). It is documented for the Chimbu area, at least, where a Patrol Officer, L. G. Vial (1935: 13) described the strains caused in outlying areas by the shortage of women and pigs, both of which had 'migrated' into the richer areas near European settlements. Even in 1953 there was unrest in Siane over the tendency for wives to desert their husbands and go to richer villages, nearer the source of European valuables.

As women and pigs became scarcer in the areas of Siane some thirty miles from European settlement, and as valuables became more common near the settlements, women and pigs increased in value relative to shells and axes. Where, in the indigenous situation, bride-prices had been of two or three broken pieces of gold-lip shell and a few other *neta,* now bride-prices increased steadily and even in western Siane had doubled by about 1940. While the first visitors 'bought' pigs for a few *tambu* shells, later travellers found single axes or large gold-lip shells insufficient.[5] By 1953 the period of rapidly increasing prices seemed to have passed, and rates were high and stable, but parties of natives still came from the north-east trying to exchange single axes or shells for the pigs of the supposedly unsophisticated locals. They were unsuccessful. But Siane groups who went twenty miles to the south-west into uncontrolled territory sometimes *were* successful. Increased prices were just reach-ing the uncontacted tribes to the far south-west.

[5] An exception to this rule was Mr J. L. Taylor. In a personal communica-tion he said that during the War, when trade goods were scarce, natives in Komunku and Yamofwe often killed ten or more pigs when he camped for a night, even though he could give no shells in exchange. This was not done for other Europeans and from my conversations with the Yamofwe people I feel that Taylor's personal 'credit' was so great that he did not need to return any payment. The route taken by the first expedition through the area is still known as 'Mr Taylor's road'.

There is no direct evidence of how higher exchange rates and bride-prices spread from the centres of contact. The simplest re-construction would picture a gradual spread of a few miles each year. In one year a village five miles from a centre of European settlement, and still using uninflated exchange rates, might lose numbers of women (as brides or as deserting wives) to villages nearer the centre, but would gain numbers of valuables. Later, when the loss of women caused strain, they might recoup their losses by taking brides from villages farther out and giving low bride-prices, while refusing to let girls go to the more contacted villages, except for high bride-prices. The richer villages would not be unwilling to pay these higher rates (in fact they may well have provided some of the impetus for the inflation), since to be known as people who make large presentations was to gain in prestige. Fairly soon the two villages close to European settlements would reach a balance in numbers of women exchanged and in the size of bride-prices they would pay. The imbalance and strain would be transferred to the relations between the second village and a third set of villages farther out. Gradually the new balance would spread even farther, and strains would be set up in more distant areas. The fact that uncontacted natives twenty miles to the south-west of Siane were adjusting exchange rates in 1953, when a major change in the wealth of Siane had occurred in 1951, suggests that the inflation spread about ten miles each year. It will be noted that the increase in rates did not merely tend to equalize the flow of women between groups; it also served to distribute the new stocks of valuables more rapidly than would have been possible with low payments.

The process of inflation also strengthened the position of the 'big men'. Previously, a young man could hope to 'produce' a few valuables, through the pigs his wife raised, and these would steadily repay the contributions he had received towards his bride-price. Now the numbers he could produce were swamped by the dis-proportionate numbers flowing in as ceremonial payments to those already participating in *gimaiye* activities—the 'big men'. They could make larger payments, and more grandiose gestures of reconciliation at peacemakings, from what they received. Their reputations for generosity increased, and as a result they received even larger payments from others. Their stocks of valuables grew as the inflation grew, while the stocks of less venturesome, younger men remained static. Although the 'big men' produced nothing, their wealth and power grew, as did the wealth and power of entre-preneurs during the Industrial Revolution. Inflation made the Siane situation into one of boom.

But although prices increased, this did not necessarily mean that stocks of goods owned increased at the same rate, nor that all the increase was due to the obtaining of new goods from Europeans. Even without any increase in the total number of valuables in circulation, the same inflationary effect on prices could have been produced by an increase in the velocity of circulation. In fact it seems unlikely that the goods distributed from the Government centre at Benabena can have doubled the stocks of valuables owned by natives over several thousand square miles. Yet a small increase in the supply of one valuable—steel axe blades—did soon lead to a large increase in the velocity of circulation of all valuables.

Steel axe blades soon became distributed, at least in small numbers, over all the Siane area, by means of the ceremonial exchange described. Accurate dates for this distribution were not obtainable, but the rate of ten miles per annum, suggested above, would indicate 1936 as the date when axes began to be common. First they went into the hands of 'big men', who used them both for exchanges and for production. When 'big men' obtained more than one axe, although this was nominally a *neta*, or valuable owned as personalty, other men, observing its use as a tool, could ask to borrow it, in the same way as they could borrow other tools. Where previously two markedly different types of object had performed the two separate functions of use and ceremonial presentation, now both functions were performed by one object. The ownership of steel axes gradually became universal among adult men, and their use in ceremonial presentations diminished. By 1953 they were rarely so used within the Siane area, although they were used by Siane men as presents to uncontacted natives.

The effect steel axes had in cutting the time needed for subsistence activities from 80 per cent of a man's time to 50 per cent has been described. The time saved could have been used to make larger gardens and to produce more food, but it was not. Instead, other activities increased.[6] Warfare was one of these. During the period from 1938 to 1945 three large wars occurred in the central Pira Valley, in which villages were burned and clans exiled. The histories I collected described only four burnings during the previous twenty-five years, and the wars had involved only two clans on each occasion.[7]

[6] The same pattern has been observed throughout eastern Melanesia. Thus Belshaw (1954:60) comments that in eastern Melanesia the reaction to a greater ease of production was to produce the same amount, using less time, and to use the time 'for activities which were not materially productive'. He does not analyse the implications for production of these other activities.
[7] These figures do not claim to be exhaustive, but the same trend has been remarked for other areas following first contact with Europeans, not merely

Time was also spent in *gima* activities. The number of rites of passage cannot have increased greatly, but the number of participants at ceremonies did. Before 1933 only the immediate lineage groups of bride and groom plus one or two 'big men' from their men's houses would attend a wedding. By 1953 whole villages participated *en masse* in the festivities. Previously, men who spent 80 per cent of their time in subsistence work did not have time to join in the discussion of ceremonials for members of other lineages. Now they not only had the time but they also had more valuables to contribute, and so they were free to increase their participation, and thereby to increase their prestige. As I have indicated previously, those who did not actively participate in *gima* activities were left behind in the competition for prestige, and the power difference between 'big men' and 'nothing men' increased.

Larger ceremonies also meant that more guests were entertained and more pigs killed to feed them. The demand for pigs increased, and their exchange value, relative to shells, increased further. Pig-stealing became a more frequent cause for fighting. That pig production increased is suggested by informants' comments that more pig-houses outside the villages are now being built in the interval between Pig Feasts. Before 1945 this tendency towards scattered residence would clearly have conflicted with the insecurity caused by increased warfare. But the presence of such a conflict might well explain the welcome given in 1944 to Europeans, who brought a relief from the tension.

It would be expected that luxury visiting also increased during this period. I was told of visits by groups of southern Siane men to their Yamofwe friends who were building the airstrip at Goroka during the war. Men from southern Komunku clans told of visiting their trade-friends who lived near the Lutheran mission at Asaroka. Whether these visits represented an increase in frequency, I do not know. But from the stories of what was brought back by such visitors—a leather belt, and a European cigarette, for example— the pattern of visiting would seem to have been the same as that I observed between contacted and uncontacted natives.

In 1953 I saw two parties from areas previously visited by only one or two patrols visiting Siane groups in which there were numbers of youths who had returned from indentured labour. The visitors appeared 'naked', wearing no shells or cloth. To the sophisticates, coloured handkerchiefs, machetes, leather belts, plastic

---

in Highland New Guinea (cf. Leahy and Crain 1937:214) but throughout the Pacific. Wars on the scale seen in 1938-1945 would have rapidly devastated the whole Siane area.

bangles, and beads were all just 'small things'—luxury articles that could not be used in bride-prices or to exchange for pigs, but which could be given as gifts to the visitors. But the unsophisticated natives from the far south-west greeted these objects with screams of admiration and thanks, far louder than is normal for a visitor saying farewell. Surreptitiously, also, the visitors picked up the lids of tin cans which I had thrown away, or scraps of coloured paper. This amused the blasé men of the village nearest to me, who commented, 'They don't know the white men's ways yet'.

When the sophisticated hosts had previously visited uncontrolled territory, they had brought back with them quantities of *roi* oil. When they gave back handkerchiefs, pieces of cloth, machetes, or even axes, they felt they were making an equal, or even a favourable, exchange. The unsophisticated visitors presumably thought of these novel European commodities as 'valuables', and their joy in receiving them was joy at being given valuables in exchange for luxuries. Clearly this was how Siane men had regarded such things as leather belts ten years previously. Yet by 1953 their standards of value had changed. It was no longer true to say that the categories of valuables and luxuries were permanently fixed and mutually exclusive. Uncertainty had entered the trade-friend relationship when luxuries could be given and valuables received, and when goods, thought of formerly as valuables, turned out after a time to be only luxuries. The changes in the pattern of luxury visiting during the period of indirect contact can be interpreted as introducing uncertainty into the standards of exchange value.

But there was also a stabilization of new exchange values. By 1953 the new standards were well fixed in Siane, but the recency of their stabilization was demonstrated by the hopeful visits of natives from the north and east. They brought round trinkets of many kinds, trying to exchange them for valuables or native luxuries. As I have said, the visits were usually unsuccessful, and the Siane men were quite incensed. 'They think we are *bus-kanakas*', they said, using the insulting word for an unsophisticated native. The new exchange rates did not involve an evaluation in terms of money, but they closely paralleled the values of goods at trade stores. Large shells, either gold-lip or green-snail, headbands of cowries sewn on bark, and six-foot lengths of coloured *laplap* cloth became the units of *neta* or valuables, driving out the dog's-tooth necklaces and cassowary egg-shell beads, which are not seen any more. Mirrors, spotted handkerchiefs, whistles, white plates, plastic bangles, leather belts, and other similar articles eventually became *kevora neta* or luxuries.

In 1953 the new standards were becoming established farther south. In January some Siane men asked to take an axe of mine, as they went on a visit to the far south, in order to obtain a pig for me to kill. They themselves took a few beads. They returned without a pig, saying that there were no men without axes, but with several chickens obtained with the beads. Another group of men succeeded in obtaining a pig, but said that southerners really wanted shells and not axes for pigs. Yet another group which went visiting in August obtained no pigs, and only a few chickens, and complained that the previously ignorant southerners now knew how much chickens were worth.

Summary

The period of indirect contact between Europeans and Siane could be generally characterized as mainly a period of gradual change in the native standards of value. The gradualness of the change seems to have been accompanied by a lack of 'anomic' symptoms such as occurred in other areas of the Eastern Highlands. Groups near Asaroka who had early direct contact with Europeans showed stubborn resistance to European innovation and the building of roads (Simpson 1954:121). Groups in the southern Dene-speaking area had less experience of European goods and naïvely accepted a Cargo Cult introduced by native evangelists from Kainantu in 1947 (Salisbury 1958). The local prophet convinced them that if stones were heaped inside a house and watched over by himself and all the young girls of the villages, they would turn into shells. Sticks similarly treated would turn into rifles, which could be used in tribal fighting. Siane men visited the cultists, criticized such stupid behaviour, and told me with glee how the cultists had been discomfited when they tried to shoot their wooden rifles against the police who arrived to settle the outbreak.

Beside the value changes, the greatest change in Siane in the period of indirect contact was the great florescence of ceremonial and warlike activity. The activities themselves were not new, but new commodities were adapted for use in them, while the amount of time spent on them and the volume of goods handed over increased tremendously. The increase can be seen as the autonomous form of reaction to two key changes extraneous to Siane—the increase in the supply of valuables, and the technological change to the use of steel axes. The first change without the second would have produced a slight increase in the number of valuables owned and exchanged, the second change gave people increased leisure and enabled them to participate more in ceremonial and political activities. Economically, the change appeared as inflation in bride-prices and as a greater velocity of circulation for valuables. The effect of the inflation was to pull together larger groupings to participate in ceremonial exchanges and to increase the power of the 'big men' relative to the power of the 'nothing men'. It was a period of 'boom'.

5

DIRECT CONTACT WITH EUROPEANS

IN LATE 1944 native warfare, which had been increasing since 1938, reached a climax as the victims of earlier wars sought their revenge. Simultaneously a dysentery epidemic struck the area. How far the warfare was actually blood-feuding to avenge dysentery deaths, believed caused by sorcery, I do not know, but at this time some *bosbois* of non-combatant groups decided that arbitration by the Europeans, whom they had previously visited, was necessary. Fortunately, a military administration (ANGAU) patrol in the nearby Sinesine area was soon able to provide medical assistance. From this time dates the establishment of medical aid posts, periodic patrolling, and the formal recognition of *bosbois*, but in the villages there was little break in the way of life which had grown up in the preceding twelve years.

The first patrol[1] gathered together all visible native weapons and burnt them in one fire on the site of the present Government Rest House of Pira on Emenyo territory. The patrol leader 'bought' many pigs with gold-lip shells, and gave a large feast in which all the fighting tribes joined. A semi-permanent aid-post staffed by native medical assistants was set up a little farther north, and the epidemic was brought under control after some villages had lost up to 20 per cent of their adult male populations.[2] It will be seen that the patrol leader occupied the traditional native role of 'big man' and mediator in the fighting. He ensured that the warring parties exchanged pigs and contributed himself to the peacemaking payments. Later patrols strengthened this idea of the European being equal to a native 'big man', and the term *we namfa* is still often used to describe a patrol officer.

The early patrols gave gifts to 'big men', tacitly recognizing them as *bosbois* by giving such objects as rings, belts, and articles of clothing. Much of this 'recognition' was indiscriminate and its later withdrawal, when the regular administration appointed *luluais* and

[1] I was never able to establish the name of the patrol leader, although his native name of '*Masta Nom*' is almost legendary in the area.
[2] Figures collected from one village showed a ratio of one female death to five male deaths. This anomaly may be due to female deaths being forgotten or considered not worth mentioning, but the figures are otherwise reliable.

*tultul*s,[3] caused heart-burnings. But the gifts were given in regular *gima* form by the representatives of European groups to representatives of native groups. Since Europeans appeared like wealthy *gima* partners it became politic to be on good terms with them. Whenever a patrol arrived, native 'big men' would hasten to give presents of pigs, and to receive presents of shells in return. The pigs would be received by the patrol leader, who handed them over to his police constables to kill, cook, and distribute, just as a *bosboi* does when a pig is given to his men's house. Even in 1953 the position of a European as the 'representative' or 'father' (*merafo*) of the group of carriers, policemen, servants, etc., who come with him (his *lain*, in pidgin) is still important. The larger his *lain*, the more he is respected.

Acceptance in an indigenous role also gave patrol leaders a right to expect hospitality from tribes among which they stayed. Even now, in the unsophisticated south-west, a European is greeted by a whole village bringing gifts of (literally) tons of food. There is little obligation to make more than token return gifts. But Europeans always do make a direct return, which is not of commodities of the same nature as foods, or 'things of no account', but of commodities which are 'little somethings', luxuries such as salt or tobacco and paper. In some instances minute amounts of valuables such as cowrie shells or beads may be given. Here again commodities are used for activities for which, in the indigenous economy, they are inappropriate. *Kevora neta* are exchanged for *faivya neta* in a way that flouts the native definition of these categories.

But if European behaviour in an entertainment situation flouts some native standards, it conforms to others. Native hospitality is reciprocated by the Government[4] when people go from the villages to the Government centre as village officials, witnesses in court cases, hospital patients, or as stretcher-bearers. The District Officer gives the native a note to take to the 'compound', which houses labourers working on the roads or awaiting planes to take them to the coast for indentured labour. The visitor receives food and a bed, and no return is expected.

Government patrols also act as though giving luxuries in return

[3] The terms for Government-appointed village headman and for his deputy, who is nominally also an interpreter.

[4] And also by missions to natives of the same faith. The first question asked of me on the two occasions when Mount Hagen natives passed the house where I was staying was whether I was *popi, taratara,* or *sevende* (Roman Catholic, Lutheran, or Seventh Day Adventist). The visitors were at a loss and left when I said I was none of these. Siane men with me told me that they were Lutherans and would have asked me for food and shelter if I had been Lutheran.

for 'help' (as in the native luxury nexus) when a patrol moves from one Rest House to another. The baggage is carried by local natives who are not paid, since carrying for the Government is a legal obligation under native ordinances, but when the destination is reached the carriers are usually given some sort of 'entertainment', such as sugar cane to drink. They line up and receive a small luxury gift, such as tobacco or newspaper to roll cigarettes with, before departing for home. The presentation parallels the giving of luxury gifts to a returning party of trade-friends. In short, patrols immediately fitted in with the native luxury and *gima* activities, and did little more than confound slightly further the rigid classification of goods.

Then money was introduced into the area. Some coins had long been owned as rare valuables: I saw American dimes and Japanese coins, and was told of German pre-1914 marks.[5] Medical assistants and police recruited from the north-east of Siane earned substantial sums from the Government, and knowledge of 'shillings' and 'notes' spread on the Goroka Plain.[6] Some knowledge of 'shillings', presumably from the early use of coins as valuables, spread into Siane before the pidgin term did. *Kifana* or 'stone' was the only term I heard in 1952, but the pidgin term *silin* began to be used when more men returned from indentured labour.

During the period 1948 to 1952 coins must gradually have lost their status as rare valuables, for by 1952 only a few older conservative men continued to maintain great secrecy as they revealed their possession of a few coins. Most men carried coins with them in an empty tobacco tin and would display them every time they opened the tin to bring out matches or a piece of paper. Now a departing visitor is commonly given a coin as a parting gift. When a quarrel within a village is settled, one party may kill a chicken 'to make the belly all right', and this gesture is reciprocated with a gift of a few shillings. Coins are often given in the same situations as are handkerchiefs, beads, or leather belts. In short, coins have become accepted as *kevora neta* or luxury commodities. Only among the more sophisticated natives is there much comprehension of the values of different sizes of coin. Pennies (of which few are in circulation) are often added to threepences and sixpences, and a sum of

---

[5] Roberts (1935:7) also reports finding German 5-mark pieces in the Wahgi Valley.

[6] Simpson states that money was first introduced in the Goroka Plain about 1948. The actual date is unclear, for the stories of medical assistants and policemen indicate that money has been in use in Goroka since wartime days. 1948 was the date when the Goroka native hospital began purchasing vegetables from local natives for cash.

six coins is often called 'six shillings'. Such a collection of coins is felt to be equivalent to two chickens, handkerchiefs, or belts—to two units of *kevora neta*. Three shilling pieces, or about the cost of a belt or handkerchief in Goroka, are becoming increasingly accepted as the standard for a *kevora neta*.

Pound notes (and a few ten-shilling notes) are now also current in Siane, but are usually kept locked away in valuables boxes. They are publicly displayed when clipped to a pole as part of a bride-price being carried from village to village. Youths returning from indentured labour told me that they had brought back pound notes 'to buy shells with'. Certainly in 1950 a pound note would have bought a large gold-lip shell or a full-sized axe at a trade store. Even in 1953, when the prices of shells had more than doubled, natives from Siane still took single pound notes with them to Goroka, intending to buy a shell. Pound notes have, in short, become equated with 'valuables', and in the enumeration of a bride-price a pound note is counted as one unit *neta*. It must be repeated that it is only paper money that forms a valuable; coins, particularly shilling pieces, form luxuries. Most Siane natives do not treat the two types of money as interchangeable.

In 1950 the first few indentured labourers went from central Siane to work on the coast. They returned to their villages in the middle of 1951 and were soon followed by a much larger group who left for work in the goldfields. The second group returned to Siane in January 1953, soon after my arrival in the field. A third group of about the same size left in July 1953. These men brought with them larger quantities of money than had previously been known in Siane. They also brought back other goods, new attitudes, and new habits. Already in January 1953 a ritual had been established to welcome them on their return, ostensibly to re-incorporate them in native life, but which served also to absorb their earnings into the *gima* system. Before describing this ritual and its effects, it is necessary to describe what indentured labour involves.

At any time, though most commonly after a party of labourers has recently returned and a census patrol has established that the village manpower is at its normal strength, a group of men (mostly between the ages of 15 and 20) from one or more villages may travel to the District Office in Goroka. There the District Officer checks with the village census book that the men are over age 16 (an impossibility) and that their departure will not deplete manpower in the village by more than 25 per cent. The men 'sign' a labour contract and go to the Government compound, where they are medically examined and inoculated and receive an issue of clothing, blankets, and eating utensils. They wait there, working on public works projects, until a private employer engages them to work on the coast or in the goldfields for an eighteen-month period. In accordance with Government regulations a labourer is paid 15s. a month minimum wages,[7] plus housing, clothing, tobacco, and liberal rations of food. Five shillings of his pay is given him in cash each month, and a lump sum of nine pounds or more is given at the end of his indenture. His food and clothing are strange in native eyes—rice and tinned meat are staples, and a cloth *laplap* and singlet or possibly a pair of shorts the universal wear—while sleeping in ventilated houses under blankets, eating when the European-style noon time lunch bell says so, and smoking European tobacco rolled in newspaper are all novelties. The labourer watches more sophisticated natives playing guitars and harmonicas, gambling with cards at *laki,* and peroxiding their hair. He uses European tools to perform unskilled jobs, and may even help in a European house and learn some of the mysteries of European housekeeping.

On his return to Goroka he is kept in nominal quarantine isolation, but word passes to the villages that the youths whose departure was mourned by the slashing of earlobes have now returned. Villagers trek in thirty miles, bringing sugar cane and sweet potatoes for their 'brothers', and return carrying the wooden boxes which contain the purchases the labourers have made. After three weeks the labourers are free to return to the villages, carrying what they have bought with their final payment—usually shells and such articles as footballs, which they wish to keep with them.

As the labourers enter their village the women scream and wail, literally as though the youths had returned from the dead. They are now 'hot',[8] and go straight to the men's houses where they are secluded and not allowed to touch food which women's cooking has made 'cold'. For three months they must have no sexual contact with women. On the day of their return they cook their own food, using cooking pots or tin cans which they used on the coast. When the other villagers have assembled in the men's house clearing, they open their valuables boxes, amidst screams of amazement and delight. They then distribute about half of their goods, giving one or more valuables to the lineage heads of their own men's house, a little more to the village *luluai,* and something to the 'big men'

---

[7] This 'basic wage' was increased in May 1956 to 25s. For a native's account of his experiences while an indentured labourer see Salisbury (1956c : 477).

[8] In the same way in which newly initiated boys are said to be 'hot' (cf. Radcliffe-Brown 1922).

of other men's houses. They do this, using the *gimaiye* ritual, as if these were presents being made to members of foreign clans.

On the next day each returnee's lineage head kills one or more pigs and presents them to the youth, who reciprocates by presenting one or more gold-lip shells. Mother's brothers, wife's brothers, brother's wife's brothers, sister's husbands and even unrelated 'friends' come to visit, wailing in loud mourning until presented with pork to eat. Each 'mourner' receives a small gift on his departure. At this time the returnees have 'cooled' sufficiently to eat pork. Visitors continue to arrive for several days, the returnees emerge to play football, and eventually start making gardens and eating food brought to the men's houses by their mothers and wives. When they recommence cohabiting with their wives the event passes without comment or ceremony.

The ritual has many resemblances to the ceremony of initiation, and clearly symbolizes the incorporation of non-members of the clan into the body politic. The *gimaiye* presentation stresses the non-membership of the returnees, who must 'buy' membership in the clan. On being readmitted they are immediately involved in clan obligations to 'help' by the killing of pigs on their behalf. Most significant in an economic analysis, their stocks of valuables are immediately redistributed throughout the clan, but mainly to the 'big men', *bosboi*s and *luluai*s.

Table 3 shows how one typical youth aged 19 distributed his *kago* (as the goods in a valuables box are called in pidgin), together with an estimate of their cost price at a coastal trade store. It will be seen that the monetary value of the *kago* is over £12, while the youth earned only £13. 10s. during his period of indenture. He had spent only about one pound for articles which he did not bring back. The few older labourers aged 25 brought back fewer goods, and presumably spent more during their indenture on luxuries, payments to women, and compensation to other groups with whom they fought,[9] but these figures are typical for the youths who form the majority of the labourers. It will also be seen that the labourer keeps for himself about four valuables (shells, pound notes and *laplap*s), five or six luxuries (handkerchiefs, belts, beads, shillings, etc.), and some articles for personal use (shorts, footballs, machetes, etc.). In addition, he usually has some part-worn clothing which he is wearing, and a few used articles which he carries in a small bag round his neck or leaves beside his bed. These articles include cups,

[9] Only quarrels with other Highland natives are settled by payments, and the group of men who departed from Emenyo tribe for indentured labour in July 1953 specifically asked *not* to be sent with other Highlanders so that their earnings would not be dissipated by making such payments.

TABLE 3

Distribution of Goods Brought Back by an Indentured Labourer

Recipient	Article	Cost*
		s. d.
the *luluai*	1 *laplap*	6 0
	1 feather headdress	3 0
the *luluai*'s son	1 tin of ointment	2 0
the *bosboi* of his men's house	1 *laplap*	6 0
a lineage head of his own men's house	1 axe	8 0
another of the same	1 *laplap*	6 0
another of the same	1 handkerchief	1 6
another of the same†	1 axe	8 0
	1 handkerchief	1 6
a 'big man' of another men's house	1 *laplap*	6 0
another of the same	1 *laplap*	6 0
another of the same	1 *laplap*	6 0
another of the same	1 *kumkum* shell and 3s.	8 0
another of the same	1 handkerchief	1 6
his own lineage head‡	1 gold-lip shell	30 0
	1 *laplap*	6 0
his own mother's brother	1 *laplap*	6 0
a true-brother's wife's brother	1 axe	8 0
a lineage brother's wife's brother	2 *laplaps*	12 0
his own mother	1 handkerchief	1 6
Total distributed		133 0
The youth kept for himself:	1 handkerchief	1 6
	2 *laplaps*	12 0
	1 pair scissors	5 0
	some white buttons	2 0
	2 leather belts	6 0
	1 machete	7 6
	1 pair shorts	7 6
	1 gold-lip shell	30 0
	1 football	15 0
	1 pound note	20 0
	four shilling pieces	4 0
Total kept		110 6

* My estimate of the cost of the articles at a coastal trade store.
† Who had looked after the labourer's widowed mother during his eighteen-month indenture.
‡ His *yarafo*, who killed one pig and gave it to him.

knives and forks, sticks of tobacco, and quantities of newspaper issued by his employer, and things like combs and razors acquired variously.

Besides the material goods the labourer brings back, he has also acquired new habits and new standards of evaluation of goods.

Labourers wear as normal clothing their singlets and *laplap*s, they smoke trade tobacco rolled in newspaper in preference to uncured leaf wrapped in banana leaves, and use soap regularly for washing. They play football and are prepared to wear out the balls; many of them have kerosene lamps and need fuel and wicks; they treat belts, hats, shorts, beads, peroxide, 'lollies', and face-powder as luxury articles to be consumed if they are available, and not just as curiosities belonging to white men.

The supplies of these goods which a labourer brings back are not inexhaustible, and he usually retains a few shillings for buying more at the trade stores in Goroka. His pound notes are explicitly retained for the purpose of buying shells, but many a labourer came to me, when the stream of visitors had continued for some days, and shamefacedly asked me to *sensim* (pidgin for to 'change') a pound note into shillings. Supplies of luxuries had been exhausted, and more were needed to give as gifts to departing visitors. Changing money into units of lower denominations is normally unthinkable to a native. Even at a trade store no native bargains for what he will receive in exchange for the coin he presents to the storekeeper. He puts down his coin and says '*bis*' (beads) or '*sore*' (salt) and is presented with an equivalent in beads or salt, even if the coin he puts down is a shilling and all he needs is three pennyworth of salt. He distributes his surplus to his friends, and never asks merely for the salt he needs, plus ninepence in change. This is partly because the very idea of changing does not occur to him, but partly because, even among returned labourers to whom the practice is familiar, there is an element of shame in exchanging valuables like pound notes for luxuries like shillings, and shillings for trifling small coins. After several months some returnees changed more pound notes. The reason was the continual drain on cash resources occasioned by the visits of other returnees. They had to be offered trade tobacco since they would be insulted if offered the native product, and their food had to be salted with salt bought from trade stores in one shilling packets.

For the labourers, then, although they clearly distinguish pound notes as valuables, and shillings as luxuries, there is no longer a certainty that valuables must be used in *gima* activities, and luxuries for entertaining. A new sort of economic choice has been introduced by the fact that money has both forms and can be subdivided into smaller units in a way a shell or headdress cannot. The occasions when such a choice had to be made were limited in 1953 by the scarcity of pound notes in circulation. But since the use of money in bride-prices and for entertaining is likely to increase, if the experience of other areas of Africa and the Pacific is followed (cf. Hunter 1936: 193; Fortes 1936: 38; Keesing 1941: 127), the choice is likely to become more common. Further implications of this choice will be discussed later in this chapter.

A more obvious effect of the return of labourers is the vast increase in the stock of goods owned in Siane. This increase has affected stay-at-homes as well as labourers, as can be seen from Table 4. In fact the stay-at-home lineage *yarafo* listed was youngish and not yet a real 'big man'. If he later becomes a 'big man', he will presumably be richer. The richest man resident in Siane, a stay-at-home *luluai*, into whose box I only glimpsed, owned at least 17 gold-lip shells, 5 green-snail shells, 5 bird-of-paradise plumes, and numerous *laplaps*. It can be seen that going away to do indentured labour does not make a person wealthy in Siane society, and does not serve as a channel by which unimportant men can make themselves important. Wealth still flows into the possession

TABLE 4

Goods Owned by Two Men of the Same Age (25)
of Antomona Clan, Emenyo Tribe*

Lineage Yarafo who had not been to the Coast	Value†		Unimportant Returned Labourer of Same Age	Value†	
	s.	d.		s.	d.
3 gold-lip shells	90	0	9 *laplaps*	54	0
5 *laplaps*	30	0	1 towel	7	6
1 towel	7	6	1 machete	7	6
1 pair shorts	7	6	3 spoons	4	6
1 football	15	0	1 tin face-paint	1	0
2 spoons	3	0	2 belts	6	0
2 strings beads	3	0	1 roll newspaper		6
2 boxes matches		6	1 small knife	3	0
1 reel thread		6	1 bag containing	2	6
1 singlet	7	6			
1 machete	7	6			
2 bars soap	1	6			
2 rolls newspaper		6			
1 large knife	4	0			
1 mirror	3	0			
1 leather belt	3	0			
1 tin box containing	8	0			
Total	192	0	Total	86	6

* Both men also owned 3 feather headdresses to which no cash value could be attached.
† Estimated cost of purchasing at coastal trade stores.

of those who are active in *gima* activities, and the differential between 'big men' and 'nothing men' has not been reduced.[10]

The amount of wealth now possessed can also be compared with the size of payments which are now made. A bride-price given by a comparatively wealthy northern group (see p. 98) included 20 unit *neta*, 14 of them gold-lip shells; one from a relatively uncontacted group comprised 9 gold-lip shells, 2 cowrie shell headbands, 3 bird-of-paradise plumes, and 2 *laplap*s plus 3 small green-snail shells and an opossum fur, or 16 large unit *neta*, and 4 smaller *neta*. These give about the range of variation as between areas of different wealth, while the range of variation in bride-prices paid on behalf of different individuals of the same clan is somewhat less, since the payments are corporate clan payments, reflecting the prestige of the whole clan.

Exceptional cases where a clan takes no corporate responsibility show the importance of this factor. In the case described on p. 102 a bride-price contributed by many men of the groom's clan was refused by the bride's clan. It amounted to 11 gold-lip shells, 2 cowrie shell headbands, 5 plumes, 1 *laplap* and 2 pound notes, plus 5 green-snail shells (21 large *neta* plus 5 small *neta*). The groom enlisted in the police but the bride eloped to his village and insisted on marriage despite her own clan's opposition. The boy's father tried to collect another bride-price, but only three lineage heads of his own men's house contributed 8 gold-lip shells, 1 plume, and 24s. The other men said 'It is not our affair. The youth is now a Government man. They should provide his bride-price.' When the clan's prestige was not involved, few men contributed and the bride-price was low. I assume the payment was accepted only because the girl was adamant, but the case shows that it is possible, though unusual, for two or three lineages to contribute enough to make a small payment.

All the payments at a wedding have inflated in size since 1933. The bride's decoration consists of some 6 gold-lip shells, 7 green-snail shells, and numerous plumes, headbands, handkerchiefs, and *laplap*s. The presents to the bride's mother 'to stop her crying' amount to almost as much. The bride's clan takes about 4 pigs to the wedding feast, and the groom's clan entertains their guests with about 6 pigs.

For the birth of a first child a father kills some 6 pigs, and presents about 3 gold-lip shells, 3 green-snail shells and other smaller objects

---

[10] Alternatively one could say that the 'big men's' authority is effective in enforcing the distribution of valuables, though there are challenges to this authority which will be discussed in the next chapter.

to the child's mother's brother, who has previously brought 2 pigs 'as gifts for his sister's son'. At the haircutting-weaning ceremony 1 gold-lip shell and 1 small *neta* is all that is presented, along with luxuries and a pig. At an initiation 3 gold-lips, 5 green-snails, 4 *laplaps*, and 3 feather headdresses might be presented. The mother's brother's clan gives one last 'gift' at a funeral, consisting of about 2 pigs, 2 gold-lip shells, a *laplap* and 2 axes, and this is returned by a presentation of the same number of valuables and about 4 pigs.

The total of these typical payments indicates that a married man with one son and one daughter now has to make payments amounting to about 28 gold-lip shells and over 30 other valuables between his marriage and his death. Most of these payments occur during the early years of his marriage, when he is aged under 30 and his children are less than 8 years old. For the rites of passage during this period he must kill more than 30 pigs. The possessions of a young man, even of a lineage *yarafo*, could not possibly (even if return payments are calculated) finance the making of payments on this scale. The balance must be provided by older men, whose receipts from payments must be commensurate with their provision of 'help'. This dependence on older men is an important factor in their maintaining control over youths, and incidentally in forcing them to distribute the very valuables which are the basis of the older men's power.

So far the changes described have been consequent on direct contact with Europeans and have been changes in the luxury and *gima* nexuses of activity; no mention has been made of changes in the subsistence economy. The all-important technological changes occurred earlier, but direct European contact has brought some further small changes. The first patrols distributed seeds of most European vegetables to supplement native diets. These European vegetables have been eagerly grown by natives to please their European visitors and to have the appropriate food to offer them. Only cabbages, tomatoes, and potatoes are eaten by natives. In exchange for the gifts of food made to European visitors, the natives receive small quantities of salt and other luxuries. The consequences of this exchange of subsistence commodities for luxuries have been mentioned.

As yet there has been little attempt to increase the amount of luxuries obtained by planting larger areas of European crops. This can be related to two factors—the limited market, and its unpredictability. Government patrols occur only about twice a year, and consist of about twelve persons (a Patrol Officer, native police, interpreters, etc.). Visits by the missionary or the agricultural ex-

tension officer are newer phenomena, happen a little more frequently, but entail fewer visitors in each party. The Government
centre at Goroka is thirty miles, or two days' walk, away and the
maximum load that can conveniently be carried is thirty pounds
per man. Thirty pounds of vegetables fetch 2s. 6d. when sold to
the native hospital, and this is small return for four days of hard
walking.

Thus the potential market in Goroka is used only when natives
have to go to the Government centre for other reasons, such as to
be witnesses in a court case. It is hardly possible to plan production
in advance of such occasions. Similarly, the date of arrival of
patrols or visitors is unpredictable, though it is true that there is
a greater likelihood of a patrol during the four drier months of
the year. The luxuries obtained from such patrols' demand for food
are thus regarded as windfalls, disdained by the men for the most
part, but eagerly sought after by the women, the *amfonka* of the
vegetable produce.

But the men's disdain is largely a function of the smallness and
uncertainty of the market, as I realized after I had provided a
consistent market for the women's vegetables for several months.
On one or two occasions I also bought bundles of firewood from
women, but refused bundles which men brought later in the afternoon. The village *luluai* remonstrated with me, complaining that
as men were unable to obtain luxuries from me by bringing food,
I should give them a chance by buying wood from them alone,
and not from women. Subsequently I noted that it was the men
who brought in most European vegetables, while women only
brought native vegetables. At first, men had brought only sugar
cane, bananas, eggs, and chickens, while women had brought *all*
vegetables. I could not determine whether this marked a change
in the native concepts of ownership of vegetable produce or whether
it was a temporary phenomenon. In either case it indicates that
the establishment of a regular market for cash crops could lead
to a new delineation of property rights over food, with men owning
cash-crops, and women subsistence crops. The fact that axes are
used during the cultivation of the recently introduced crops of
passion fruit and coffee clearly marks them as 'male crops'. Even
though axes are not used for the cultivation of, say, cabbages, the
fact that men wish to treat them as male crops may lead to men's
participation in their cultivation.

There are also some indications of possible changes in land tenure.
Although the main trend in cultivating gardens has been to clear
the same number but lower on the slopes, informants also say that

more pig-houses are built nowadays. Many of these pig-houses are built on mountain ridges, and small gardens are cleared nearby from the virgin moss-forest. These gardens provide phenomenal crop yields, but entail so much work in clearing that they do not form part of the regular sequence of garden clearing. Single individuals do the work in the intervals between their assistance in communal garden work. They often live in the pig-houses and seem to be of two main types: young men, who are not lineage *yarafo*, are not wealthy, and who are newly cohabiting with their wives, or older men aged about 40, often with young children, who, though influential, have not become *bosbois*. These are the men who have the least to gain by remaining in the centre of clan activities and the most to gain from independence. It may be that they mark a trend towards individual ownership of the land they clear and of its products. If so, they may be the first to be affected by the establishment of a market for cash crops.

Summary and Prospects

Direct contact with Europeans has made little change in the subsistence activities beyond the changes made in pre-contact times by the introduction of steel tools. Luxury and *gima* activities have not changed in nature, but have increased in frequency and in the number of goods involved. The goods introduced by Europeans have been incorporated into the pre-existing native categories, just as Europeans have been incorporated as 'big men'. Indentured labour has been incorporated as an experience to be undergone by youths between the ages of 15 and 20, when they would otherwise have little employment, and it serves to provide goods for the increase in *gima* activities. Although the trend towards concentrating power in the hands of 'big men' has increased with the increasing inflation (and also with the importance of Government-appointed *luluai*s as permanent village representatives), there are also more possibilities for individuals or lineages to work independently of the village organizations. The greatest change has been the introduction of money, first as a substitute for valuables and for luxuries, and later as a medium of exchange for obtaining goods from trade stores. As a medium of exchange it has effected a further breaking down of the rigidity of the native standards for classifying objects, which started during the period of indirect contact.

What can be predicted about the future direction of change, from a theoretical consideration of existing changes? There is little likelihood that ceremonial payments will cease to be made. No feast is complete without the killing of pigs, and display is of great importance, as when shells and coloured cloth are carried on a pole and displayed as an offer of bride-price. Shells and pigs are likely to remain of great importance, though money is likely to bulk larger in ceremonial payments. At present it is rare for as many as five one-pound notes to be included, even by a highly European-ized village, in a bride-price worth £30. Money, as notes, was first accepted for use in payments since it was rare and could be dis-played, though less spectacularly than shells. But a main function of payments is the alignment of one corporate clan against another, thereby emphasizing the solidarity of each group, their mutual distinctness, and the possibility of inter-marriage. Clan solidarity and the relative influence of individuals within the clan are ex-pressed by the contributions to payments. If articles that are less easily displayed, of less rarity, and divisible into smaller units are used in payments, less ceremony is likely to attend their collection and handing over. Clan solidarity will be ritually stressed less often, the relationship between payer and payee will become less of a corporate relationship, and the rules of clan exogamy will be less enforceable. If such a trend were accompanied by a continued increase in the wealth of 'big men', who alone could finance pay-ments, a division of the existing clans into small 'empires' ruled by dictatorial 'big men' would be predicted. Such an organization would resemble that described for the Mount Hagen tribes (Vicedom and Tischner 1945).

Luxury gift-giving is, at present, a matter of individual ties to 'friends', and is concerned with obtaining goods for personal in-dulgence or with widening one's social contacts. If, with the break-down of distinctions between luxury and *gima* commodities, such gift-giving became imbued with the suspicious effusiveness now found in *gima* presentation, another sphere would be available for the self-aggrandizement of 'big men'. If, on the other hand, the pattern of friendly luxury giving were extended to the exchanging of what are at present valuables, this might lead to a general individuation of social relationships of other kinds. This would accord with the decrease in clan solidarity, already indicated, and with the trend towards lonely residence by individuals. It would be accompanied by a decline in the power of the 'big men' and a refusal by returned labourers to distribute their earnings.

These are the possible effects of a breakdown in the clear-cut categorization of commodities, of an increase in the convertibility of commodities for use in different types of activity, and of the introduction of money. It must be noted in passing that it is not the characteristics of money—of being storable, a repository of value, and generally acceptable—or a standard of value that have made its introduction critical. All these were possessed by the valuables and luxuries for which it substitutes. Its divisibility is the characteristic that has made money usable in many contexts.

The trends expectable from a consideration of *gima* and luxury activities in Siane thus lead in two directions: towards a progressive atomization of society into small groups of lineage or nuclear family size, or towards a consolidation of groupings round 'big men', who wield power through their *gima* activities. The critical factor in deciding which trend is more likely to prevail is whether the power of the 'big men' increases or declines.

Much the same two opposing trends, with the same critical distinction, can be predicted from a consideration of the subsistence nexus of activities. At present the centralized unity of clan groups of 200 people has generally increased, although with steel tools single individuals can clear gardens independently, and the entire labour force of the clan rarely needs to be mobilized for the performance of any single productive task. If some new productive tasks requiring the organization of a large labour force were introduced (e.g. the operation of a coffee drying plant, or a co-operative transport and marketing scheme), then the 'big men' would be eminently suitable to perform the managerial and entrepreneurial tasks. Presumably their power would then increase, but they would contribute to a further increase in village solidarity.

The alternative possibility is that no new tasks will be introduced but that there will be a steady increase in the importance of cash crops grown by existing techniques. As long as land is plentiful this could well lead to increasing cultivation of individual gardens, a decreasing dependence on the village as a source of labour 'help', and a relegation of the village to the status of a ceremonial centre. Divorcing the organization of productive activities from the organization of ceremonial activities would involve a decline in the importance of the 'big men'. On the other hand, if a land shortage develops, the land rights possessed by lineage heads, many of whom are 'big men', may prove critical, especially if coffee trees provide the most important cash crop. At present there is no conflict between the lineage trusteeship rights to land (exercised principally by the lineage head) and the personalty rights of individuals to the boundary *tanket*s, since lineage heads frequently redistribute personalty rights and all lineage members have trusteeship rights. Trees, regardless of their planter, come under the jurisdiction of the trustees of the land. If a material advantage could be gained by refraining from distributing title to personalty, it would be expected that lineage heads might so do, thereby strengthening their position *vis-à-vis* other members of the lineage. Since the lineage land would be in continuous use under trees there would be no question of other clansmen using it in virtue of clan rights to usufruct, which would tend to fall into abeyance. The land would become 'enclosed', and each lineage would tend to become independent of others, while each lineage would be under the effective control of its head, who would control the labour of lineage members and their wealth. He might well use the lineage wealth to obtain larger numbers of wives to further increase the labour supply and also his own possessions. This eventuality, indicated as it is by changes in the three nexuses, appears on the face of things to be the most likely future course of change. Confirmation of this is given by the situation near Goroka in 1953, where there was a market for cash crops and some shortage of land. Plural wives were an economic asset, and one man, who 'paid' his nine wives as though they were wage-labourers, had become privately wealthy, even by European standards.

The description of Siane economic life so far has focused on the way in which it has changed, and of how these changes can be seen as a steady progression from an indigenous basis. New tools gave people free time to indulge in a vast increase in ceremonial activity, and when Europeans arrived they were incorporated as participants in that activity. New goods were quickly absorbed into the native activities, while indentured labour became an easy way of increasing the supply of new goods and of using up some of the free time of youths. The use of money as a 'new good' has now begun to make further changes. Superficially, too, the main impression is of change: more decorations and clothing are worn; men have boxes full of valuables and luxuries; ceremonies are more elaborate; the young men play football when their fathers would have fought wars; many men have travelled by air to the coast, while few older men had travelled more than ten miles from home. Unquestionably, native life is richer in colour, in variety, and in material possessions.

Yet underlying the changes, the structure of society and its activities remain formally the same—there may be slight changes in the attribution of authority, but the groupings are the same: 'help', although it may now mean a loan of cash, is still given to clan-mates and forms the basis for recruiting work groups and distributing food; luxury and *gima* activities are conducted with the same partners and towards the same ends. What has changed

are the resources available and the method of allocating them
between the same competing ends as existed in 1933. It has been
an economic change. As further changes occur, if my extrapolations
are correct, they will be changes in groupings, changes in the
authority structure, changes in the type of activities performed—
they will be social changes. Such changes will be the subject of
later studies. At this point I shall break off the description of the
economic changes that have occurred to see how interpreting them
either in more traditional economic terms, or at least in more
theoretical terms, gives a fuller understanding of how a technological change has produced economic changes, which in turn have
led to changes in the basic structure of the society.

6

CAPITAL INVESTMENT DURING
ECONOMIC CHANGE

IN ECONOMIC LITERATURE much of the discussion of 'economic development'—the term commonly used to refer to the raising of *per capita* real income (cf. U.N. 1951:3)—is concerned with the rate of capital investment in non-industrial societies, relating the annual production of those societies with both their capital stocks and their rates of investment. It is clear that large outputs are correlated with both large stocks of capital and high rates of investment; implicitly many economic studies and the efforts of overseas governments to promote investment in non-industrial societies appear to assume a direct causal connection between an increase in capital investment and an increase in *per capita* real income. The higher income then gives greater saving, and hence investment. On general grounds one could predict that a lowering of the price of capital relative to labour—as would occur if a more efficient form of capital were introduced—would also lead to a greater use of capital in production, capital being substituted for labour. Major factors preventing the adoption of cheaper forms of capital would be a lack of education (U.N. 1951:4), overpopulation, and a large labour surplus (cf. Frankel 1953:100), or the high initial outlay required.

This chapter examines three somewhat simplistic propositions based on these lines of reasoning (which would appear valid for western societies undergoing economic growth), to see how far they are relevant to the Siane during their economic change, and what increased insight they give into what happened. The propositions are (1) that producing a larger output requires a larger capital stock, (2) that it also requires (or produces) a higher investment rate, and (3) that capital, which costs relatively less, would tend to be used to an increased extent in production.

To do this, 'capital' will need to be defined in such a way as to make it measurable in Siane. The measures will, of necessity, be approximations and estimates, so that calculations based on them will be of qualified accuracy, and Siane data will be forced to fit concepts that may or may not be relevant to the actual behaviour in Siane. Much of the chapter, then, is an academic exercise in seeing how far one can translate and use traditional economic concepts in analysing a specific case. Yet the generalizations that result from the analysis may be simply stated, and they are not basically dependent on the elaborate calculations preceding them. It is hoped that the reader will bear with the technicalities for the sake of the conclusions.

The Concept of Capital

Many anthropologists and sociologists have attempted to apply the concept of capital to the analysis of non-western economic systems, and have emphasized different aspects of it. Early writers looked for capital either in objects similar in form to the tools or possessions in western society or in 'commodities which, by their own inherent nature, cannot merely maintain themselves, but increase themselves' (Thurnwald 1932: 109) and which in non-western societies take 'two main forms; capital in plants and capital in domestic animals' (ibid.). Firth (1939) stressed that capital is a stock of goods and services, which is used in the productive process by being 'immobilized' (i.e. not used by the entrepreneur for immediate consumption) and 'used . . . to meet any . . . changes in the productive situation' (p. 273). He described the accumulation of capital on the Polynesian island of Tikopia 'by surplus production over immediate requirements rather than by abstinence *per se*' (p. 274), and differentiated between fixed capital (canoes and similar objects in Tikopia) and liquid capital or 'goods used to initiate production and repay participants in the process' (p. 305). He was chiefly concerned with stocks of food kept to pay workers while building canoes for chiefs. Weber (1947: 192), while emphasizing the productive nature of capital, was more concerned with its use as a measure 'in terms of which the means of profit making are valued. Profit, and correspondingly loss, is the difference between the valuations (of the stock of capital) as revealed by the initial balance, and that drawn at the conclusion of the period.' For Weber, money was essential for the concept of capital to be applicable.

All of these elements in the concept capital are commonplace to economists, but even for them the primary concern with the accounting aspect of capital leads to some controversy over what is, and what is not, capital. Fisher (1906: 106) distinguished capital from 'income which follows later' in the form of enjoyment. Frankel (1953: 51), confronting the problem of measurement in non-western societies, says that it is impossible to differentiate income and enjoyment, and that all we can do is to measure consumption, or, for accounting purposes, place some goods on a capital account, and then transfer them somewhat arbitrarily to an income account before they are actually consumed. Capital in its real sense refers to goods at one stage in the productive process, and these goods are not fixed but 'need replacement' (p. 10). Kuznets (1953: 47) deals with the distinction between capital goods and finished products, where one good may be a finished product for one entrepreneur and yet capital for another, who buys it to produce other finished products. Kuznets avoids the problem by considering the point of view of only one entrepreneur at any one time. Yet another distinction made by economists is between capital goods and consumer's goods. Capital goods 'enable the community to satisfy its wants more fully in the future, by augmenting the future output of consumer's goods and services . . . and contribute indirectly and not directly to the satisfaction of wants' (Benham 1938: 146). They involve a 'renunciation for the time being, of consumption, . . . with the incentive to waiting being the promise of an increase in output' (ibid., p. 147).

In Siane a definition of capital in terms of money is clearly unusable and the definition must be stated in real terms to apply to material goods or to services. Nonetheless, the accounting aspect of a monetary valuation must not be lost sight of, and some substitute will be needed. In real terms, then, capital will be defined as a stock of goods, present before a productive act is performed, used in production, and 'immobilized' from direct consumption while the act is in progress. The act of production is designed to add to the stock of goods (including services), some of which is eventually dispersed by being transformed into income, which is then consumed. As Kuznets (1953: 201) and others have shown, such a definition can include naturally occurring goods (resources) and produced goods, and both tangible goods and intangibles such as knowledge. In practice, resources and intangibles are not usually included in measures of the stock of capital, since they are difficult to express in the same accounting terms as other items of capital, and are almost constant and of importance mainly when they change—when resources become exhausted and knowledge increases. Both are ignored here, though it is clear that an increase in knowledge did occur in Siane during the period analysed.

Consideration of which goods in Siane are covered by this definition is aided by the fact that many distinctions necessary in a complex economy are irrelevant in Siane. Entrepreneurs do not hand over finished products to other entrepreneurs for use as capital goods, unless we consider valuables as capital. Valuables, at first sight, are not capital, since they produce nothing; they will not,

therefore, be treated for the moment. Given a slightly looser definition, however, there is a sense in which they can be considered
capital, and this will be discussed later. Finished goods used for
production are tools either made by the entrepreneur himself or
obtained in finished condition from outside the Siane area (e.g. axes
from the north-east). When owners take goods from their stocks
(remove them from their capital account), the objects are immediately consumed by the owner and others (become part of the
income account) and do not form part of anyone else's capital
account.

The most obvious capital goods in Siane are those that form
fixed capital—the 'durable instruments of production' (Knight and
Hines 1952:102). Men's tools are almost exclusively axes; women's
tools are digging sticks and bone needles. Less clearly capital are
objects such as houses and clothing, which represent a stock of
goods that is not immediately dispersed or consumed. They may
be considered capital, however, since they 'produce' services for
their owners while they exist, and the term consumer's capital is
often applied to them in western society. For accounting purposes
they can be regarded as on capital account until they are destroyed
(and become income) and are replaced by a new capital investment.
Initially, depreciation—an accountant's way of spreading the income
over a longer period—is ignored, because assuming an even rate
of capital formation, and, at least in the short run, no changes in
capital stocks, depreciation merely serves to halve the value of the
stocks. It would do this for each period of account we choose to
consider.

The third category of capital commonly distinguished—liquid or
working capital—comprises goods an entrepreneur must hold in
stock during the period of production: raw materials, half-finished
goods, finished goods awaiting dispersal, and stocks to pay for
labour, etc., during this period. In Siane labour is not paid, but
half-finished goods are in evidence as gardens that have been improved by clearing and planting, by fencing and weeding, and that
have not yet begun to be converted into income by the harvesting
of crops. Other forms of working capital are trees that have been
tended but have not yet borne fruit, and stocks of bark fibre owned
by women.

Listing the items of real capital in Siane is simple compared with
the task of measuring the disparate items so that they can be added
to give a single index, as is given by a money assessment in other
societies. As Frankel (1953:29-50) and Kuznets (1953:192-212) have
shown, even using monetary measures has its pitfalls when one

144 FROM STONE TO STEEL

wishes to compare different societies or the same society at different times. The index I propose to use for Siane is the labour cost of the various capital goods, though with the understanding that this index may only be useful for Siane and that its use to measure capital stocks and investment at different times presents problems to be discussed later.

Apart from the practical consideration that labour cost is the only measure readily available, there are justifications for its use. Capital in monetary societies is usually assessed at cost, and the figure so obtained is then subject to depreciation, which is being ignored here. But time is the only resource that can be used for competing ends in Siane: the cost of any activity is what has to be forgone by using the time for that particular activity. Time, then, is *the* Siane measure of cost. At different moments (e.g. when a Pig Feast is in progress) a unit of time may represent a larger cost (since people are extremely unwilling to forgo eating pork), but an average cost can be assumed in calculations dealing with aggregates. So, too, the fact that different individuals have different abilities and their 'time costs more' can be neglected in Siane. All men practise the same skills to some extent, and each man's work is considered as help, which is repaid by another man's help, even though the productivity of the two men may be quite different. Time, in short, is treated as being standard for all men.

Capital Ownership in Siane

The capital goods owned by a typical ward group of seventeen adult male workers, nine youths, seventeen wives (a working force equivalent to forty adults) and their dependent children and old people can be listed. As a corporate group they own one men's house. The separate lineages own about twenty women's and pig houses, and have improved some twenty strips of land, each about 30 by 60 yards, which have not yet begun to yield income. The men own individually about twenty axes and their clothing of thirty net aprons. The women own about thirty net carrying bags, eighteen bone needles, and thirty bark-cloth skirts and string aprons. Other working capital is represented by trees and stocks of bark fibre.

To build a men's house, thirty men work for three days erecting the structure, and another six men thatch it in one day. Materials for the house are collected over a long period, and much old material is re-used, but I estimate that thirty men could collect the materials in two days, while thirty women collect the thatch straw in one day. A men's house thus represents a cost of 186 man-days of labour diverted from other uses.

Three men can erect a woman's house in a day, and one man thatches it in another day. I estimate that a man takes three days collecting materials, while his wife spends a day collecting thatch. The house costs eight days of work. This figure and that for men's houses would have been somewhat larger when stone tools were used, but against this can be set the fact that fewer pig houses were built then.

I could not observe the manufacture of stone axes, but Vial (1941: 160) gives the following times for the manufacture of ceremonial stone axes around Mount Hagen.

> It takes from half an hour to all day to chip out a good blank [of stone], . . . the polishing takes about three days; the carving of a wood handle a day; the weaving of the cane binding and other decoration two days. . . . An ordinary axe would take less time for the stone is smaller and thicker and it could be chipped out more easily, and the polishing is less accurate. The handle has none of the decoration of the ceremonial axe; it is held together by a rough bark binding.

My own observations confirm that at least a day is needed to shape a handle, and another day to make an adze binding. Six days would be a fair estimate of the cost of a work axe, including the transportation of the stone from the quarry to the village. Needles take about a day to fashion from cassowary bones. A woman takes about three full days of work to make a net-bag or apron, and a man takes a full work day to make a bark-cloth skirt. These objects are made during odd moments of the day, but my estimates are based on time spent in continuous work.[1] To buy a steel axe at a Highland trade store in 1953 required about 12s.,[2] or what could be earned in twelve days of casual labour for Europeans.[3] The time

---

[1] A purist might argue that, since these are odd moments, they cost nothing. I justify my assigning a cost partly in terms of the entire days that are occasionally spent doing such work and partly in terms of the fact that people could, theoretically, sleep or do nothing. The cost is then the leisure forgone.

[2] The difference between this figure and that used to compute the cost of items bought at a coastal trade store is due to the high cost of air-freight on all goods carried into the Highlands, including those needed for subsistence by storekeepers. In the present context, it is the price in the Highlands that is important. In Table 3 what is relevant is the sum actually paid by an indentured labourer.

[3] I use the current rate for casual labour, rather than one-thirtieth of the monthly pay of an indentured labourer, because, although casual labour can rarely be performed by a Siane man, the indentured labourer receives board, lodging, and clothing, as well as cash.

taken to produce needles, axe-handles, and string-bags has probably not changed with the introduction of steel tools.

Clearing and fencing a strip of land took one man twelve days in 1953. He then spent another two days in planting, while his wife spent twelve half-days. Weeding during the period of growth takes the wife about fourteen half-days. The capital represented by this labour is dispersed as soon as crops begin to be harvested, but is then replaced by the improvement of other land. It is a stock in hand, not producing income at any one moment but continually being replaced as income is withdrawn. The stock of working capital in trees and bark fibres I should guess cost some eighty days of work, weeding and clearing undergrowth, or stripping and shredding bark.

When stone tools were used it took three times as long to clear and fence land. This would mean that these jobs took about thirty-six man-days for each strip, although planting and weeding probably took the same amount of time as they do now.

The number of capital goods owned when stone tools were used was approximately the same as the amount owned in 1953, when the introduction of new capital goods such as spades, bush-knives, and European-style houses and clothes was only beginning. Table 5 lists these goods and summarizes the calculations of cost in both stone-using and steel-using times.

The meaning of these figures can be put in commonsense terms if we relate them to the 'national income' of Siane, or to the cost of what is consumed each year. The total cost of all goods and services consumed (over the long term and thus ignoring savings from year to year) is 365 days per worker. For a ward group with a labour force of forty men and women the aggregate income costs 14,600 man-days. In stone-using times the capital stocks of the society represented about 12 per cent of one year's income; in steel-using times they have shrunk to about 10 per cent of the national income. At this point the relevance of the definition of capital as 'stocks of goods which must not be used for immediate consumption but must be immobilized during the productive process' becomes clear. If in stone-using times a village were forced to abandon all its tools, houses, and gardens (as could happen in warfare), it would have to spend 12 per cent of a year, or a month and a half, re-creating its capital before it could obtain any 'income' or goods for consumption. In 1953 a ward group could re-create its capital and be ready to obtain income after 10 per cent of a year, or just over a month, if it were fed and housed during that period.

It may be argued that this apparent *disinvestment* is in fact

produced by a change in value of the units of measurement. The
stone-using capital stocks are expressed in 1933 man-days; the steel-
using stocks are in 1953 man-days. The cost of a man-day, expressed in terms of the goods produced, has changed between the
two periods, four 1953 days producing what needed five days in

TABLE 5

*Amounts and Estimated Labour Costs of Capital Goods Owned by
One Siane Ward Group*

Type and Amount of Capital Owned	Cost of Capital in Man-days			
	Stone-using times		Steel-using times	
	Per unit	Total	Per unit	Total
Fixed capital				
20 axes	6	120	12	240
18 needles	1	18	1	18
		—		—
		138		258
Consumer's capital				
1 men's house	186	186	186	186
20 women's houses	8	160	8	160
30 men's aprons	3	90	3	90
30 women's skirts	1	30	1	30
30 carrying bags	3	90	3	90
		—		—
		556		556
Working capital				
Improvements to land by—				
fencing 20 gardens	36	720	12	240
planting „ „	8	160	8	160
weeding „ „	7	140	7	140
trees and bark fibre		80		80
		—		—
		1,100		620
Total		1,794		1,434

1933. On this basis the 1933 capital stocks could be calculated as
worth only 1,435 (4/5 × 1,794) 1953 man-days, or virtually the same
as the cost of the 1953 stocks. The difficulty of changing units of
measurement has no simple solution, but in the present instance
it is safe to say that capital stocks have not increased in the period
of technological change, but have either decreased or remained
constant.

The problem of changing units does not arise in considering how
far capital has displaced labour in the productive process, since

this involves comparing capital costs at one time with labour costs at the same time. Thus in 1933 capital stocks costing 1,794 man-days were used in production with 80 per cent of 14,600 (i.e. 11,680) man-days of labour—the percentage of the year spent by men and women in productive tasks. This gives a ratio of 1 unit of capital to 6·5 units of labour (or to 13 units if one depreciates the capital). In 1953, 1,434 man-days of capital were used with 9,161 man-days of labour (50 per cent of the 23 men's time and 80 per cent of the 17 women's time) or about 1 unit of capital to 6·4 units of labour, virtually the same ratio again as in stone-using times. Capital stocks, relative to labour used, have remained constant. Capital has not displaced labour in production, but the use of both factors has declined at the same rate. This has resulted in a form of 'techno-logical unemployment', but this, it must be noted, has not hindered the acceptance of the new technology.

Table 5 also draws attention to another change in capital stocks implicit in the technological change—a change in the pattern of capital ownership. In 1933 the largest single unit of capital was the men's house, owned by the corporate ward group, while the next largest units were improvements to land, ownership of which was vested in the lineages. Individually-owned capital consisted of small items such as clothing and tools costing little for each unit. In steel-using times the importance of the lineage-owned units of work-ing capital has decreased sharply, while individually-owned items of fixed capital have increased in importance; the men's house still remains the most important unit of capital. One of the important functions of any corporate group (cf. p. 75) is to maintain intact capital aggregations which individuals acting alone might disperse. The changes in the pattern of capital ownership may thus be linked to the changes in importance of the various groupings mentioned previously. Individually-owned capital has become important as society has tended to fragment into individual units; lineages may decline in importance if the capital they own becomes less im-portant; the concentration of power in the hands of 'big men', who form the nuclei of ward groups, is associated with the importance of the men's house as the largest single unit of capital in Siane.

Capital Investment in Siane

None of the preceding discussion has concerned the rate of capital *investment,* or the formation of new capital. If it is assumed that capital is replaced at a steady rate and that Siane entrepreneurs (being the consumers of their products and the providers of their tools) replace capital goods as they wear out, it is possible to calculate, from a knowledge of the life of each article,[4] the average cost of capital replaced every year.

Steel axe blades last several years. The fact that German axes were reported in the Highlands in the 1930s, although German goods ceased to be imported in 1914, suggests that sharpening with sandstone prolongs the life of an axe beyond the three or four years' expectation when carborundum is used. I should estimate twelve years as an average life for a steel axe. Stone axe blades chip easily, are quickly abraded by sharpening, and are probably worn out in a year and a half. Axe-handles need replacement each year. Bone needles last indefinitely, as does men's dress, but women's skirts need replacement about every eighteen months. Net bags last about three years. Men's houses are rebuilt every three years, as are women's houses in the village, but new pig houses are needed more frequently, because cultivation sites change about every two years. Working capital is constantly being replaced, but never varies in total amount and can be ignored in a consideration of capital formation. Table 6 presents an estimate of the amount of capital investment made each year by a ward group, based on these figures for the life of capital goods.

These figures show the same order of change as do the figures for the amount of capital stocks. Expressed in terms of labour cost, the annual rate of capital investment in steel-using times is only four-fifths the rate in stone-using times; instead of spending 2 per cent of the total national income in capital investment, as in stone-using times, now only $1\frac{1}{2}$ per cent is so spent. As has been noted earlier, these differences may be more apparent than real, in view of the changing cost of time, but it is clear that Siane prosperity has not been accompanied by any dramatic *increase* in the rate of capital investment.

The difficulty of changing units of measurement may again be avoided by relating the amount invested each year to the annual real product. In stone-using Siane the subsistence production of a men's house group represented 11,680 man-days work (cf. p. 148) of which 276 were for capital replacement—one day in 42. In steel-using times subsistence production represented 9,161 man-days, including 216 days of capital replacement—again one day in 42 or no change in the rate of investment. Although this is the overall replacement rate, the replacement rate of axes, considered by themselves (i.e. their cost per unit output), has declined. In stone-using

[4] Firth has calculated similar figures for the Tikopia (1939:256), which can be compared with the present figures.

times a day's output cost 1/117 days of labour replacing axes and handles; in steel-using times the figure is 1/230. Steel axes cost only half as much.

TABLE 6

Annual Replacement of Capital Goods Needed by a Siane Ward Group

Type and Amount of Capital Goods	Amount Needing Annual Replacement in Man-day Units			
	Stone-using times		Steel-using times	
	% replaced*	Cost†	% replaced*	Cost†
Fixed capital				
20 axes	66·7	80	8·3	20
20 axe handles	100·0	20	100·0	20
		100		40
Consumer's capital				
1 men's house	33·3	62	33·3	62
20 women's houses	40·0	64	40·0	64
30 skirts	66·7	20	66·7	20
30 carrying bags	33·3	30	33·3	30
		176		176
Total		276		216

* Based on the estimates of the life of articles given in the text.
† Obtained by taking percentages of the totals given in Table 5.

The Propositions

The preceding calculations permit the relevance to Siane of the original propositions to be assessed. It is clear that present-day Siane prosperity has not required any great increase of capital stocks to produce it, nor has it required or been accompanied by a higher investment rate. Nor has the decrease in the cost of capital per unit output led to any substitution of capital for labour in production. The propositions, which relate primarily to economies which are growing without any technological change, do not necessarily apply to societies involved in technological change. In such societies the problems of finding comparable units of measurement which are present in any study of two economies become even greater. Whatever allowance is made for this difficulty, however, does not radically alter the picture of no capital changes yet increased prosperity in Siane.

But although the propositions themselves are inapplicable to the Siane case, the analysis they occasioned does throw light on the process of change. Firstly, the ratio of investment to output for an axe-using bush-fallow agricultural economy may be compared with the ratio of gross capital formation to national product in societies with other technologies. The Siane ratio was 1:42 or 2·4 per cent: Kuznets (1960:72) shows that highly industrialized countries such as the United States have an average ratio of 21·3 per cent, ranging down to a ratio of 11·4 per cent for countries mainly dependent on subsistence agriculture but having cash-cropping and large extractive industries as in Nigeria. The Siane case clearly extends the application of the generalization that high income countries have higher rates of capital investment. But the absence of change in Siane capital stocks would seem to indicate that technological change (or an increase in knowledge) may be more effective than any massive capital infusion in *producing* a higher income (a conclusion Kuznets [p. 74] arrives at by considering the small difference in investment ratios between the societies he studied).

Secondly, the analysis suggests where to look for determinants of the observed direction of change and level of investment. Several possible courses of action were open regarding the level of investment. The Siane could have maintained comparable capital stocks and produced more goods with the same amount of effort. Instead there was a decision to limit subsistence production to roughly the same amount as before (a reasonable decision since a man can eat only a certain amount of food) and to divert effort into other activities. Even given this decision, alternative courses were open. Relatively *more* axes could have been obtained, to allow youths to participate in the easier work involved in the use of steel axes; *less* axes could have been used if each man had decided to work part-time and share axes with other men. In fact a decision to limit the possession of axes to adult men and to continue with each man owning an axe—a decision to maintain the existing division of labour between men, women, and youths—determined that the same proportion of output was earmarked for capital replacement. This could alternatively be phrased as a decision to continue to *consume* the same proportion of output as before. The Siane 'propensity to consume' (Keynes 1936:125) and the factors affecting it, need to be studied equally with their saving.

Another part of the analysis has pointed in the same direction. When describing the overall change in Siane I have described them vaguely as being 'more prosperous'. I have not said 'their income has risen' as the term 'income' has been used solely to refer to material income. In terms of goods produced there has been no *measurable* change. On the other hand the increase in output needed to cope with the increased amounts eaten at the more numerous ceremonials would be of the order of 4 per cent—too small to be measured. Production of craft goods has certainly increased from virtually nil in stone-using times, but again it cannot be measured. Consumption of subsistence and luxury goods has almost certainly increased to some extent and it might perhaps be fair to say their income has risen.

Most evident as an index of Siane prosperity, however, is the increase in their leisure, ceremonies, travel, and the dressing-up and use of decorations these activities demand. Some economists have discussed treating such services as 'welfare income' (cf. Frankel 1953: Essay 3) but with indeterminate results. The Siane have chosen these activities as the alternative to increased income in goods, and a consideration of the capital investments made in these activities must be made—the subject of the next section. To anticipate the argument there, capital investment for the production of services, for which demand was income elastic, rose markedly, while capital investment for the production of goods for which demand was relatively inelastic did not rise. The nature of demand and the propensity to consume again appear crucial to a consideration of change. Why investment in services should be important at the stage of economic change occurring in Siane, and what are the factors inducing a demand for services—these are the topics of succeeding chapters.

Valuables as Capital

The foregoing analysis has considered capital solely in terms of subsistence goods; in fact much of the wealth of present-day Siane is in valuables, and time and energy is spent in amassing stocks of these objects. Valuables have been omitted from consideration as capital because their use produces no increment. It is possible, however, to treat the valuables as a stock of working capital, producing services at the ceremonies in which they are handed over. The nature of these services will be considered in Chapter 8, but for the moment the assumption that they are produced can be regarded as heuristic, to be accepted in order to see how far the changes in the use of valuables lend themselves to an orthodox economic analysis. In real terms, the services produced by a ceremony could be performed by the labour of the participants, without the use of any valuables as capital, but this consideration will be ignored, and the use of capital in the *gima* nexus of activities analysed in the same manner as was the use of capital in the subsistence nexus.

Firstly, stocks of capital were low in stone-using times. 'Big men' owned one or two broken shells each; unimportant men owned fewer—either none at all, or possibly one. Now a young lineage head, whose years of financing are ahead of him (cf. Table 4) owns three shells and numerous smaller valuables, and unimportant men also own valuables.

Much, but not all, of this increase can be attributed to the returning labourers. Assuming that the figures given in Table 4 represent average amounts now owned, the estimated cost of stocks owned in 1953 by a typical ward group of six 'big men' and twenty youths or unimportant men was about £140. This is more likely to underestimate than to overestimate, since the lineage *yarafo*, whose stocks are listed, probably owns less than an average 'big man'. To estimate the stocks held in 1950, before indentured labourers began to contribute supplies of valuables, the amounts brought back in 1951 and 1953 must be subtracted. If one labourer returned in 1951 and four returned in 1953, and if each brought back £11 worth of valuables, a total of £55 worth would have been provided by them, and £85 would have been accumulated before 1950 by means of *gima* exchanges. This could be considered as some sixty gold-lip shells (purchased on the coast at 30s. a shell) and could be compared with the amount presumably owned during stone-using times, about twelve broken shells. The capitalization of the *gima* activities thus increased about five-fold during the period of indirect contact and autonomous economic growth. The amount of labour employed in *gima* activities also increased from about 6 per cent of a man's time to 18 per cent, a three-fold increase.

Here, then, is a situation where the hypotheses proposed at the beginning of the chapter prove valid. New capital was made available, and was accepted. If the services produced by the use of the capital can be measured by the number of people at ceremonies, then the output and the income of services have increased greatly, as have the stocks of capital. The new capital, because of its productivity, has been used increasingly in the productive process, while the use of labour has declined relatively, though not absolutely. One crucial difference between the behaviour of capital in *gima* activities and in subsistence activities appears to have been a highly elastic demand for the services produced by the *gima* activities; another, that a single unit of *gima* capital can be used over and over and so can employ indefinitely large amounts of labour. In these terms the Siane have taken what Frankel (1953:98) says is 'the best way to accumulate capital'. By investing in this form of capital rather than in subsistence capital they are making 'the best use of that factor which is most abundant, i.e. labour—[not displacing] it by capital which is relatively scarce'. By promoting general economic activity (even if not directly stimulating production) they are performing a type of pump-priming analogous with the burying of banknotes or the building of pyramids cited by Keynes (1936: 129) as a way of stimulating a boom in a monetary society.

The remaining section of this chapter will deal with ways in which the promotion of general economic activity is beginning to have an effect in increasing the accumulation of productive real capital. The way will then be clear to discuss the changes in demand which have been adduced as efficient causes for the stability of subsistence investment and the rise in *gima* investment.

Capital Changes after the Return of Indentured Labourers

The first part of this chapter has analysed capital changes in Siane after steel tools were introduced, and up until 1950. With the return of youths from indentured labour new types of capital investment (mainly consumer's capital) have become available, as, also, have some new forms of production.

Returned indentured labourers use *laplap*s, not only as valuables, but as clothing, together with singlets and shorts. One torn blanket may be retained by them; they use basins and bowls for serving food, and they own kerosene lamps, which provide services over a long period. Other indentured labourers and some village officials are beginning to copy European methods of house building, and are making houses raised slightly off the ground, with walls of woven cane some six feet high, doors that open on hinges, and beams that are held together by nails.

There has also been a slight increase in the number of fixed capital goods owned. Many men now own a machete (pidgin *busnaip*) as well as an axe, for use in clearing undergrowth. A few spades are kept by village officials,[5] and are used when Government work is to be done on roads or rest houses. Spades are not brought back by indentured labourers, probably because the garden work, in which spades might be useful, is women's work. Men do not turn the soil and so do not feel a need for the tools that would make it easy.

Each of these new capital goods requires for its purchase a lump

[5] These spades are Government property, for use on Government work days, but they have been written off by the Administration.

sum of about 6s. It is difficult to retain large sums of money (see pp. 130 et seq.), in view of the frequent obligations to entertain visitors. It is even more difficult to accumulate a lump sum by selling occasional small amounts of produce or by casual labour. Most of the new capital goods can only be obtained by indentured labourers, who then distribute them to other members of their clan.

The typical ward group, as a result of four of its youths (or one-sixth of its male members) having newly returned from indentured labour, now owns some ten machetes, two lamps, three enamel basins, and three worn blankets, and some ten of its stock of 'valuable' *laplap*s are in use as clothing. These goods would be valued at about £9, but, from the point of view of the ward group, they have been acquired at negligible cost. The youths who left the village would only have spent one-fifth of their time productively, if they had stayed (cf. Appendix B), yet they would have eaten a full share of the food. Such capital is thus a windfall accumulation.

But to replace this capital as it wears out requires more effort. Machetes, basins, and lamps last until the next windfall arrives when the next group of labourers return. But clothing wears out in use, as do blankets, and lamps require maintenance and fuel to remain useful. In all some £5 would be needed for replacements each year, but this replacement does not seem to be made. The number of *laplap*s or pairs of shorts I saw being worn declined steadily during the eleven months after the return of the indentured labourers; lamps without wicks or fuel, and blankets with huge holes became increasingly common as the year wore on. The money kept by the labourers does not keep their newly acquired goods serviceable.

In short, returning labourers do not increase capital stocks as much as they could. Since the money they retain is dissipated in entertaining visitors and is not used for purchasing valuables, as is intended, they affect the supply of capital principally by the goods they bring back with them and distribute immediately. These goods, as has been shown, are mainly valuables which form capital only for the *gima* activities. This is a form of capitalization encouraged by native society and for which saving is approved; newer forms of capital, though they are accepted if they arrive as windfalls, are not maintained by allocating a proportion of income to their replacement.

Tendencies towards Individual Accumulation of Capital

Thus far the valuables of the returning labourers have been treated as supplying capital for the *gima* system and as going into the hands of the owners of capital in the native system—the 'big men'. But from the figures of Tables 3 and 4 it is clear that a proportion of the goods brought back are accumulated by men who would not be capital-owners under the indigenous system. I shall now consider this and other types of accumulation of capital which would have been impossible in the native system, and shall show the extent to which these new accumulations are used 'productively'.

Returned labourers, most of whom are between the ages of 15 and 20, do not all enjoy distributing their earnings. They feel they have worked more strenuously and continuously than do people in the village and that they are entitled to some reward. They complain especially of having to give gifts to distant affinal kinsmen, who are unlikely to make any return. Yet another complaint stems from the native pattern of sharing any object a fellow clansman is not using at the moment. Hats, footballs, clothes, and lamps are borrowed and worn out by the more numerous stay-at-homes, who are less careful, less knowledgeable, and less scrupulous about personal hygiene. Returnees remark bitterly about 'dirty, ignorant *kanakas* who break things and make clean clothes filthy'.

The most that a returnee can retain is about £5 worth of valuables and cash, but even this amount has some important effects on the native economic system. It represents about one-fifth of a bride-price, earned either before marriage or soon after. In the native system a youth could only begin to accumulate valuables as his wife raised pigs for him, unless he was a lineage *yarafo* and received payments for his sisters. He would owe all his bride-price and would not be able to join in the councils of the clan until he had repaid his indebtedness and was contributing to the payments of others. Now the labourer can be free of debt sooner and is thus less dependent on the contributions of older men. Since the need for the support of others in making payments is a major sanction for obedience and sharing, the indentured labourer is becoming freer to behave as he wishes and to flout authority and custom. As yet the revolt is limited to complaints, and no serious breakdown of the native authority system is impending.

What could happen if independence were achieved is indicated by what happens to those who leave the villages to find more permanent employment. They are not detribalized, in the sense of becoming isolated urbanized individuals, but retain ties with their villages, where their wives may reside and where they keep *merafo* land rights. They visit their homes on holidays, and occasionally send messages by letter or messenger. They work mainly in Goroka, as police constables or medical orderlies for the Government, as servants for Europeans, or as mission helpers. Only twenty-five men were so working in a population of 6,000 covered by my census, but they seemed to be among the most active and intelligent men in the society. They receive schooling in the police or medical service, and most medical orderlies can read and write pidgin. All such workers learn European skills; they earn regular pay, which increases with experience; they copy European techniques of organization and management. These techniques are one of the major forces for change. No native can directly order any other in the indigenous system, but police constables give orders in parade ground style. Medical orderlies order the draining of potentially malarial swamps or the carrying of patients to hospital, and will use force to ensure that their orders are carried out. House servants hire younger boys (pidgin *manki*) to do chores for them, and give more peremptory orders than do their masters, while if they visit their home villages with their masters, they are distant and aloof with their clan-mates.

Although these men can become wealthy, strong pressures are applied to make them distribute their wealth. All fellow-villagers who come to town stay with them and expect to receive presents on departure. Visits are arranged to coincide with the monthly pay-day. Few workers bring their wives to Goroka, and the remainder must give presents to the men who make houses and gardens for their wives. Having no resident wife means the employee has no ready way of feeding guests; no garden with tobacco in it. He must either incur his employer's displeasure by using his supplies (as often happens), or he must use cash to buy tobacco, salt, and food, and as a gift when the visitors depart. If a gift is brought by the visitors it is usually food, such as sugar cane, for which the worker has little use, since he is liberally fed by his employer.

Natives in employment recognize this drain on their wealth, and try to obtain employment at a distance from home. Those who cannot, use subterfuges to disguise their wealth, often saying that their employer only gives them five shillings a month, concealing the fact that a lump sum is being held for them. One constable from the northern edge of Siane, who had been employed for about ten years in Port Moresby and other distant areas, had been able to place about £600 in two Savings Bank accounts, but still was able to appear poor. My own servant, whose village was thirteen miles from my house, got me to confirm the same excuse, which he often gave to his visitors. He planned to use his money as productive capital, after I left, but had to adopt another subterfuge to prevent his accumulation from being dispersed. He wished to breed chickens for sale in Goroka, and let it be known that he was buying birds on my behalf. He told any visitor that the birds in his chicken pen belonged to me and could not be killed for entertaining. Unfortunately his desire for quick returns led him to sell his fattened hens rather than wait for eggs and chicks, and marauding dogs completed the collapse of his venture.

Another man—the paid Government interpreter for the Siane area—thought of buying chickens and pigs in less sophisticated southern groups and selling them in Goroka for a profit. Through me he bought several pounds of beads, but prevented his wives from demanding that he share them only by saying that the beads were mine and that he was buying chickens and pigs on my behalf. He talked of setting up a trade store, but his trading was largely unsuccessful as, he said, natives would have been prepared to trade with a European but would not buy from another native.

These examples bring out another point—that permanent workers have been taught how to make money in a market economy, and have learned techniques for organizing and controlling other natives. If they can accumulate and retain capital, they are the people best trained to become individual entrepreneurs, and this is what they plan to do. The policeman with £600, perhaps the wealthiest man in Siane, planned to buy a jeep to carry produce into Goroka. Many men spoke with admiration of a native from a village near Goroka who has nine 'wives', to whom he gives periodic large gifts for working a market garden. He sells produce to the Government hospital and police barracks, and at one point in 1953 had cornered so much of the supply of sweet potatoes that the Administration had to send out trucks to buy his produce instead of waiting for him to bring it in for sale. In addition, he has provided capital for some small native gold-washings, including one in the south-east of Siane territory. He is said to be *'man olosem masta'*—'a native who is like a European'. To be like him (even though he is not a Siane), to accumulate capital, and to use it productively in an individual business is the goal of the few educated Siane. It is a goal that is opposed by the native system of sharing.

Corporate Capital Ownership

The fact that individual capital accumulation is difficult may be attributed in part to the fact that in the indigenous system all large capital items are owned corporately. The possibility of introducing new productive tasks, requiring a large labour force and presumably corporately owned capital has been mentioned (see Ch. 5) as potentially leading to greater village solidarity. In fact there have been trends in this direction.

As has been indicated, the main obstacle to growing cash crops has been the poor connection between Siane and a dependable market. In 1952 the Agricultural Extension Department introduced passion-fruit and coffee as crops which it would be financially advantageous to grow, and when I arrived natives clamoured for an airstrip, where Europeans could buy their produce and fly it out to Goroka and the coast. Their visions of wealth if an airstrip were provided may have been magical ones, but when the Government decided that an emergency landing ground was needed in the south of Siane, all the nearby Siane tribes went to work on the task of levelling an area, every week on Monday, the Government work day. The airstrip was not quite completed when I left the field in November 1953, but represented twenty days' work by some ten tribes, or 2,000 men. If it proves an economic proposition for a European to operate a trade store and purchasing station there, and to fly out native produce, the airstrip will represent a corporately owned capital investment in the marketing of cash crops.

A similar investment to the north of Siane is the jeep road completed in October 1953 by local native labour, with European supervision and with Europeans building the bridges. At first there was native opposition to the seemingly pointless work on the road, especially since the broken stone surface was uncomfortable to walk on barefoot. But after the first jeeps travelled the road, and the first purchases of produce were made by travellers, opposition vanished: natives now work on the road every Monday without supervision. This work can be regarded as maintaining corporately-owned fixed capital.

Some investment in roadbuilding occurs in the rest of Siane on Mondays, but none of the tracks are passable to wheeled vehicles. Some progressive villages have levelled long stretches, but other groups are apathetic. Since difficult engineering work would be needed to connect the tracks with the jeep road, it is unlikely that the improvements will be turned into a profitable investment. Nevertheless, improvement of transport and communications is the most important means of investment to assist cash-cropping, and it is a means which puts capital in the hands of large corporate groups.

The other aspect of novel capital investment has been the growing of new crops that are relatively easy to transport to market.

Passion-fruit began to yield in 1953. Visiting Europeans (including myself) were able to consume the small 1953 crop, but the 1954 crop promised to greatly exceed the local market, and the opening by an Australian firm of a plant in Goroka to pulp and export passion-fruit juice was planned to coincide with the harvest. But since only 1d. a pound was paid for native-grown fruit, Siane natives did not carry any fruit in to Goroka in 1953. There was talk of raising the price, but by November 1953 this had not taken place.[6] If an increase in price makes passion-fruit an economical crop, then the planting of vines and the construction of supports will be another novel form of capital in Siane, albeit individually owned.

A few coffee trees in Siane bore berries in 1953 and there was a prospect of some economically significant production in 1954. In 1953 world coffee prices were at a peak, and it was possible to offer native growers 1s. a pound for dry berries in Goroka. The prospect of a return of 30s. for carrying one load into Goroka certainly acted as an incentive to plant coffee trees during my stay,[7] and many natives went to the Government nurseries for seedlings and instruction.[8]

Since young coffee plants need extensive care to provide them with shade and shelter, they are a good form of investment for people with a labour surplus. At first such investment was on an individual basis, men planting single seedlings beside their wife's house and treating them with the care given to special flowers. The same pattern was followed with passion-fruit vines, which were planted singly and allowed to climb over nearby casuarina trees. One village, however, under the leadership of a progressive *luluai*, set up a nursery, some thirty feet square and complete with artificial shade, drainage, and deep-dug soil to grow coffee from seed. In 1953 a site was prepared for planting out the trees in rows, con-toured around the hillside, and using *Crotalaria* as a temporary

[6] By 1958 the price paid had risen to 3d. a pound, and the total crop of the Eastern Highlands yielded 12,000 gallons of pulp (*South Pacific Post*, 27 Jan. 1959) which I estimate at about 120 tons of fruit. Prices paid were later reduced to 2d. a pound (*S.P.P.*, 27 Feb. 1959), for fear of overproduction and opposition from Australian growers, despite the tariff of 8s. 3d. per gallon.
[7] Since 1953, of course, there has been a world slump in coffee prices, but by 1959 the price of New Guinea coffee was stabilized at 4s. to 4s. 7d. in Sydney (*S.P.P.*, 17 Apr. 1959). European growers had said that at a price of 3s. 9d. in Sydney it was almost only worth burning the crop (*S.P.P.*, 27 Jan. 1959). The effect of the price changes on native production is not clear.
[8] Some time before the Government introduction of *Coffea arabica*, the Lutheran mission distributed seedlings of *Coffea robusta* to their native evangelists. The result is that, without detailed inspection, purchasers of native coffee cannot be sure it is 100 per cent *arabica*. Unless the *robusta* can be eradicated, native coffee will inevitably fetch a lower price than it otherwise would.

shade. Two other villages were following this example, but less efficiently.

The establishment of the efficient nursery was a clan project, with groups of plants owned by particular lineages. The holes for planting the trees were dug by lineage members on land of which they were *merafo,* but the whole plantation area was continuous, as is a large clan garden, and was surrounded by a fence built by the whole clan. In other words, the indigenous system for organizing large enterprises was employed, using communal labour and having individuals or lineages owning crops and improvements to land. To the extent that large work-groups are necessary for starting coffee growing, the power of the clan as a capital-owning group may be expected to increase; to the extent that profits accrue to lineages, they are likely to increase the importance of the lineage as a capital-owning group.

7

CHANGING DEMAND

THE PREVIOUS CHAPTER has indicated that although changes in capital investment accompanied economic development in Siane, the determining factors affecting what changes actually took place were those concerned with the nature of demand for products and services. Goods that could be used in *gima* activities to provide a form of services which were in demand were eagerly adopted, even though not materially productive. Other goods that were materially productive were accepted but not fully used because they produced goods for which the demand was inelastic. The question is thus whether these different patterns of changing demand can be interpreted as a consistent part of a single theory or whether they are idiosyncratic curiosities.

To answer this question it is possible to look, on a microscopic level, at how demand changed in response to a change in potential supply, analogous in a small way with the change in potential supply caused by the steel technology. The change in supply was occasioned by my own presence in Siane, since, in my isolation from European settlement, I had to give the Siane European goods in exchange for most of my food, fuel, and services. Previously there had been no local source of European goods—the Lutheran mission store fifteen miles away in Dene territory was open irregularly for an hour a day, while the Goroka stores were two days' walk away. The goods I supplied did not form a significant proportion of all the goods consumed by the tribes I dealt with. I cannot measure their importance relative to garden produce, nor the effort spent in obtaining them, but I feel sure it was negligible, just as the presence of one additional person in Siane must have caused only a negligible increment to the amount of food produced by 6,000 people. But this relative unimportance means that the goods I supplied were marginal: easy to dispense with and therefore most susceptible to any changes in supply or in other factors. Changes in the types of goods demanded from me provide a sensitive index for studying the factors affecting demand.

Setting up the Experimental Situation

When I started to record what goods were demanded from me I did not foresee that the records would be important theoretically, so that a description of how I collected my data will enable the reader to evaluate how far they are independent evidence, and will also enable the validity of the conclusions to be assessed.[1]

I arrived in the Highlands at Goroka airstrip in November 1952. At that time the 'town' of Goroka consisted of some storage huts near the airstrip and a recently abandoned Government office, all built of native materials, together with a dozen or so wooden buildings with metal roofs, including a new Government office, bungalows for Government officers, and five trade stores attached to the houses of their European owners. To the north of the town was a native police training barracks, a native hospital (including many huts for quarantining labourers newly returned from the coast), and the compound for Government-employed native labourers. There were also houses for the Europeans in charge of these native services. Outside the town but within a restricted radius were about a dozen European farms and several mission stations. Centrally situated between the town, the native section, and the Agricultural station to the west of town was the Goroka Sports Club, the largest building. During the ensuing year great building programmes were undertaken, most houses were covered with metal roofs, street names were posted, and a 'pub' completed the picture of civilization (cf. Simpson 1954: 115). But in 1952 Goroka was a small frontier community of little over 100 inhabitants, having little direct influence on native life and contributing little to the supply of European goods to an area occupied by 100,000 natives.

I was told by the Assistant District Officer, the Agricultural Extension Officer, and by Dr K. E. Read, an anthropologist who was then working with the Gahuku people near Goroka, that the people near Pira Rest House, thirty miles or two days' walk from Goroka, were 'quite different from the Goroka natives'. They had been visited by five patrols, and there had been tribal fighting in 1947. There was no mission in the area, which had only recently been declared controlled. The country was rich, and plenty of pigs and food could be bought. I decided to make Pira Rest House my headquarters.

More specifically, I asked what I should take to pay for native food and services. People who had visited the Siane area within

---

[1] Only after my return from the field did I compare my experiences with those of Firth (1939:377) in Tikopia. His list of exchange rates shows the phenomena I observed in Siane: distinct categories of demand, and a variation in demand even in a stable monopolistic market. He does not fully explore the implications of these phenomena, and in a sense this chapter might be considered an attempt to explore more systematically hints given by Firth.

the preceding six months agreed that the natives wanted small *tambu* shells, beads, newspaper, twist tobacco, and salt. Natives nearer town, they said, would accept threepenny pieces in payments, but there was no demand for cash in Siane. I asked at the trade stores, and was told that plastic bangles, face-paint, small knives, and axes were acceptable gifts. Large gold-lip shells were much desired but had become much more expensive and were out of stock. I laid in supplies of all these articles, sufficient, as I hoped, to last me for three months.

I also wished to know how much to pay for goods and services. Here I had two guides. Firstly, the Government bought much native produce for feeding policemen and hospital patients and had fixed prices and procedures for purchasing. Each day a native orderly waited at a large shed near the hospital with a huge spring balance (*klok* in pidgin), weighing net bags of produce which women brought, and paying for them in cash. The rates he paid were listed on a grimy sheet of paper as $\frac{1}{2}$d. a pound for native vegetables such as sweet potatoes, yams, taro, bananas, and native spinach, and 1d. a pound for European vegetables of all kinds. He used only silver coins in payment, paying to the nearest multiple of 3d. I decided to adopt the accepted system, and habituate unsophisticated natives to the Government's methods. I was told that in the bush I needed to pay only a fraction of these sums, as natives would give me loads of produce for trifles, but I decided to pay the Government rates, except that as my spring balance was marked in 4 lb. and 8 lb. units it was easier to show one 'mark' as equivalent to 3d. for European vegetables, and two 'marks' as equal to 3d. worth of sweet potatoes.

In the second place, the Native Labour Ordinance prescribes what must be paid to long-term contract workers, in cash and kind, the minimum cash payment being 15s. per month at that time. The prevailing rate for casual labour was 1s. a day plus food. In the third place there were customarily fixed rates for eggs and chickens sold in Goroka of 3d. each for eggs and about 5s. for chickens. I adopted these prices and found them acceptable in Siane.

When I asked how much *trade goods* to pay for food, the answers were vague—'Give them a spoonful of salt or a few beads for a *bilum* (net bag) of sweet potatoes'. I decided to base what I paid on the cash value of the food and the cash price for the trade goods when bought at a store, so I surveyed the trade stores for what 3d. would buy. My remaining doubts were allayed, as everyone told me I could live off the country, and that natives would accept whatever I did, since I would be the only European in new country.

I needed personal servants, but within a day of my arrival I was approached by two natives who had heard I might go to Siane, and who asked, through the employer of one of them, if I would employ them. I was warned that employing local men would cause difficulties, for their relatives would strip my cupboards bare, but these natives came from Yamofwe tribe on the northern edge of Siane, and although they spoke the same language, they had no ties with the Pira area. They had both had considerable experience of Europeans, one as a cook and the other as a medical orderly, and I paid them well above the minimum rates when their work proved satisfactory. It proved fortunate in the present connection that they were 'foreigners', for it meant that their pay did not form part of the income of the nearby village, and so did not bias the demand figures this chapter discusses. Six months later one married a local girl (cf. p. 103) and left to avoid his affines, after which I continued with only one servant, as I had no further need for a second as an interpreter.

My biggest problem was to transport my stores to Pira, but with the help of Dr Read I obtained the services of forty-five carriers from his Gahuku village. Provided with what I thought was an adequate supply of small coins to pay the carriers, I cheerfully set out on the first 3,000-foot climb between Goroka and Siane.

Disillusionment set in. After we had forded the Upper Asaro River, which was shoulder deep and swiftly flowing, the carriers refused to move unless I made an advance of pay; half-way up the mountain, when my own resistance was at its lowest, came demands for higher pay; at the mountain top they left me and only twenty local men would help me; we had to move half my goods at a time, from their village to the next: at the next village a new set of carriers had to be recruited, and so it continued. In what was supposed to be an unsophisticated area the only payment demanded was 'money'. My servants were invaluable in seeing that nothing was lost, but the thirty-mile journey took three full days. At the Rest Houses where I camped immense quantities of food were brought by the natives, and I felt compelled to buy all of it 'to establish rapport'. Round my fire in the evenings I was always told 'Don't go to Pira. It is a cold place. Stay with us. We will look after you.' I began to realize that I was being treated as a source of easy income, to be exploited to the limit that I would allow.

When I arrived at Pira, near Antomona clan village, Emenyo tribe, the 'exploitation' continued. Vast supplies of vegetables were brought in, and I felt obliged to purchase them; my house was invaded by local 'big men', who all expected favours—especially tobacco; when I asked natives what they wanted in payment for produce they always said *kifana*—the native word meaning 'stones' but also used for 'coins'. If I said I did not want any vegetables, I was told 'I have brought them a long way, just to give to you. I will not take them back. Accept them for nothing.' But I knew that a 'free gift' in Melanesia usually demands a return gift.

The climax came when a village arrived, led by its *luluai*. All the men had brought huge cabbages weighing about ten pounds each, while the women had brought net bags of potatoes. The heap in front of my door contained, at an estimate, a quarter of a ton of cabbages and half a ton of potatoes. Ruin faced me if I continued to buy everything, and I decided to take a stand. A crowd of five to six hundred people had assembled. I accepted a few vegetables as a token, but made a speech in pidgin pointing out how small my household was, how I wanted to stay for a year and buy produce but could not if too much was brought, and how the 'white man's way' was to buy goods as he needed them, giving an immediate and fair return as was indicated by the *klok*. I handed over a few beads as the equivalent of what I had taken, and waited, expecting a riot. Instead there were appreciative murmurs from all sides; the *luluai* who had brought the produce made a speech in Siane and held out his hand for me to shake. In pidgin he said he wanted to do things according to 'the white man's way'. That evening the crowd in my house told me that people were bringing food just to take advantage of me, that I should just take what I wanted, and that I was silly not to have done so before. From this time, a week after my arrival, my position as a steady small market for native produce or services and as a small supplier of European goods was, I think, established. I had learnt many lessons the hard way, for my supplies of coin and trade goods were much depleted, but my understanding of my own role was clearer.

During this period I tried to keep records of what was brought to me. I hoped thereby to find differences in the types of produce from different areas and so obtain a measure of the European influence on the different groups; to record my expenditures in case an account of my fieldwork grant was needed; to find whether there were differences in the goods demanded by different groups. By questioning everyone who visited me I hoped to learn the native language, the names of groupings, and the way in which I was being fitted into the native society. I fell into a routine of sitting in my doorway typing notes and talking to, or medically treating, anyone who came, whether he brought produce or not, and within a few weeks I had been visited by and had shaken the hands of several thousand Siane from most of the tribes, so that some of my hopes were fulfilled. My other hopes proved vain, however, but I realized that the figures I had compiled might be used for an analysis like the one that follows.

I also realized that if I was to keep records, standard exchange rates were needed so that each transaction could be noted down as, say, 'Komunku man, wood, 3d., paper'. I accordingly fixed my rates for the remainder of my stay primarily in agreement with trade-store rates, so as not to damage my relations with other Europeans or make natives distrust them, but I also made them slightly lower so that natives would prefer to take trade goods rather than cash (in fact I need not have worried about this). Lest rates like 3d. for two teaspoonfuls of salt be considered exorbitant, the high cost of freight must be borne in mind. A 56-pound bag of salt cost 23s. 4d. on the coast; air freight to Goroka at 11d. a pound added 51s. 4d.; three natives took about four days to go from Pira to Goroka and back collecting the salt and were paid 10s.; five or six pounds of salt were usually lost in the rain. The cost per pound delivered was 1s. 8d. The rates I used throughout my stay are shown in Table 7. For the present analysis the importance of the fixity of rates lies in the fact that the changes in quantities demanded cannot be seen as reflecting changes in the rates.

Nor do the changes reflect inadequate supplies of particular goods, for, with two important exceptions, I always maintained sufficient quantities. These exceptions occurred during my first month, when my stocks were unexpectedly depleted and I had to return to Goroka to re-stock, and for a few days at odd intervals when I was

TABLE 7

Exchange Rates of Trade Goods and Cash Used for Purchasing Native Produce and Services in Siane

Article	Unit	Cash Equivalent	
		s.	d.
Glass beads	teaspoonful		6
Small cowrie (*tambu*) shell	teaspoonful		3
Salt	2 teaspoonsful		3
Newspaper	¾ of a double sheet		3
Twist tobacco	stick		9
Face-paint	teaspoonful	1	0
Hard soap	tablet	1	0
Plastic bangles	each		9
Razor blades	each		3
Needles	each		3

unable to collect my supplies on time. The importance of these periods will be shown later. I ceased keeping records before the end of my fieldwork, when my imminent departure caused my stocks to run down and the Siane to stock up.

After my return from Goroka at the end of my first month I adopted a different procedure for purchasing supplies, one more in accordance with native practice but for which I felt I needed the approval of the Administration since it might have infringed against regulations on 'Trading with Natives'. When I was 'given' supplies, I immediately presented the seller with a coin. If he later said he would prefer, say, beads, I would give him beads instead. Many natives were embarrassed about converting (cf. p. 130), and there was often several days' delay before this was done. I was sometimes in doubt whether I was converting the same person's cash into goods. In the figures in Tables 8-13 I subtracted the value of goods given in exchange for cash from the sums of cash given to the individual or group during the preceding two days. At no time did I give more in goods than I had previously given in cash. The new procedure not only speeded up my purchasing (its main aim), but introduced more natives to the use of cash and permitted them an unforced choice of what goods they wanted.

My daily routine during fieldwork illustrates my position in the native economic system. As I ate breakfast, men from nearby villages called on their way to the gardens for medical treatment or to sell eggs and pawpaws. When I returned from work for lunch I was greeted by people from distant groups with net-bags of produce and wounds needing patching. I took some produce from each person, though rarely all they had brought, accepting all purely European vegetables such as radishes and peas. Visitors sat, talking and smoking my tobacco as I ate lunch, typed up notes, and asked them questions. As we shook hands on their departure at about 3 p.m. they would shyly ask to exchange their coins for trade goods. By taking only token amounts I tried to discourage people from distant villages bringing me unusable amounts of, say, sweet potatoes. This did decrease the flow of visitors from distant groups but never stopped it. My attempts to discourage were only partially successful at first because what I, in my status as European, was able to refuse at the front door had to be accepted by my cook, as a Siane, when 'given' to him at the back door. His return 'gifts' either came out of his salary or from the household supplies of salt (cf. p. 157). It was only when I told my cook that all gifts should be given to me as the household head—his *merafo* or 'father'—that he was able to refuse gifts.

By about 3 p.m. the women of nearby villages were returning from the gardens with sweet potatoes, and stopped to give me some. At first I took eight pounds—the minimum amount purchaseable with cash—from the first few and none from the rest, giving their babies a lick of salt as consolation. Later I realized that all merely wanted some salt for the evening meal, and it became a custom for each woman to leave a tuber at my house in return for a morsel of salt. These transactions are not listed in my records, but would serve to increase the recorded amount of luxuries consumed by nearby clans. They illustrate my status as a 'member of the clan', being 'helped' with a small share of the food, and 'helping' with a share of the flavouring.

My next visitors were groups of youths carrying five or six bundles of firewood, who would leave one with me in exchange for a half-sheet of newspaper for rolling cigarettes. As I burned only two or three bundles of wood a day and was always offered more than I could use or store, my relationship with the youths became similar to the one I had with the women. We both helped each other, and accounts of our transactions were not kept.

The men returned about 5 p.m. and stopped at my house to smoke and discuss the day's events, while I asked any questions which had arisen during my typing of the day's notes. They brought chickens, bananas, yams, sugar cane, and large logs and took payment in goods or cash. Even at ceremonial times, when no one stopped at my house, I was not short of food, for my household was included in the distributions, which I attended.

My participation in ceremonials started early, when I observed several weddings in distant villages and was presented with legs of pork. These provided meat for my household for several days. About two months after my arrival a pig belonging to Waifo clan, Komunku tribe, broke into a garden near my house and was killed. The owner of the pig came to me literally with tears in his eyes, saying that he had no cause for distributing pork, and wondering what to do with the carcase. A crowd had gathered to hunt the pig, and some men suggested I could buy the animal and pay off my debts. I was sympathetic towards the owner, and thought this was a happy accident from my point of view (when I grew suspicious of the 'accident', I realized it was better to let sleeping dogs lie). I paid 15s. for a thinnish animal which was cooked and distributed at a ceremonial *gimaiye,* repaying all my debts and providing meat for some friends I wished to honour. The cash I paid for it can be seen in my records (Appendix C) as an abnormal amount received by Waifo clan. After this I received some fresh meat almost each week; I kept a list of who had presented meat to me, and when my debts mounted I mentioned my interest in making a distribution. It usually happened that a pig was 'accidentally' killed soon after, and brought to me for disposal. The cash I paid for pigs is included in the tables. Participating actively in distributions brought home to me their function in giving a more regular supply of pork in a society where storage is impossible, the informal sanctions of obligation when one has not reciprocated a payment received, and the satisfaction of being 'one up' when one's own presentation has not been returned.

I also paid for services, which were offered more frequently than they were needed. Men from the nearest village often asked if they could go to Goroka to collect my mail and groceries. Every two or three weeks I sent a man who could speak pidgin and could conduct my business at the airstrip or District Office, but he would take a friend (or several men if he was to collect stores). I paid such parties 1s. per man per day, and gave them tobacco, matches, paper, and some small change to exchange for their food. Most parties were from the nearest village, except when there was a ceremony in progress, at which times more distant villages vied for permission to work for me and earn money. When I went on journeys and needed carriers more men volunteered than were needed to carry my boxes, and I paid only the needed number. Even so, others came too, living off the food I bought and the pork I received, and enjoying the visits to distant parts under my protection.

In short, my presence was fitted by the natives into their own economic system. My wants needed little effort to satisfy but provided natives with an opportunity to convert their existing surpluses of time and produce into more desirable commodities, which they had previously been unable to obtain. Where my wants conflicted with traditional activities (for example, when a death put a taboo on anyone leaving a village), the traditional activities were preferred. I was a means of supply, not a creator of demand. The total amount supplied was limited by the amount of goods I wished to buy, but within this limit natives had a free choice of which commodities to take. The price of each commodity was fixed, so that a supply/demand analysis would lead one to expect that the relative amounts demanded of each commodity would be fixed by the prices of the commodities and by their relative attractiveness (or in Hicks's [1939] terms, by the indifference curves relating the commodities together). If there proved to be changes in the relative amounts demanded of different goods, these changes would have to be related to extra-economic factors. My position as a monopolistic supplier rules out the presence of other markets as being one of these factors; I propose to consider as factors the degree of previous contact with Europeans, the relative distance from the source of supply, differences in social status, and differences in the absolute number of transactions previously recorded.

Categories of Demand

It was brought home to me during my first month with limited supplies that demand was not completely specific. Natives did ask for a specific good at first, but if their first choice was unobtainable they seemed equally satisfied with any one of a set of goods, but would refuse offers of goods outside that set. If a native asked for beads and I had none, he would then ask for cowrie shells, bangles, and face-paint, and take whatever I offered first, but would refuse any other article. The sets of goods were the same for different people, and were constant over time, on the few other occasions when I was temporarily out of stock. I shall refer to these sets as 'categories of goods'. Some goods, which I did not stock since I rarely gave out sufficient cash to enable a man to purchase one of them, appeared to form another category. Natives from distant groups often asked for these goods, which included *laplap* cloth, leather belts, machetes, and enamel dishes. When I replied I had none, they often accepted razor blades or matches, indicating, perhaps, that all these goods actually formed one category. Some of the cash I paid to carriers was used to purchase such goods at trade stores, but I have recorded only the fact that I gave carriers cash. I have used my knowledge of what was bought to interpret the meaning of an increased demand for cash.

The categories of goods were as follows:

Category A Bangles, beads, small (*tambu*) shell, face-paint, and face-powder.
Category B Newspaper, salt, twist tobacco, and sugar and tea for some returned labourers.
Category C Matches, razor-blades, tinned meat, kerosene, lamp-wicks, needles, nails, small knives.
Category D Soap (for which nothing except cash was substitutable).
Category E Cash.

It must be noted that the categories have been set up on the basis of the demand behaviour of the Siane. Within each category the goods are competitive, or substitutes for one another (cf. Hicks 1939: 42), yet the demand for any good of one category is independent of the demand for any good of another category, except in so far as a large proportion of the total purchasing power is used to obtain one commodity. Cash forms an anomalous category in that it was always acceptable in place of goods of any category, yet on some occasions no goods could be substituted for cash. Yet an approximately similar set of categories could be made in terms of the use of articles or of their inherent qualities. Category A goods are used on ceremonial occasions, as gifts or as decoration; category B goods are luxuries, used mainly for the entertainment of visitors; category C goods are all hard goods of novel types, unrelated to any indigenous commodities. Soap replaces the pumice (as I think the stones shown to me as 'native soap' were) with which natives used to wash before Europeans arrived. Washing was not frequent, but was enthusiastically indulged in as a regular procedure whenever Siane men crossed a deep river. One could say that natives fitted the introduced commodities into the native categories of *gima*, luxury, and regularly-used goods, and had a separate category for other goods. I shall use the categories listed throughout my analysis and refer to them as 'valuables', 'luxuries', 'soap', 'hard goods' and 'cash'.

Table 8 shows the total number of transactions I had with each group during the period for which I kept records, and the categories of goods demanded, expressed as percentages of the total demand. The groups are listed in descending order of nearness to me, with the clan outside whose village I lived at the top. The people living nearest obtained most goods, and those living farthest away the least. In economic terms, the demand for goods varies inversely with the cost or effort involved in walking to obtain them, as would be predicted from theory.

But there are anomalies, such as the relatively small demand in nearby Feramana clan and Fowe tribe and the relatively high demand of Rofaifo clan and Raya tribe. One could rank the groups in order of 'degree of previous Europeanization' (using such criteria as the number of European-style houses owned, the readiness with which coffee and passion-fruit were adopted, and the amount of clothing worn), and this ranking correlates highly with the rank order of number of transactions.[2] I would rank the groups in order

[2] The number of transactions could also be correlated with such variables as nearness to sources of European influence, the personality of *luluais*, the age structure of villages, or the number of returned labourers. All are different aspects of 'Europeanization', and are beyond the scope of the present study.

(1) Rofaifo clan (most
    Europeanized)
(2) Roanti clan
(3) Antomona clan
(4) Waifo clan
(5) Aranko tribe

(6) Raya tribe
(7) Feramana clan
(8) Ramfau tribe
(9) Fowe tribe
(10) Duma tribe
(11) Gai tribe (least Europeanized)

TABLE 8

*Transactions with the Different Clans of Siane Area during
Ten Months of 1953, and the Categories of Goods Demanded
in Payment for Produce and Services**

		Group Differences in Demand				
Clans, in descending order of proximity to anthropologist	*Total transactions per clan (about 200 individuals)*	*Total transactions in each category of goods*				
		A Valuables	*B Luxuries*	*C Hard goods*	*D Soap*	*E Cash*
	Units of 3d.			%		
(1) Antomona (Emenyo tribe)	2,171	35	22	7	9	27
(2) Feramana (Emenyo tribe)	506	51	25	9	7	9
(3) 2 clans of Fowe tribe	25	38	24	24	14	–
(4) Rofaifo (Komunku tribe)	798	25	26	10	29	10
(5) Waifo (Komunku tribe)	446	12	30	5	18	34
(6) Roanti (Komunku tribe)	207	23	21	7	32	18
(7) 3 clans of Aranko tribe	183	51	20	3	18	9
(8) 4 clans of Ramfau tribe	62	56	6	7	4	27
(9) 2 clans of Raya tribe	104	35	15	20	22	8
(10) 4 clans of Duma tribe	70	61	10	6	23	–
(11) 6 clans of Gai tribe	22	79	6	1	15	–

* This table is a summary of Table III, Appendix C.

Raya and Rofaifo are higher in this table than they are in Table 8,
while Feramana and Fowe are lower. In fact, the correlation between these ranks and the rank order of number of transactions

is higher than that between proximity and number of transactions.[3] In other words, previous Europeanization is a greater determinant of the level of demand for European goods than is the ease of obtaining them.

Degree of Europeanization is associated not only with the total demand for goods, but also with the pattern of goods demanded.[4] Table 9 shows the average patterns of demand of the most contacted, the least contacted and intermediate groups, and shows that the intermediate groups are also intermediate between two contrasting patterns. The least contacted groups take more than half of their goods as valuables and only small quantities of other goods; the most contacted take less than a quarter as valuables, exactly a quarter as luxuries, and higher amounts of both soap and cash; all groups demand about one-tenth of hard goods. These two basic patterns—an unsophisticated demand for valuables, and a sophisticated demand for goods of all types, especially luxuries—should be noted, as they will recur throughout the remainder of this chapter.

TABLE 9

Goods Demanded by Groups Arranged in Order of Extent of Previous Europeanization

Groups	Total Transactions in Each Category				
	A Valuables	B Luxuries	C Hard goods	D Soap	E Cash
			%		
4 most-contacted	24	25	7	22	22
3 medium-contacted	46	20	11	16	9
4 least-contacted	58	12	9	14	7

Note: Because of rounding, figures may not add to 100.

'Degree of Europeanization' is a convenient rubric under which to subsume many factors. These include the saturation of indigenous demand, the learning of new patterns of demand, and the 'income effect' described by Hicks (1939: 32) and analysed by Duesenberry (1949), whereby the fact that people with high incomes and people

[3] The coefficient of correlation, rho, between transactions and Europeanization is ·81; between transactions and proximity it is ·7. Both coefficients are significant at the ·01 level. Between proximity and Europeanization rho is ·53, which is not significant, as would be predicted.
[4] The pattern of goods demanded is also related to proximity to me, but to a less marked degree.

with low incomes save and consume different amounts has important consequences in times of generally rising incomes. I shall deal in turn with these and other specific factors influencing demand. First I shall treat length of contact with myself as a type of Europeanization, and consider how the demand patterns changed following longer contact with me. Table 10 shows how the demand pattern of the group most affected by my presence changed over time. Since period 2 shows a pattern almost exactly that of least-contacted groups, while periods 5 and 6 show that of most-contacted groups, my presence can be considered as having the same effect as previous Europeanization.

TABLE 10

Patterns of Demand for European Goods for Antomona Clan, Emenyo Tribe

Period*	Average Number of Transactions Each Day	Total Transactions in Each Category of Demand				
		A Valu- ables	B Luxu- ries	C Hard goods	D Soap	E Cash
	Units of 3d.			%		
(1) 17 Dec. 1952- 1 Jan. 1953	9	33	2	–	–	65
(2) 2 Jan. 1953- 17 Jan. 1953	11	65	7	5	10	12
(3) 18 Jan. 1953- 16 Feb. 1953	8	62	11	–	5	22
(4) 17 Feb. 1953- 13 Mar. 1953	8	61	20	3	13	3
(5) 14 Mar. 1953- 25 May 1953	7	24	32	8	10	26
(6) 26 May 1953- 6 Oct. 1953	7	23	26	10	11	30

* My records only show the dates when I started and completed each page of accounts. Each page represents an average of two weeks' transactions. In Table 10 and succeeding tables the two-week periods have been added together when the overall demand pattern did not change.

But the figures for this group show anomalies, the explanation of which is important for an understanding of why demand changed. In period 1 much cash was demanded, although little-contacted groups do not typically demand cash, but ask for valuables. The amount of soap taken is fairly constant, although it would be expected to rise as does the demand by most-contacted groups. There is a steady but slow rise in the demand for European hard goods,

the demand for which does not vary with degree of Europeanization. Consumable luxuries reached a higher level of demand in
period 5 than is found even in most-contacted groups, but fell off
in period 6.

The first reason for anomalies is that the figures in Table 9 are
aggregates, averaging the distinctive features of different periods.
The unexpected demand for cash in the first weeks of my stay was,
in fact, general and is masked in the figures for least-contacted
groups; the same is probably true of the declining demand for
luxuries in the latest period; the reason why the demand for soap
was unaffected by my presence but varied according to the amount
of previous contact with Europeans will be discussed later (pp. 181-2).
It was not because of a lack of an example of its use.

The early demand for cash *might* be interpreted as a demand
for a storable medium of exchange when it was not certain that
I was staying. But my observations suggest this was not the explanation, since little of the cash was eventually used to exchange
for other goods. Since this demand was immediately, and almost
exactly, substituted for by a demand for valuables, and since small
coins were increasingly used in compensation payments, it appears
that cash was first demanded as a form of valuable. It was only
later that I saw it used as a medium of exchange, when the cash
I gave was used to purchase large European goods from trade stores.
In other words, cash changed from being in the valuables category
to being in the hard goods category, at least among contacted
groups, by the end of my stay. The increase in hard goods taken
by Antomona clan (Table 10) is thus comparable with the increase
in cash shown by the most-contacted groups (Table 9).

In short, the patterns of demand by Antomona clan extend the
patterns already described for other groups. There is generally what
I call the 'Uncontacted pattern', which is predominantly a demand
for valuables, but the valuables may be either cash or objects such
as beads. The final pattern, which I call the 'Contacted pattern',
involves a demand for a diversity of objects, but there is a distinctively high demand for European hard goods or for cash to buy
them with. Intermediate between these patterns is one where the
demand for valuables drops and the demand for hard goods has
not yet risen, but the demand for luxuries is extremely high. This
stage is disguised by the figures that apply to long periods; I shall
call this the 'Native Luxury pattern'.

Other clans passed through the same stages of demand as did
Antomona clan, though more distant groups did not pass through
all of them. The detailed figures are given in Appendix C. Briefly,

Rofaifo clan, a Europeanized group, showed the cash type of Un-contacted pattern until 1 January; the valuables type of Uncontacted pattern till 16 February; the Native Luxury pattern till 13 March; and the Contacted pattern until October, though hard goods and not cash were demanded. In this group soap constituted 42 per cent of the total demand in the final period. The sequence and timing of the various stages was the same as for Antomona clan.

Clan Waifo had fewer dealings with me and took longer to go through the same stages. Their Uncontacted demand, cash type, lasted until 30 January; the valuables type until 13 March; the Native Luxury pattern till 2 August; and the Contacted pattern till October, a demand for cash predominating.

Clan Feramana was a conservative group but had many dealings with me. They took cash and valuables equally in an Uncontacted demand which lasted till 13 March. A transition followed until 26 May, after which time their demand followed the Native Luxury pattern.

Ramfau tribe was both conservative and non-interacting. From December to October their demand followed the Uncontacted pattern, with a gradual transition from a predominance of cash to a predominance of valuables, and a tendency to increase their demand for luxuries towards the end of the period.

These changes in demand patterns have been treated as due to the *length* of contact with myself, and hence as a learning of demand. They could be treated as due to the *amount* of contact with me, and hence as a progressive satiation of previously pent-up types of demand. The similar lengths of time taken by Rofaifo and Antomona clans in making their changes suggest that a certain minimum of time is necessary and that learning plays a part. But the fact that the change from the Uncontacted to the Native Luxury pattern occurred in most groups soon after they had had 175 transactions with me implies that there was some standard demand for valuables that had to be met before demand turned to a different commodity. I shall return to these two topics later.

These changes can also be considered from the point of view of the elasticity of demand for each separate category of goods—by the degree to which demand for each category changed in response to an increase in the supply of goods. The demand for valuables, either as cash or in more traditional form, was the most elastic. It was not infinitely elastic but fell off progressively after about thirty shillings' worth (70 per cent of 175 transactions) had been acquired—an average of 6d. per adult male—finally declining to 11 per cent. When the demand for valuables fell off, the demand for luxuries proved the next most elastic, but never exceeded 40 per cent of total demand before it, too, levelled off at 25 per cent of total demand. The peak demand for luxuries never occurred earlier than at least three months after the increase in supply, or until the clan had had at least 300 transactions with me. The demand for European hard goods was even less elastic and changed only when the demand for luxuries had reached a stable level. I did not stay long enough to see whether this demand also reached a peak or stable level, but I would tentatively suggest that it stabilized at 35 per cent of total demand in the clans with which I had most dealings. Within any one clan the demand for soap showed the least change and the lowest elasticity, although the level of demand varied with the level of previous Europeanization of the particular group. These changes in the aggregate demand patterns of groups and the differing elasticities of demand for categories of goods will become more understandable if the statistics describing individual patterns of demand and their changes are considered.

Individual Differences in Demand

I was able to keep records of the transactions I had with each individual from the village near which I lived. To reduce the data to manageable proportions I have grouped individuals into categories, using the native categories of social status but also distinguishing those individuals who have been away as indentured labourers and have had intensive contact with Europeans. Village officials have frequent contact with Government officials, but among those who have not been indentured as labourers the amount of contact with Europeans varies inversely with age, the youngest boys having most contact. The data are contained in Appendix D.

Table 11 lists the categories of individuals in Antomona clan in descending order of contact with Europeans. As was the case with groups, the most Europeanized people had the most transactions with me. It is impossible to say whether there is any causal relationship between these phenomena, or whether Europeanization and having transactions with anthropologists are both results of certain psychological tendencies. But it can be said that once a man starts either obtaining European goods or being Europeanized, he then tends to do the other.

But the transaction rates for a particular category of persons did not increase steadily as their contact with me increased, nor did they decrease steadily as the aggregate transaction rate for the whole village did (cf. Table 10). Table 12 summarizes the changes in transaction rates.

TABLE 11

Transactions by Different Categories of Persons in Antomona Clan
(Units, 3d. worth of European goods)

Category	No.	Transactions	
		Total	Average per individual*
Men returned from indenture in 1951	4	242	60·5
Village officials	2	124	62·0
Youths (and some men) newly returned from indenture	17	559	32·9
Youths, not yet indentured	22	591	26·8
Young childless married men	13	155	12·1
Unimportant men with children	18	170	9·5
'Big men'	15	94	6·3
Women	54	236	4·4

* The number of transactions per individual woman was too small to make differentiation of categories of women practicable.

TABLE 12

Individual Monthly Transactions in Antomona Clan, by
Social Categories

Categories	Transactions					
	(1), (2) 17 Dec.- 17 Jan.	(3) 18 Jan.- 16 Feb.	(4) 17 Feb.- 13 Mar.	(5) 14 Mar.- 25 May	(6a) 26 May- 3 Aug.	(6b) 4 Aug.- 6 Oct.
Men returned from indenture in 1951	24·5	6·0	8·2	5·1	1·6	2·9
Village officials	15·5	10·5	3·0	4·4	4·5	6·5
Youths (and some men) newly returned from indenture	1·5	2·8	2·2	2·5	3·6	6·4
Youths, not yet indentured	0·5	3·3	2·2	3·1	4·0	2·5
Young childless married men	1·1	2·4	1·6	1·4	0·8	0·8
Unimportant men with children	0·8	0·4	0·3	1·1	0·6	1·9
'Big men'	1·6	0·1	1·0	1·1	0·1	0·3
Women	1·7	0·8	0·5	0·2	0·1	0·4

The highly-Europeanized categories of person (1 & 2) had markedly higher rates in the first month than did the less-Europeanized categories (4-8), but all the latter have such low rates that a comparison between them is meaningless. During the year there was an overall drop in the demand by categories 1 and 2, a marked rise in the demand by categories 3 and 4, and little change in the demand by categories 5 to 8. It is the averaging of these conflicting tendencies that produces the steady decline of aggregate demand.

For no social category does the demand rate increase or decrease uniformly. Instead, the rates show peaks in some months, followed by dips and later by other peaks. These peaks are shown in bold type in Table 12.

It will be noted that the peaks for different groups are not synchronized. They are not an artifact caused by my increasing my demand for goods and services at certain times and so supplying more goods, or by outside events such as ceremonies or crop planting increasing and decreasing demand, since such outside events would have affected all villagers equally. The peaks could be restated in terms of individual preferences as being those times when particular assemblages or 'packages' of goods (cf. Riesman and Roseborough 1955) appeared more than usually attractive to specific individuals, and gave an added incentive for working to obtain those goods. What these packages were appears in the figures for patterns of demand in Antomona clan given in Appendix D.

Long-returned labourers (category 1) had peak transaction rates when their demand patterns were exactly those of the cash type of Uncontacted demand, the Native Luxury pattern, and the Contacted pattern. During the dip periods they show patterns intermediate to the two patterns of demand on either side. The newly-returned labourers (category 3) had peaks which coincided with a valuables type of Uncontacted demand and with a Contacted pattern; the youths (category 4) had peaks coinciding with the cash type of Uncontacted demand pattern, and with the Native Luxury pattern; the young married men (category 5) showed the cash and then the valuables type of Uncontacted pattern, while the unimportant married men (category 6) show these two patterns in the reverse order, followed by the Native Luxury pattern; the 'big men' show the cash type of Uncontacted pattern and the Native Luxury pattern; the women show only an Uncontacted pattern, in which both cash and valuables are demanded. In all cases peaks coincided with standard patterns of demand, while at other times demand patterns were intermediate and transaction rates were lower.

These standard patterns of demand, or packages of goods demanded, although primarily statistical descriptions, appear also to be standards in a normative sense. People make extra efforts to meet these standards, but once the standards are met, their demand is saturated until they find new standards towards which to strive and a new package of goods to demand. For individuals, demand changes by discrete jumps and not steadily; it is only when we study aggregate demand by groups that individual changes are masked in a general trend that appears continuous. Social categories, when studied, show individual changes occurring close enough together to be apparent in aggregate figures.

How were these standard patterns transmitted from one category of person to another? The change from an Uncontacted pattern to a Native Luxury pattern was first made by the long-returned labourers after one month. The newly-returned labourers and youths changed after two months; the 'big men' and the unimportant men with children changed after five months; the men without children and the women did not change at all. The change to a Contacted pattern of demand was made after three months by the long-returned labourers, after five months by the newly-returned labourers,[5] but not at all by other categories, although the youths were beginning to change away from a Native Luxury pattern. In all cases the new demand pattern was first adopted by the long-returned labourers and later accepted by other categories. The process of transmission can thus be described as one of teaching and learning, especially since the first 'learners' were those who were young or most likely to be influenced by the long-returned labourers.

But learning does not explain the anomalous demand patterns of the Antomona village officials (see Table 13). In the first two months the officials' pattern resembled the valuables type of Uncontacted pattern, except that they demanded more soap. While other social categories took more luxuries in the next six months, the village officials did not, but took even more soap. In the last two months, when other Europeanized persons took hard goods or cash, the officials did too, but increased their soap consumption still more. Their demand patterns might be interpreted as changing directly from an Uncontacted pattern to a Contacted pattern and

[5] This change did not coincide with a peak in transactions. I interpret this as meaning that the newly-returned labourers did not see any great novel incentive in obtaining twist tobacco, paper, etc.

omitting the luxury pattern, with the constant abnormality of a greater demand for soap. But officials must always appear washed and with clean clothes when they meet Goverment officers, so that soap is for them a necessity for remaining in office. They illustrate how the social position of an individual can affect his demand pattern.

TABLE 13

Patterns of Demand for European Goods by Village Officials of Antomona Clan, Emenyo Tribe

Period of Demand	Transactions in Each Category (%)				
	A Valuables	B Luxuries	C Hard goods	D Soap	E Cash
17 Dec. 1952-16 Feb. 1953	77	2	–	13	8
17 Feb.-2 Aug.	44	7	4	44	2
3 Aug.-6 Oct.	4	15	15	66	–

Note: Because of rounding, figures may not add to 100.

Anomalies in the demands for soap by different groups (pp. 175-6) can be understood in this light. The officials of Europeanized groups are more conscious of their position, and go to Goroka more frequently, so they need more soap. Since my dealings with Europeanized groups were often with village officials, their needs are closely reflected in my figures.

The social position of individuals and the behaviour expected of them may be used to explain other anomalies, such as the low demand for luxuries by officials. It may also explain the choice of cash or valuables in the Uncontacted pattern of demand. Thus the 'big men', the youths, and the long-returned labourers took cash, while the officials, the newly-returned labourers, and the unimportant men, young or old, all took valuables. Most categories of persons needed goods for making direct payments or for display, and so took valuables—even the Europeanized group of newly-returned labourers, who knew the value of money but who presumably had stocks of it. The long-returned labourers also knew the value of money but had long had no source of supply, so they took money, and were copied by the youths. The 'big men' could not take small valuables from me without lowering their prestige. This was shown, for example, when one, with whom I had not spoken for some weeks, came up to me as I sat typing and said

'I am sad that you have ignored me. I will kill this chicken and my bowels will cease to be sore.' He wrung the neck of a chicken he was carrying and threw it down on my table. Without a word I got up, collected four sticks of tobacco and some paper and threw them down on the table too, saying 'I am your friend. I give you this tobacco freely.' We shook hands, and sat down. As we talked he confided that he really wanted beads and not tobacco, so I substituted beads. This is an extreme example of how 'big men' avoided lowering their prestige. Another method was to take scarce and important valuables, as cash was at the beginning of my stay.

8

ECONOMIC VALUES

Value, as used in modern economic writings, means always value in exchange. It is inevitably relative, since the value of one thing must always be expressed in terms of another; there can be no such thing as 'intrinsic' value in the modern economic sense of the term.

F. Benham, *Economics*

IN TRADITIONAL economic theory value is a concept derived from observation of exchange situations, and is operationally defined as the amount of a commodity, X, that is given in exchange for a commodity, Y. By defining the concept in terms of how it is measured, economists can omit reference to the 'commonsense' implications of the term, while also taking advantage of them. These implications are that individuals have positive feelings towards the commodity, and that it is these feelings that provide the incentive to exchange. Other concepts, such as 'utility', 'satisfaction' and 'wants', similarly derived from the observation of exchanges but not directly measurable, are used to refer to these feelings. They are related with one another *ex definitione*, satisfaction being the state when wants are filled, and utility the potential of a commodity for giving satisfaction or for filling wants. Though value is not defined in terms of these concepts, utility economics shows that it tends to equal the utility of the last unit of a good that is obtained, or the 'marginal utility'. Indifference curve analysis attempts to avoid using the concept of utility, which is not measurable, by substituting 'preferences', which are. As Norris (1941: Ch. 2) has shown, this substitution does not eliminate the concept of utility; it makes it implicit where before it was explicit. In its analyses, however, utility economics is not concerned with the commonsense validity of these concepts, but with the manipulation of the quantified measures of them.

Where the mathematical manipulation of these measures shows that theory based on the assumption of the commonsense validity of these concepts does not fit all the facts, new, *ad hoc*, commonsense concepts are added. Thus 'changes of taste' explain changes in demand, or it is argued that 'demand for luxuries is elastic, while demand for necessaries is inelastic'. Similar *ad hoc* concepts have been used in the preceding chapter in the analysis of demand; this chapter will try to show how they are systematically related to the basic standards of evaluation in Siane society, and how a recognition of different types of utility (all related to one another in a systematic way) would render the economic anomalies of Siane demand quite predictable.

Among early economists, Marshall did try to trace the relationship between wants and the bases for evaluation in the society, and to discover regularities in the relationship. He talked of 'man's wants in the earliest stages of his development' (his biological wants), of 'wants adjusted to activities' which form the basis of man's 'standard of life', and of wants associated with a 'standard of comfort', which he stigmatizes as artificial and gross (Marshall 1925: 86-91, 689-90).[1]

Anthropologists have often tried to classify wants, considering them as 'culturally accepted needs' (Nadel 1942: 334), rather than as needs in the abstract, but their classifications have not generally related the wants or needs to economic behaviour. Malinowski's (1944) well-known classification of 'primary' and 'derived needs' is a case in point. Nadel's discussion of Nupe 'needs' (1942: Ch. XX) is an exception. He distinguishes 'basic needs' (roughly those of food and shelter), but points out that these include a need for artifacts with which to produce food and shelter. Then there are needs which constitute 'more or less fixed demands on resources, which are involved in institutions and customs, and which are accepted with little variation, irrespective of status or wealth throughout the society'. Thirdly, he distinguishes commodities wanted by 'the élite', and also desired by 'the common man' because the élite wants them, even though they are not necessary to the maintenance of life.

Nadel's second category corresponds closely with Marshall's 'wants adjusted to activities', as is seen, for example, when Nadel says 'cultural requirements include the clothing expected of a family head' (p. 354). His third category can be compared to Marshall's category of 'wants associated with a standard of comfort', but Nadel also notes that 'expenditure of wealth in any form also represents expenditure for the sake of status and prestige at the same time' (p. 358). The relevance of such classifications to economic behaviour appears in Nadel's comments about 'fixed demands on resources', for if demands are fixed, alterations in price and supply will not produce the effects predicted by formal economic theory.

[1] For a fuller analysis of the assumptions about individual behaviour made by economic theorists, and a discussion of Marshall's treatment of wants, see Parsons (1937: 129-300), on whom the present analysis leans heavily.

The concept 'value' can be related to wants, since the satisfaction of wants constitutes an end for behaviour, and value is 'the preference quality assigned to an object in virtue of a relationship between means and ends' (Firth 1951:42). Value in a monetary society can be measured because, whatever the desired end, some quantity of money can be found which is preferred to any specific object as a means of attaining that end. Since amounts of money can be compared on a basis of size alone, values (or incentives to exchange) 'can be arranged in an order of intensity' (Robbins 1935:86) and can be treated as varying only in size. In non-monetary societies there is no such unitary measure of value in terms of which comparative worth is expressed. My use of time as such a measure does not correspond with any native usage, and involves many assumptions that may not be valid in other societies. Firth (1939:377), while pointing to the same lack of a unitary series of exchange values in non-monetary Tikopia, has also used an artificial measure for purposes of analysis. Early writers, however, stressed this lack as a failure, due to historical accident or 'primitive ignorance', to develop a unitary standard such as money, which *ought* to be present. Even writers like Nadel (1942:339) assume that there is an *implicit* unitary standard when they use such phrases as 'wants placed higher or lower on a scale of cultural values'.

In Siane there is not even an implicit unitary standard, for no situations occur in which a Siane man can express in an exchange a preference for, say, shells against houses or against nuts. Siane men can express their preference for shells as against feathers, and in quantitative form. So, too, they can compare quantitatively their preferences for oil as against nuts, or for sweet potatoes as against sugar cane. Only in the case of valuables (cf. p. 96) did I analyse what this preference scale actually was. It would require much work to establish other scales, but it could be done.

Since value is assigned to an object by virtue of the object's relationship to the attainment of an end, the *scales* of value indicate the relative closeness of that relationship, while the fact that objects are *not* measured by the same scale of values indicates that they are used for the attainment of disparate ends. The assignment of value in Siane society could, of course, be better understood if the disparate ends of the society were known. But to talk of ends would require an interpretation of motives in Siane society, so, to obviate the speculation involved in such an interpretation, I shall discuss the *uses* to which objects are put and the benefits that accrue from their use. I shall try to establish the standards for assigning preference to, or for valuing, objects in Siane by analysing the uses to which they are put.[2]

Standards of Value in Siane

In Chapter 3, the uses of goods have been described in terms of the three nexuses of activities in which they are used—the subsistence, the luxury, and the *gima* nexuses. What benefits accrue to people during these activities, and what are 'uses' which form the central foci of these nexuses?

At first sight, subsistence activities involve the use of commodities to keep people alive. But they also involve much more than this. They involve the use of goods to produce tools and capital goods and (through such institutions as 'help') the use of goods to maintain the productive organization of society. Classifications of needs have run into difficulties trying to separate the need for food to stay alive from the need for tools and from the need for maintaining productive organization. Marshall did not explicitly differentiate the second need; Malinowski grouped the second and third as 'derived needs'; Nadel grouped the need for tools with the need for the objects they produce, and, like Marshall, grouped the use of goods to maintain productive organization with their use to maintain all social activities.

The Siane themselves do not make any such distinctions when describing the use of subsistence goods. One phrase *'namo orufero ne'* ('it is my job') can be used to describe any subsistence use of goods, from a man working on a garden to a woman cooking, from the preparation of new axe handles to the making of a prescriptive speech initiating garden work by a lineage head. The common element appears to be the continuing obligation to perform these tasks. In short, subsistence goods are used for the fulfilment of continuing obligations. It will be remembered that the analysis of the term *umaiye* (see Chapter 3) was also in terms of the lasting obligation to use, for the benefit of any fellow-clansman who needs them, any goods over which one has trusteeship rights, one's labour, and any personalty one is not using at that moment. After one man has 'helped' another, for example by making an axe-handle, the recipient of the help gives food to the other man, and after eating, both men say *'sene muruna yowo ne'* ('our bowels and livers are

[2] I am indebted to Dr W. E. H. Stanner for suggesting the term 'standards of evaluation' to describe the central concept in this analysis. Any errors in the use of his term and in my justification for its usage are my own.

even') to signify that there is no change in this balance of mutual obligations, which might conceivably have been caused by a net gift of services by one party.

Food is the commodity most often used as a token or a symbol of continuing relationships, for reciprocating gifts of labour, services, or material goods. Most commonly it indicates common member-ship in a group, for the Siane say *'namo wenena weneneta faivya umaiye'* ('we help our own people freely with food'). Food given to strangers indicates that the stranger is, momentarily at least, treated as a member of the same group. Ritually this is clearest in the wedding feasts, where gifts of food symbolize the bride's becoming a member of her husband's village. Food, then, is given by in-dividuals to preserve their membership in productive groups; its acceptance by other individuals serves to maintain or enlarge the group itself. So it is with the use of other subsistence goods.

An analysis of why only certain foods are used to symbolize group membership shows that it is not the mere fact of edibility or the universality of use that makes them into subsistence goods with this symbolic meaning. All Siane eat salt and pork, yet they are luxuries and *gima* commodities. Small birds and rats are treated as subsistence goods, although only boys eat them and adult males will not touch them. Similarly, men's aprons and women's skirts are subsistence commodities in the way they are produced and the way they are exchanged as help, yet women cannot wear men's dress, nor men women's, except in ritual transvesticism.

The first exception suggests that cultural standards define some foods as universally indispensable, and so they become subsistence goods, while dispensability leads other foods to be treated as special. The second exception suggests that goods that are defined as in-dispensable, even if only for a single clearly-recognized social status, also become subsistence goods. Not merely are such goods *used* by people with that status, their use (e.g. of the appropriate cloth-ing) is necessary to indicate that a person has the status and to maintain him in it. Thus soap is now a subsistence commodity because being clean is a hallmark of a village official, who would lose his job if he did not use soap.

The foregoing statement of the use made of subsistence goods can be refined, then, to say that they are used, not merely to fulfil all the culturally defined obligations incumbent on each individual if he is to remain a member of society (and *ipso facto,* alive), but also to indicate his particular accepted status in society and to maintain him in that status. Nadel (1951:67) has called 'diacritical' those goods and activities used to indicate status but not necessarily involved in carrying out the duties of that status. Subsistence goods, one would conclude, are evaluated in terms of the extent to which they are used both as 'diacritical' goods indicating accepted statuses and in carrying out status obligations.

If the use made of subsistence goods is examined, not from the point of the individual using them but from the point of view of society as a whole, this statement can be re-phrased. Subsistence goods, if they are used to maintain each individual in an accepted social position, serve to maintain the existing organization of the whole society, the accepted relationships within it, the basic consumption level it enjoys, and the stock of capital goods needed to support that consumption level. In short, subsistence goods are used to maintain what Marshall calls 'the standard of life'—a standard that has variant forms for each accepted social position, but which every individual must maintain if he is to retain his social position.

In the earlier discussion of the use of valuables the apparent meaninglessness of *gima* activities was considered, but it was noted that men hand over valuables to obtain women from other groups; more correctly, they obtain *rights* over women and their children, rather than women as chattels.[3]

But it is not rights over women that are transferred when net payments are made at peacemaking ceremonies by the side which has killed or insulted more of their enemies. Yet rights of a different nature *are* transferred. Any killing or insult obliges the offended party to seek revenge, but accepting a payment removes the obligation. From the point of view of the group expecting vengeance to be wrought upon it, making the payment gives it a right to expect immunity.

Even less specific are the rights obtained by presenting pork to non-relatives (other than *emona we*) at a Pig Feast, by presenting abnormally large bride-prices, or by the presentation of valuables by returned labourers. All these presentations are described with great pride by their donors, but that pride is not based on the expectation of obtaining any specific rights or an equal return. A bride would be obtained if the bride-price were of normal size, and the labourers would be accepted back however many goods they brought with them; people say they hope the recipients will *not* be able to return an equivalent payment.[4] What is immediately

[3] On the limited rights, which are the counterpart (the *mona*) transferred when specific payments are made, see p. 96; on the religious aspect of these transactions see pp. 34-5.
[4] To be sure, the recipient of the present feels obliged to return an equivalent one. Much has been written, following Mauss (1951), about the compulsions underlying this obligation. The present analysis sees the initial present as

received by the donors is a compliment—either a full-throated roar of *'mika-mika-eee'* ('ground') to compliment the fertility of the donors' soil, or a flattering speech of acceptance. The compliment acknowledges an unspecific obligation in addition to the more specific obligations to repay. In an exchange of large material valuables for specific rights, compliments form the small change of obligation.

In inter-group situations, then, valuables are used to exchange for rights and to set up obligations. The obligations may be as specific as that of producing two children; somewhat vague, as that of accepting insults without demanding vengeance; or as diffuse as the acknowledgment that givers of valuables have better land than the recipients. The common factor in these obligations is that they are created where no obligations existed before and that they raise the power of one group to control the activities of another group. In Mauss's terms (1951:72), giving valuables puts the donor in a superior or *magister* position and the recipient in an inferior or *minister* position, from which he can escape only by returning an equivalent of the valuables. This power to control may be actively exercised or merely asserted in a 'holier-than-thou' attitude by the donors until their valuables are returned. In its most general form this power is prestige; when people informally recognize others as superior it constitutes 'social ranking' (Homans 1950).

Both informal prestige and rights specifically acquired are contrasted with the lasting control that some people or groups exercise over others, that is recognized as legitimate (cf. Weber 1947), and that is vested in specific social statuses. This is usually termed authority, and constitutes a fixed relationship between individuals. No increment to this authority is added by giving *gima* goods to a subordinate—when a father gives goods for his son's bride-price, he still has the same authority *qua* father as he had before. By contrast, what is obtained from the use of valuables is power that is not inherent as authority in the person's existing social position. I shall term it 'free-floating'.

Valuables are used to obtain free-floating power within a group, when contributed to the payment of others. The contributor gains power in the form of an increment to his informal social ranking, although in formal Siane ideology he still occupies a social position no different from that of any other individual. Another use of valuables to obtain free-floating power within a clan group occurs

given in exchange for the right to feel 'one-up' (cf. Barnett 1938). The donor hopes to retain this right, but the recipient knows the only way to avoid being 'one-down' is to return the present.

at some rites of passage (e.g. at the weaning ceremony when a child becomes a clan member). Where the child had only a certain number of rights as the incumbent of his former position, by the giving away of valuables in his name he acquires new rights, and a new social status which he must maintain through his subsistence activities.

Clearly, then, individuals use valuables to obtain new power or new rights that they did not previously possess by virtue of their recognized positions in society. This power may be obtained as one of a group that corporately obtains rights from other groups or as an individual who changes his social ranking within his own group. Valuables are exchanged for power, and a scale might be established equating each valuable with so many *quanta* of power, thus enabling the 'flow' of power in the society to be measured. Clearly there are practical difficulties, however.

An alternative is to look at the use made of valuables in terms of their function for society at large. The exchange of valuables, by virtue of the limited stock existing, functions to ensure an equal distribution of women between groups. In view of the foregoing, this analysis can be extended to say that the exchange of valuables functions to ensure an equal distribution of rights of *all kinds* between groups; within groups it functions to give some prestige ranking and authority structure in an otherwise anarchically democratic society. The clan groups in Siane, it will be remembered, are each sovereign, recognizing no group as permanently superior; yet they must interact in order to gain wives and reproduce themselves. Somehow the power of different groups must be regulated. This is what the use of valuables does.

The earlier analysis of the relationship between the circulation of valuables and the exchange of women explored the economic implications of an increase in the stock of valuables: women 'flowed' towards the source of supply of valuables, but rights over women increased in value relative to *gima* goods until the flow slowed down. If valuables equal power in general, the same analysis indicates the possibility of a similar inflation of the value of power and a similar flow of power into the hands of richer people. Within each group this did occur, as an increase in the power of 'big men'. Yet because the stocks of power in the society are limited—people will voluntarily obey powerful men just so far before they feel slighted and demand 'their rights'—the process of unequal distribution of power can go only so far before inflation causes a new equilibrium to be reached. The power of the rich will be stabilized at a slightly higher level than before.

If, on the other hand, the total stock of power or unassigned rights is increased also, the unequal distribution could proceed much further. In concrete terms, if the size of groupings increased, control over material resources became greater, or new ways of controlling other people were invented, then in a society like Siane where token valuables can be exchanged for power, the difference in power between rich and poor could become much greater. Many authors have described the way in which larger societies with greater control over material resources and complex ways of controlling people tend to have a greater number of social strata (e.g. Sahlins's analysis of variations within Polynesia, 1958). The Siane material indicates a mechanism by which this would automatically come about, given an equation of power and prestige with material tokens, without any exploitation of the poor by the rich. But the same material also suggests that the greater degree of social differentiation and the larger social groupings will remain stable only if new productive activities are introduced providing greater wealth for everyone, employing the larger groups of workers, and utilizing the organizing abilities of the power-*élite*.

The earlier discussion of luxury activities described the way in which luxury goods, though primarily used for entertaining, were also for self-indulgence; by the use of these goods diffuse personal relations are set up between individuals who have no clan obligations to each other, and each individual gains articles to use as he wishes.

The setting up of such ties, or 'friendship', is evident in many uses of luxuries not previously discussed. Thus I frequently gave children a lick of salt, in the same way as Siane men commonly give children luxuries. Although I gave the salt primarily to see the children's obvious pleasure, in fact I obtained the friendship of their mothers. So, too, the way in which Siane men carry half-smoked cigarettes behind their ears acts to initiate friendships. At first I thought the custom was solely because native cigarettes soon go out when lit, and thus protect even strong stomachs from the effects of the virulent native tobacco. But it also means that whenever Siane men are walking along a road and pass a fire, they pause, light a cigarette, take a few puffs and talk to whoever is sitting by the fire, before passing along the road. If a passer-by has no cigarette he merely takes a cigarette from behind the ear of a man sitting by the fire, takes a few puffs, and then returns it. This is the commonest way of striking up casual acquaintanceships and hearing gossip in Siane.

The use of luxuries for self-indulgence can be clearly distinguished

from the use of subsistence goods to satisfy wants or needs. If a
Siane man has no subsistence goods he says he has 'nothing' and
he cannot perform as an ordinary member of society. He may have
nibbled nuts all day, but will say he has eaten nothing if he has
had no sweet potatoes; if he has no net apron to wear, he will not
dare to leave the men's house, but whether he wears a red and
white neckerchief is entirely a matter of his personal choice.[5]
Although Siane men will tolerate being without tobacco, they will
complain bitterly about it. This probably indicates that tobacco is
changing from a luxury commodity to a subsistence commodity.
The way in which objects change categories, and the effect such
changes have on their evaluation, will be discussed later.

But to say that luxuries are used merely to obtain friendship or
sensual gratification is to oversimplify. They are indeed so used,
but on occasions such as the entertaining of affines they are lavishly
used in what appears to be an effort to impress the visitors. Individuals who are not 'big men' provide large quantities of luxuries
on such occasions, and frequently anoint their children with oil in
what appears to be an effort to gain prestige through an ostentatious
display of luxuries. It is not a successful effort, since only men who
are active in the *gima* nexus are accorded prestige by others, but
no one prevents a man from acting in this way, if he wishes so to
use his luxuries. Or again, men working permanently for Europeans
away from the villages use luxuries to entertain fellow-clansmen,
although the obligations incumbent on them as clan members
would only demand the use of subsistence goods. They have chosen,
of their own free will, to work away from the village, and they use
luxuries to maintain permanent ties they do not wish to sever.

In fact, almost every possible kind of use is made of luxury
goods on some occasion. On no occasion is their use socially demanded, but on every occasion it is permitted. They seem to be
used to meet the 'random wants' of the utility economists, and the
particular 'want' that is met on any one occasion is a matter for
personal choice by the individual. If he is not satisfied with the
gratification provided through the use of subsistence goods in his
accepted social status, or if he is not satisfied with the prestige he
has obtained by using the accepted prestige tokens, he may use
luxury goods. More generally, luxuries give the individual a chance
to behave according to whim, instead of according to social dictates;

[5] I am indebted to Dr D. L. Oliver for the suggestion that the categories of
goods could be distinguished in terms of the sanctions compelling their use
rather than of the standards by which they are evaluated. Such a social
analysis would complement the present economic analysis, especially where it
treats the social functions of activities, but will not be made here.

it is a matter of chance that such whims usually involve the gain-ing of friendship or sensual gratification.

From the point of view of society at large, the use of luxuries has several functions. Firstly, it gives dissatisfied persons a per-mitted means of obtaining satisfaction outside the framework of the role structure of society. Secondly, since goods classed as luxuries may be used in whatever way the individual chooses, aberrant in-dividuals will sometimes, by random chance, think up new uses for old luxuries and will be allowed to use them in this way. If new goods are classed as luxuries, they too may be used in new ways. Some of these innovations may be beneficial, and since they are permitted as luxury uses they may eventually become more gener-ally accepted. Thirdly, luxuries are used to set up individual ties, outside the hard and fast framework of clan relationships of for-mality and hostility. As Eisenstadt (1956:96) has shown, such friend-ships preserve the society from too rigid divisions, preserve peace over wider areas, and permit the introduction of new goods and new ideas. In all these ways the social function of the use of luxury goods is to ensure society against too great a rigidity in its traditions or in its formal organization.

To sum up, the use of goods in the different nexuses of activity enables three standards of evaluation used by individuals in Siane society to be isolated. Subsistence goods are valued in terms of how they enable each individual to maintain the activities appropriate to his existing social status; valuables are valued in terms of the free-floating power they enable the individual (or group) to obtain; luxury goods are valued for their use in enabling the individual to behave according to his whims and not according to social dic-tates. From a social point of view, subsistence goods are used to maintain the existing role structure of the society; valuables are used to balance and distribute the free-floating power present in society; luxuries are used as an insurance against excessive rigidity.

New Goods

The preceding analysis has been of the use of goods present in indigenous Siane society. The use of the terms 'luxuries' and 'valuables' for the goods I supplied has tacitly assumed they were used in similar ways. I have already shown why soap can be con-sidered a subsistence commodity. My assumption needs some justifi-cation for the other two categories, and the standards used for the evaluation of cash and hard goods also needs consideration.

The valuables I supplied—bangles, beads, cowrie shell, face-paint and face-powder—were not *neta,* used in *gima* activities. They can justifiably be called valuables because they were used to obtain other rights over people. Boys took bangles and face-paint and used them to impress girls and to persuade them to do what they wanted; men took beads to pacify turbulent wives and so to obtain permission to visit them at night; men took beads to wear and to obtain prestige within the village. The rights these valuables were used to obtain were favours on *awoiro* visits or from wives and prestige within the village, rather than the more important rights obtained through the use of *neta*. My use of the term luxuries needs less justification, since the goods I supplied were used in exactly the same way as native luxuries, with one exception. Sticks of tobacco were sometimes kept as a medium of exchange and as a store of wealth, especially by returned labourers who had no doubt learned the habit on the coast where the practice is common. Not merely could the tobacco be used for entertaining purposes, whenever needed, but it could also be exchanged fairly freely with other natives for whatever commodity was desired at the moment. Such a use added further to the individual's choice of how he used his luxuries.

Matches, razor-blades, kerosene, lamp-wicks, knives, needles, and nails have no counterpart in native society, and cannot be classed with any native goods in terms of their use. That they were not valued in terms of their novelty is proved by the fact that demand rose as the novelty wore off. The common characteristic in the use of these commodities is that they all imply the ownership of other, larger, European goods. Nails are only needed for building European-style houses, needles sew European cloth, small knives do fine craft work for which axes are too clumsy, wicks and kerosene are incidental to owning a lamp, and razor-blades imply (but do not demand, since Siane men often shave holding a blade tensely between the fingers and painfully scraping) a razor. Matches are widely used on many occasions, but their use becomes imperative when lamps are to be lit.

All of these larger European goods are forms of consumer's capital investment of a type that was not present in the indigenous system. In a sense the goods are luxuries, since the services they will provide are over and above those provided by the corresponding native subsistence goods. From another point of view, they are used as power tokens. Little boys who ran errands for me asked for matches rather than salt, and then lit the matches one by one in front of an admiring circle of other small boys. Youths with kerosene lamps were the leaders of *awoiro* parties when there was no moon; the *luluai* who built a European-style house using many nails received most commendation from Patrol Officers on the state of his house and village. In a sense, too, these goods are becoming subsistence goods as they become formally *required* of the occupants of certain social statuses. Almost all *luluai*s have European houses, and leadership in youths' peer groups—the training ground for future 'big men'—almost always involves the possession of a lamp.

I propose, therefore, to treat the larger European goods as a special category—that of 'novel capital investments'. Introduced as luxuries, they have acquired a use as goods conferring prestige, and soon they will be used as part of the requirements of formal social statuses—as subsistence goods. When this happens the services they provide will not be over and above those contained in the basic standard of life, but part of it. The standard of life will have risen, and the novel capital investments will have provided the productive basis for changing the standard of life. Although the goods I supplied are not themselves novel capital investments, they constitute the maintenance needed to keep the new investments providing services. They provide an index of the new investment taking place, and I propose to consider the demand for these goods as indicating the demand for the capital goods themselves.

In summary, the goods I supplied were evaluated using the standards existing in the native society, but a fourth standard, that of the use of a commodity for making capital investments of a novel type, appears in the evaluation of what I have termed hard goods. Cash, and to some extent tobacco, are beginning to be demanded as a means of exchange, or a way of comparing different standards of evaluation.

The Nature of Commodities

Much of the preceding analysis has implied that the reason any particular commodity is evaluated in terms of one standard is merely a matter of the culturally determined classification of that commodity as a subsistence, valuable, or luxury good. In fact there are regularities relating the intrinsic natures of goods with the standards by which the Siane evaluate them.

Subsistence goods comprise consumable food and durable capital such as clothing, shelter, and tools, all of which are related to the physical means of survival. Although there is no clear reason why the goods used to symbolize and maintain different statuses in the society should be the same goods, this is in fact the case. The differences between social statuses in Siane are phrased in terms of differences in the style of houses, clothes, and tools—a man without an axe is a 'man who is like a woman', for example. The village official is marked by his wearing different clothing and having a different style of house. Siane men now differentiate a Siane from a Gahuku by stressing that the Gahuku eat taro, wear different clothing, and live in houses with only two central posts. Food and the men's house are also the symbols used to maintain the labour supply and to ensure the cohesion of the group and the continuance of the way of life among the southern Bantu of Africa (Richards 1932); Radcliffe-Brown (1922, 1939) has phrased the same point in terms of 'the social value' of food. The symbolic significance of and the social value attached not only to food but to styles of clothing and housing needs more general investigation.

Goods are classifiable as power tokens if the owner can destroy any possible utility or productivity they might have for him—a task made easier if the goods are not utilitarian in the first place. The goods must be difficult to produce, and the stock of them must be relatively small and must increase only slowly. They must be relatively storable and transferable, since they give power only when someone can be found who will accept them and who will allow his behaviour to be influenced by receiving them. Yet another characteristic implied by their use is that they must be relatively homogeneous and measurable. Confusion in measuring who has bought which rights over whom could disrupt all social relationships. The publicity of *gima* transactions and the unitary nature of valuables facilitates accounting and prevents confusion.

Any economist will recognize that this list of characteristics almost exactly characterizes commodities that serve the function of money. 'The characteristics of money are homogeneity, portability, divisibility and durability. . . . It is a store of value and a standard of deferred payments' (Gregory 1935:501). Divisibility is the main additional characteristic of money. In Siane money was quickly accepted as suitable for a prestige token, and only later was it used in other contexts and its other characteristics recognized. This similarity in the intrinsic qualities of prestige tokens and of money lies behind the long and somewhat sterile controversy among early anthropologists (cf. Malinowski 1922; Mauss 1951; Belshaw 1954:13) as to whether the *kula* objects of the Trobriands are money or not. This similarity in intrinsic qualities, plus the fact that prestige tokens are presented ceremonially, also lies behind the evolutionist's statement that 'the monetary functions of all objects used as means of exchange and standards of value, before the introduction of coins, originated from their use for religious

purposes' (Viljoen 1936:228). Here it is sufficient to point out that
as the general type of object used as a prestige token is a non-
productive, scarce, durable, portable, homogeneous article like a
shell, money is admirably suited to being given away in exchange
for power; it is because it is divisible that it can serve other
functions.

The characteristics determining that a good be classed as a luxury
are less easy to specify, but if the goods are to be used whenever
the whim of the owner decides, they must clearly be storable. If
they are not to form part of the universal, indispensable, consumption pattern they need to be scarce. If they are scarce they must
be transferred from the producer to the ultimate consumer, and
need to be portable. In Siane the scarcity is related to the production of luxuries in areas each of which specializes in different
products. The foregoing characteristics differentiate luxuries from
subsistence goods, but not from prestige tokens. What differentiates
them from prestige tokens is the fact that they are usually physically
consumed, and thus require the constant production of new luxuries;
prestige tokens are not directly consumable and their production
is limited. In these terms, cash, as it becomes easier to consume
through use at trade stores, and easier to produce through wage
labour or cash crops, is becoming a luxury in Siane rather than a
prestige token.

The fourth category, that of novel capital goods, is distinguished
from subsistence capital goods only by the novelty of the goods.
The sets of intrinsic characteristics apparently determining the
classification of goods in Siane are summarized in Table 14.

TABLE 14

*Qualities Present in Commodities which are Associated with their
Use in Particular Activities*

Activities	Qualities
Subsistence capital	Plentiful, durable, fixed, productive
,, consumption	Plentiful, consumable, portable, utilitarian
Prestige	Scarce, durable, portable, non-useful
Luxury	Scarce, consumable, portable, utilitarian
Novel capital investment	Scarce, durable, fixed, productive

Values in Other Non-monetary Societies

The four standards of evaluation isolated analytically for Siane
are recognizable analytically in the economic behaviour of many

societies. But many other value standards might be recognizable
also. The important features of these four value standards in the
Siane system is that they can be seen as exhaustive and underlying
all transactions, while the transactions in which each standard is
used form a nexus of activity which is distinguishable both analytically and *empirically* from nexuses using other standards. I would
maintain that these same value standards are exhaustive and useful
for the analysis of economic behaviour in other societies. I would
also maintain that the clear division of economic behaviour into
different nexuses is common in societies where the distinctions have
not become blurred through the introduction of money. To support
this statement I propose to bring some comparative evidence.

All simple societies perform subsistence activities 'built upon a
use of or close relation to primary resources, [and having] con-
comitant systems of capital accumulation and indebtedness, of
marketing and distribution' (Firth 1951:88). As many authors have
shown, in such societies these activities are often inextricable from
the activities between kinsmen. Even where specialized political
offices are connected with entrepreneurial and redistributive tasks
(e.g. the *ariki* in Tikopia [Firth 1939]), the rewards given to the
occupants of these offices form part of the accepted system of distribution of the society. They are customarily made in kind (i.e.
subsistence goods). Most writers stress that, although planning is
involved, subsistence activities follow a traditional and relatively
unvarying pattern.

Many writers have distinguished systems of ceremonial exchange
and trade from the subsistence activities (Malinowski [1922, 1935]
wrote separate books about the two nexuses), but have often treated
the distinctions as fortuitous and have tried to show that both
form one single 'economy', motivated by a search for 'utility'. I
wish to show, not only that prestige activities are distinguished
from subsistence activities, but that luxury (or trade) activities are
distinguished from both by the natives themselves.

The classic example of an exchange of valuables is that of the
kula system of the Massim and Trobriand Islands (Malinowski
1922; Fortune 1932; Tueting 1935; Belshaw 1955). In this system,
chiefs and important men present non-utilitarian arm-shells to the
chiefs on nearby islands on one side, and shell beads to the chiefs
on the other side who give them arm-shells in exchange. There is
a circular clockwise flow of beads around the islands and an anti-
clockwise flow of arm-shells. These objects are termed *vaygua* (a
term comparable with the Siane *neta* and having a relation with
the term *gugua* analogous to the relationship in Siane with the

term *kevora neta*) and are only used for exchanges and for some rare wearing. If *vaygua* are exchanged for specific services or for other *vaygua* the transaction is given a special term, *laga*. The voyages made to present *vaygua* involve great publicity and cere-monial, while the exchanges between groups within one island which result in the accumulation of *vaygua* for inter-island presen-tation are somewhat less public.

At the time of *kula* voyages Trobriand Islanders who are not chiefs conduct an extensive trade in the shadow of the *kula* ex-changes, whereby they exchange with partners for mutual profit such objects as wooden bowls, baskets, red ochre, coconuts, and obsidian. These objects are produced as specialties by different islands, and would appear to be classed as *gugua* (Malinowski 1922: 178), though the ethnography is unclear. The process of exchange is termed *gimwali*, which is translatable as 'haggling'.

Some analysts have interpreted the *kula* as a mere preliminary to bringing people together for the utilitarian trade (e.g. Thurnwald 1932: 148). But Malinowski makes it clear that the *kula* is seen as the more important by the Trobrianders; the trade is incidental. The two exchanges are further distinguished by the different goods involved, the different methods of exchange, the different people involved in the two types of transaction (Malinowski [p. 362] makes it clear that the same partners may not both trade and exchange shells), and by the sanctions ensuring that exchanges are equal. Trade for luxuries involves haggling. Exchanges of shells and beads are equal, because of 'the repayer's own sense of what is due to custom and to his own dignity' (p. 511). The rules are those govern-ing prestige exchanges in Siane. Similar systems of trade, co-existing with but distinguished from prestige exchanges, are common throughout Melanesia (Armstrong 1924; Bell 1933; Mead 1938; Wedgwood 1933; Gitlow 1947; Belshaw 1950; Oliver 1956, etc.).

They are not limited to Melanesia. The well-known *potlatch* sys-tem of the Kwakiutl of the American Pacific Northwest (Benedict 1934; Boas 1921; Barnett 1938; Codere 1950, etc.) used blankets and sheets of copper as prestige tokens, which were given away to vali-date the assumption of new statuses or prerogatives and to derogate the recipients. Codere's argument (1950:63) that it is unjustifiable to separate a 'prestige' from a 'subsistence economy' in Kwakiutl because subsistence goods were sometimes used in *potlatch*es is not convincing. When subsistence goods were so used they constituted 'fantastic surpluses above any conceivable need', and the way in which 'fantastic surpluses' are classified differently from consumable quantities has already been discussed for Siane.

Kwakiutl trade has had less attention, but it was extensive. Tribes specialized in the production of commodities such as dried halibut and olachen oil (Codere 1950: 29-30), and long voyages were made to exchange them. Boas (1921) mentions the production and exchange of viburnum berries and crab apples (p. 262), dried salal berries (p. 269) and dried herring spawn (p. 254) in similar terms. These commodities were classed as 'bad things' (as distinguished from the 'things' or valuables—Codere 1950: 64), and in modern times flour, silk scarves, dishes, and Canadian money have been adopted into this category. As with Siane luxuries, vast quantities of these goods could be used in an effort to gain prestige, but such efforts were not the normal rule.

Stanner has described similar dual systems of exchange for the Daly River tribes of Australia. The one to acquire utilitarian goods is called *merbok,* and the other, involving payments to men assuming obligations for feeding and caring for women, is called *kue.* Here the same commodities are used in the two systems, but the sanctions against default show that distinct standards of evaluating goods and transactions are involved in each. Default in *merbok* merely results in the defaulter obtaining no further goods, but default in *kue* results in the 'lasting ignominy of disrepute' since 'it is a matter of no small account to be known as a man who has given a good account of himself in *kue*' (Stanner 1934: 463). For a man to have good standing in *kue* does lead to his gaining material advantage in *merbok,* but Stanner points out that the existence of alternative standards for evaluating goods often leads to conflict over how they should be used on any one occasion.

The use of cattle as prestige tokens in South and East Africa has been described extensively (e.g. Herskovits 1926; Richards 1932: 97), and stress has been laid on the restrictions on the use of cattle as subsistence goods. The closest link between cattle exchanges and the political structure of society has been demonstrated for the Lovedu (Leach 1951). Descriptions of luxury trading in this area are rarer, but there are some (e.g. Richards 1939: 223).

This impressionistic evidence from many parts of the world is supported more clearly by the evidence of two societies for which detailed analyses are available, both of the indigenous system and of more recent changes—the New Zealand Maori (Firth 1929) and the Nigerian Tiv (Bohannan 1955). The Maori produced and consumed subsistence goods within their village units and there was 'little exchange of goods between the members of the same village'. By contrast 'transactions . . . between people of different communities were fairly common, [and] . . . exchange arose through the differences in the economic resources of the various tribes. Foodstuffs were the chief commodity which changed hands' (p. 396). Yet the list of foods so traded shows that they were not the foods involved in everyday subsistence, but were luxuries like shell-fish, shark-oil, preserved birds and forest berry-cakes. Together with ornaments and greenstone, they were traded by means of gift-exchange, but Firth distinguishes 'two salient types of exchange . . . the exchange of coastal for inland products, . . . and the movement of greenstone to the North in return for foodstuffs, cloaks and other objects of fine workmanship' (p. 402). Elsewhere he distinguishes

> the economic [form of gift exchange], in which the primary object is to acquire something of practical utility from the other party, and the ceremonial [form], in which the transaction fulfils some wider social purpose, the acquisition of goods not being the principal motive (p. 395).

Greenstone was the most striking object of the ceremonial exchanges, and Firth specifies why it was so much demanded, giving a series of characteristics similar to those I have already given as requisite for an object to be a prestige token. He continues

> [greenstone] . . . was so much used in exchange that it is sometimes said by Europeans, . . . that greenstone was the *money* of the Maori. This is quite incorrect. The stone was at no time a common measure of values, nor did it even act as a medium of exchange to facilitate transactions in other articles. It was simply the most prominent substance concerned in the reciprocal [ceremonial] exchange of gifts (p. 402).

In the terms I have used in the present analysis this could be stated as meaning that there was no common standard by which to evaluate greenstone and, say, shark-oil. Firth concludes that the native economic system 'was devoid of any finely adjusted scale of values' (p. 396); I would say that it had three scales of value, each applying to a different range of substances. I shall return to the discussion of Maori economics when I compare their economic change with that of the Siane.

The Tiv of Nigeria distinguish three, and possibly four, categories of exchangeable items, and use different terms for each category. Thus

> all locally produced foodstuffs (*yiagh*) . . . are said by the Tiv to be of a single economic kind, and immediately interchangeable. [Included in this category are] chickens and goats, . . . household utensils . . ., some tools and also the raw materials for

producing any item in this category. . . . The second important category includes slaves, cattle, white cloth and metal bars. . . . This second category is associated with prestige (*shagba*) in the same way that the first category is associated with subsistence. The supreme category of exchange values contains only one item; rights in human beings other than slaves, and particularly in women. The categories represent the fundamentals of Tiv notions of exchange and investment (Bohannan 1955:62).

Thus the Tiv value things in terms of subsistence and of power, though they also distinguish between two types of power or right. At first sight they do not appear to value things as luxuries. However, 'imported, particularly European, food is not *yiagh*', while men trade for 'goods which must be procured and traded over long distances; smoked fish, . . . camwood and kolas . . . and items such as cotton' (p. 68). Women trade for things such as 'a waistcloth for herself or small gifts for her children'. This trade is said to be 'within the monetary economy', but at least the trade for nuts and fish would seem to have existed to a limited extent previously, for with the 'pacification of the countryside . . . men's trading developed very rapidly' (p. 68). It would seem to have constituted an exchange of luxury goods.

Exchange of goods of the same category was normal and in accordance with a known system of exchange values (*ishe*). There was a possibility of 'conversion' or the exchange of goods of one category against goods of another, but this was not common. The man who obtained a prestige token for a subsistence commodity was considered successful, and his partner unsuccessful, while there was 'a strong moral quality in the rationalization of conversions' (p. 65). In our terms there are sanctions opposing a man's trading prestige for subsistence or subsistence for luxury, but supporting the man who values prestige most highly.

In these non-monetary societies the different value standards are distinguishable operationally. In a monetary society they are distinguishable analytically, as can be shown in the following example, taken from personal experience, of the valuation of a car in the United States of America. While a student my standard of life was low; owning a car was not demanded by my status, nor was it within my financial capabilities, however much I wanted the prestige or the comfort it might provide. On acquiring the status of salary-earner I needed a car, since my work was inaccessible by public transport. To achieve the new status a novel capital investment was needed. To maintain the new status I had to maintain my car and pay running costs. In 1955 the running costs of most cars (petrol,

oil, insurance, etc.) varied little and were about $400, according to
my own personal experiences and those of others (Anon. 1955). On
the other hand the annual depreciation of a car varied from $60
for an 8-year-old car to $1,000 for a brand new car, although average
annual repair costs for the same cars were $80 and $10 respectively
(Anon. 1955). The expense of maintenance thus varied from $140
($60 + $80) to $1,010 ($1,000 + $10). The low figure of $540 ($400 + $140)
represents the subsistence expense of running a car and maintaining a social status.

If I had spent the high figure of $1,410 ($1,010 + $400), what would
I have gained in addition? As luxury elements I would include the
additional comfort, the security of not constantly fearing break-
downs, and the pleasure of entertaining friends and driving for
fun. As prestige elements, I might have obtained a symbol of social
rank—the status symbolism of cars has been discussed by numerous
sociologists (e.g. Riesman and Roseborough 1955)—though this would
have been more of a factor if I had been, say, a company director
who would have felt that the 6-year-old car I did buy was not
appropriate to his position. I would also have gained some direct
power by owning a new car, as occurs, for example, when two car
owners wish to travel together. They are more likely to use the
newer of their two cars and the driver of the new car can then
decide about routes and stops. In effect, in buying a new car he
has paid for the right to decide.

The example may appear trivial, but it demonstrates the possibility of using the same four standards of evaluation to analyse
the bases for making purchases in even a monetary society (cf.
Roseborough 1957).

9

ECONOMIC VALUES AND CHANGE:
A SYNTHESIS

A CLASSIFICATION of value standards, however universal the standards might be, is sterile if it is not related to something else. It will be examined here to see how far it enables us to see regularities in the process of economic change.

Economic changes on the microscopic level were described earlier (see Chapter 7) in terms of differing elasticities of demand for different categories of goods, following an increase in the supply of all goods. This description can now be restated in terms of the standards of evaluation of those goods. Goods valued for maintaining existing social statuses and the existing standard of life showed a stable level of demand during the whole period; immediately after the increase in supply, demand for goods exchangeable for power rose markedly, but when a certain number of goods had been taken, it declined to a stable lower level. When this demand had stabilized, demand for goods satisfying random personal wants and giving a higher standard of comfort increased. When the demand for comfort-producing goods reached a stable level, there came a demand for goods to maintain novel capital investments and so to increase the standard of life.

On the macroscopic level this same sequence occurred (see the changes described in Chapters 3 and 4). In the first place, the introduction of the new steel technology raised the potential supply of goods of all kinds, since it set free time that could have been used to make any kind of good. No more subsistence goods were produced, since demand for them was stable, given the existing role structure of society. Time was spent in efforts to increase the power of each individual and group. Some of these efforts took the form of fighting to obtain power; some were efforts to obtain power through the increased use of valuables. Initially, great discrepancies arose in the power obtained by different groups, but inflation in the rate of exchanging power for valuables reduced these discrepancies until they were only slightly larger than they had been previously. The inflation increased the power 'big men' had within their own groups and increased the size of the groups that cooperated in ceremonies. The use of goods giving added comfort and personally idiosyncratic satisfaction also increased somewhat, but the greatest increase in the use of luxuries has occurred more recently, since natives have had the chance to obtain even larger supplies through indentured labour. Only those men who have had the greatest chance to obtain wealth have begun to make important novel capital investments, and so far most of these investments have been in consumer's capital goods, and few in productive capital goods.

Among the Maori (see Chapter 8) the process of change since Europeans first arrived in New Zealand appears to have been similar (Firth 1929). They first demanded objects for use in ceremonial exchanges such as cloth, bead ornaments, and, above all, axes, which resembled the greenstone *mere* more than they did ordinary work axes. There appears to have been an increase in the exchanging of rights over individuals (pp. 461n., 460n.), but more obvious were the increasing attempts to gain power through warfare, following the introduction of firearms. The Maori obtained these valuables by increasing the production of goods wanted by Europeans but not 'of primary importance in the original native economic scheme' (p. 455)—that is, luxuries such as flax and *kauri* spars, plus potatoes. Firth thinks that the time spent in producing these goods tended to disrupt the existing productive organization, but he does not consider the saving of time caused by introducing steel tools. Even more interest in luxury goods was shown in the next phase of Maori economic change, which 'was characterised by a greatly increased demand for European goods' (p. 457), mainly for clothes and tobacco but also for some soap and European foods like wheat. This period began about 1840, and by 1852 the demand was such that Government reports say that the Maori had 'started with an energy quite surprising in the pursuit of gain' (p. 460), learning new skills and organizing their marketing. During this period began the acquisition of novel capital investments to stabilize the standard of comfort as a new standard of life. By 1849 numerous flour mills had been erected and some farming equipment obtained, mostly under corporate ownership but some privately owned (p. 463).[1] 'From what has been stated so far it may be thought that the course of Europeanisation of the Maori economic system was proceeding smoothly as the result of a process of gradual replacement' (p. 464). But there was also much 'discontent which came to be focussed

---

[1] At this time money was introduced to the Maori, but its effects are not clear. The effect of the introduction of money on economic change will be discussed later.

on the matter of land'. Though part of this was because of the religious importance of the land, the loss of land to Europeans meant in economic terms a large capital loss, masked at first by the acquisition of machinery as capital. Without land a new standard of life could not be maintained; the Maori War ensued, and since then the diminished stock of land capital has supported only a part of the Maori people; the remainder have been dependent on capital owned by Europeans.

Belshaw (1954) has compiled the history of Eastern Melanesia, where a similar sequence appears to have occurred. No increase in subsistence production occurred.

> The introduction of manufactured implements [meant] the amount of labour required to perform a wide range of specific tasks decreased. The result was that more time was spent on activities which were not materially productive, rather than that the same amount of time was spent in order to increase the supply of material wealth (p. 60).

Belshaw describes these 'non-productive activities' merely as 'producing utility in non-material forms such as leisure, gossip and social activity' (p. 89), but his examples are all of increased exchanges of valuables for power and of increased trading for luxury goods (p. 125). One example (p. 131) shows how inflated bride-price payments in the New Hebrides increased the power of the old men, whose position had been threatened by the productivity of the young men. No historical sequence relating these two forms of exchange can be traced, because of the distance in time, the diverse regions discussed, and the sparse records. But Belshaw lists the major items purchased *nowadays* by natives at trade stores, and they are mainly low-priced luxuries. He also says that 'a point of satiation [of the demand for luxuries] has been reached in terms of the present culture', and points to the need for more education or higher income to raise the standard of living (p. 122). He considers that the reasons demand does not rise are that other goods are 'impossibly high priced', and that people are not trained to demand better quality goods 'of slightly higher values'. The present analysis, however, leads to the conclusion that Eastern Melanesians are satisfied with their existing level of comfort and have not yet learned a completely new standard of life which would demand novel capital investment. In a later work, Belshaw (1955) does treat the difficulties of making novel capital investment in the Southern Massim of Papua. Among these highly-educated people, village co-operatives and individuals who received large sums as compensation for war damages are actively purchasing and owning 'large items of capital equipment, notably boats and trucks [which would otherwise have been] beyond the resources of individuals' (p. 104).

Codere's (1950) methodical study of the history of the Kwakiutl shows the beginning of a similar sequence. She points out the great increase in *potlatch*ing to obtain power after the introduction of the first steel tools, and explicitly shows how fighting was an alternative means of obtaining power, which the Kwakiutl began to adopt but then discarded. The later obtaining of luxuries from Europeans is also documented, as well as some recent capital investment, but depopulation appears to have ruled out any large-scale organization or continuation of *potlatch*ing among these people.

Such regularities demand a general explanation, which I shall try to give in the form of a model of the process of change, based on this detailed description of Siane. Siane society before the introduction of steel tools might be considered as in a state of equilibrium. Demographic and archaeological evidence (Salisbury 1956a) suggests that the population had been stable in size and location for at least 100 years. Glottochronological evidence suggests that the Siane speakers split away from Gahuku speakers some 1,000 years ago, yet only thirty miles separate these groups (Salisbury 1956c). In their state of equilibrium Siane groupings corresponded almost exactly with the size of groups needed for efficient division of labour in the agricultural tasks—lineage groups were sufficient for most tasks, ward groups were suited to the larger tasks, and the limited needs for co-ordination were met by the clan group of 200. The vaguely-recognized ties between wider groups and between individuals constituted an insurance against calamities. Within the clan, the concepts of property ownership and help maintained the productive capital of the group, provided the justification for calling together labour forces when needed, and ensured that entrepreneurial tasks were allocated. The circulation of valuables ensured that able men could gain sufficient prestige within the democratic society to carry out those tasks requiring an exercise of authority and that an approximate political balance was kept between groups. The use of luxury goods prevented undue rigidity. Capital was renewed as needed by the allocation of 2 per cent of each man's time to producing capital goods, thereby maintaining both the standard of life and the indigenous structure of society.

When changes in the available technology (or in climatic conditions) make it possible for a society in such a state of equilibrium to obtain more goods, no change in the standard of life is made immediately. Demand for subsistence goods remains stable, and the amount of capital investment *shrinks* to the amount needed to produce the same amount of goods. People try to gain additional power, for which there appears the most elastic demand, either by fighting or by the use of material tokens of prestige. The work of Veblen (1899) suggests that this propensity, which he described as 'conspicuous consumption' is in fact universal. Firth (1951:144) also comments to this effect regarding primitive society. Inflation in the cost of power slows down the rate at which it is demanded and diverts the attention of less capable organizers into other, luxury, demands. Yet the effect of the activities using power tokens is to increase the size of groupings and the power of important men. With the existing productive system there is no outlet whereby the larger, better organized groups can find efficient productive employment, and if no further changes occur the society may remain wealthy, possessing a system of social statuses with little productive function but much associated ritual. Such systems are common in fertile islands in Micronesia and Polynesia.

If the increased wealth of the society does in the course of time permit the peaceful establishment of a larger, more centralized organization (I shall not consider what happens when warfare is the chosen method of centralization), further increases in wealth are used to provide luxuries. Although such luxuries may appear frivolities to an outside observer, their use has several functions. It enables the mass introduction of new techniques and goods (e.g. carrying for patrols under the guise of luxury help introduced into Siane the idea of wage labour; new crops such as passion-fruit were first grown with other luxuries in small gardens within the villages), some of which may prove worthy of general adoption. It creates a general demand for methods by which to produce new goods, and it may eventually lead to investment in novel capital goods.

If new types of investment are available, native society is now more organized than it was while in equilibrium and more able to exploit these investments—there are larger labour forces and more trained organizers available. Now, too (as was not so in the equilibrium condition), there is a demand for the products of new investment. The use of these products comes to be considered indispensable, and they become part of a new standard of life, appreciably higher than the previous one, and involving a new stable level of capital investment. Many factors can prevent the changeover from great use of luxuries to increased capital investment. One, the social pressures in the indigenous society towards the distribution of capital accumulations, has already been described for Siane. The high cost of most capital goods, mentioned by

Belshaw, is part of the same phenomenon. Yet another factor is the presence of outsiders who retain ownership of the capital investments and enable the natives to obtain luxuries without making investments. That this is an unstable condition (though originally advantageous for both parties) has been shown by recent experiences in Africa. The greater indigenous organization has no outlet to express itself, and accordingly it breaks down; natives, although relatively wealthy, have only the position of wage-labourers, and must start building up a productive organization on completely new lines, often with unhappy consequences for the capital-owners and for the wealth of the workers.

This model is advanced as an ideal of how a simple technological innovation, given time and the free play of both the human desire for power and the randomness of innovation, can eventually produce a new organization of society and a new standard of life. Some factors have been pointed out which could side-track this process, which is seen as cyclical. It might conceivably be speeded up by governmental fiat, though I would predict that only decrees which tended in the direction described would be effective.

In conclusion, some of the ways in which the process can break down are worth considering, as are some of the reasons why the different standards of evaluation in Siane and other non-monetary societies tend to favour its working. In the first place, the whole of the present study, and the ideal model summing it up, suggest that standards of life do not advance progressively; they jump suddenly from one level to another in a step-wise motion. The simple addition of a small increment to the income of all people in any country is likely to have no effect in raising that country's standard of life, since the productive organization and the level of capital investment needed to maintain the new standard of life would not occur automatically. Nor would a simple investment of new capital in a country produce a rise in the standard of life (cf. Chapter 6), since demand for the products of investment would have to be learned, and it is unlikely that provision for the maintenance of the capital investment would be made until the new products were accepted as part of the standard of life.

Secondly, where money is present the possibility of the process breaking down is increased (although the possibility of speeding up the process by governmental action is introduced). A man who has money can use it for whatever activity he wishes to, at that moment. Money provides 'a common denominator among the categories [of exchange values], which was previously lacking' (Bohannan 1955:67). Its introduction means that, even where no technological change is introduced at the same time, the allocation of the resources of the society to maintain the existing role structure, to distribute free-floating power, and to preserve flexibility is disturbed. The Tiv (Bohannan 1955) provide a good example of this. The introduction of money there has led to a dispersal of capital accumulations through, for example, the sale of land and the use for luxury purchases of the money obtained. The Tiv ruefully say 'A man can't spend a field', as the basis for maintaining their previous standard of living is dissipated. The finely-balanced Tiv system of distributing rights over women through sister-exchange marriage has been disrupted, and with it has come a disruption of the means of distributing food.

> The Tiv have come upon a simple paradox; today it is easy to sell subsistence goods for money to buy prestige articles and women, thereby aggrandizing oneself at a rapid rate. The food so sold is exported, decreasing the amount of subsistence goods available for consumption. On the other hand the number of women is limited. The result is that bride-wealth gets higher. . . . Under these conditions, as the Tiv attempt to become more and more wealthy in people [that form of wealth traditionally most productive of further wealth] . . . they are merely selling more and more of their foodstuffs and subsistence goods, leaving less and less for their own consumption (p. 70).

In a situation where technological innovation has begun the process of change, the presence of money can mean that the added resources are not employed first to create a tighter social organization, but are expended in obtaining luxuries of all kinds, or even in making capital investments which turn out to be premature. Even if a period of conspicuous luxury consumption does eventually stabilize a new form of power hierarchy, the use of money to pay for subsistence goods or for added small luxuries and the ease of dispersing accumulations of money can delay the making of novel forms of capital investment. On the other hand, the very virtue of money—that it can be stored—can also lead to hoarding and a lack of investment. Where capital exists only in the form of real goods, these goods give their owner no benefit except when put to productive use; where capital exists in the form of money, the money can be hoarded and still provide its owner with the satisfaction of knowing that he has resources available to meet any emergency that arises. From the point of view of society at large, real capital exerts a pressure to be used, whereas money capital can easily be withdrawn from use and so disrupt the steady process of capital use and replacement. As Belshaw (1955) has shown, the failure to reinvest productively the surplus of earnings over expenditure among the Southern Massim had caused their economy to stagnate despite their wealth.

Any economist will recognize that in monetary societies mechanisms exist to counter all the disruptive effects I have listed. The interest rate penalizes people who do not use their monetary capital productively. Compulsory saving through taxes and government investment in public works supplement what private investors (spurred on by differential taxes on capital investments) contribute to the real capital of the society and hence to the rise in its standard of life. Sales or purchase taxes, coupled with import duties or excise, are used to limit luxury purchases at times when effort is needed in other sectors of production. The stock market (and where the stock market fails, the takeover bid) ensures that the exchange value of the capital assets of a firm are publicly known and are not unwittingly dispersed. Banks accumulate the small savings of numbers of people and make them available as large accumulations to those who can show they will use them productively. Direct Government intervention to ensure that every individual receives his ration of subsistence goods, to determine rates of capital investment, the quantity of luxuries produced, and the organization of industry are alternative methods used by some monetary societies.

What I have tried to show in this book is that the presence in non-monetary societies of discrete scales of value, each depending on a different standard of evaluation, is not an unfortunate accident. It is a simple mechanism ensuring that subsistence goods are used to maintain a basic standard of life below which no person falls; that free-floating power is allocated peacefully, with a minimum of exploitation (or disturbance of the individual's right to subsistence) and in accordance with accepted standards; that the means of ensuring flexibility in the society do not disrupt the formal allocation of statuses in the society or the means of gaining power. In times of technological change, the fact that any good can be used to obtain only one type of value means that resources are applied (in the absence of outside interference) to the solution of the necessary problems of exploiting the new technology, in the correct sequence. A tighter organization of society is created, without changing the basic standard of life; then the general standard of comfort rises; then novel capital investment is made to raise the standard of life to a new level. In a monetary society the achievement of this essentially simple sequence requires extremely complex mechanisms, while much of the activity involved (e.g. the pursuit of prestige) appears as 'irrational', or inexplicable in terms of the economist's assumption that the pursuit of money is a single, un-differentiated spur to activity. It is hoped that this study of change in a non-monetary society may help in understanding the simple sequence underlying the complex mechanisms which Bauer and Yamey (1956) have called the *Economics of Under-Developed Countries.*

Appendix A

SIANE TRIBAL GROUPS

The following tribal groups (and their component clans) constitute what is referred to as Siane in the text. The figures for population are taken from the 1953 Government census of the Western census area of Goroka sub-district, conducted by P.O. John Thayer. The northern Siane clans became part of the Chuave census area of Chimbu sub-district following an administrative reorganization in 1953, and census figures were not available to me. In arrangement the list of groups runs from the north-east to the south-west, and then across to the east (see Fig. 1).

Tribal group	Component clans	Population		
		Male	Female	Total
Komenkaraka	6	n.a.	n.a.	n.a.
Yamofwe	4	n.a.	n.a.	n.a.
Komunku	6	n.a.	n.a.	n.a.
,,	3	383	388	771
Raya	2	259	256	515
Aranko	8	697	661	1,358
Emenyo	2	201	165	366
Fowe	2	245	234	479
Ramfau	4	845	788	1,633
Namfayufa	2	164	157	321
Yantime	6	569	502	1,071
Wanto	3	263	256	519
Nivi	2	140	119	259
Urumfa	8	639	596	1,235
Omena	3	194	183	377
Rafayufa	3	196	200	396
Yaviyufa	6	568	502	1,070
	54 clans censused	5,363	5,007	10,370
	16 clans estimated	1,589	1,484	3,073
	Estimated total	6,952	6,491	13,443

Appendix B

TIME BUDGETS

After I had observed most of the activities in Siane life, and had gained some idea of the techniques involved and the amounts of time involved in each activity, I wished to estimate the relative frequency of each activity. I tried to obtain information from eight individuals on what they did in one week, with a view to making several such periodic checks, but found it impossible to keep track of so many men. I accordingly selected a sample of twelve men, and checked the activities of three of them every day for one week. The next week I 'followed' a different three men, and so on over a period of nine weeks.

The sample of twelve men was selected on a basis of stratification in terms of social status. Three were youths (aged 13, 16 and 19); two were married men without children; three were married men (aged 24, 29 and 36) with children, but unimportant socially; two were 'big men' aged 40 and 45; and the *luluai* and *tultul* of the village (aged 35 and 29, respectively). This may be compared with the total population of the village (Antomona clan of Emenyo tribe) of thirty-four youths, sixteen childless married men, twenty-two unimportant married men, seventeen 'big men', and two village officials. Except for the category of village officials, the sample is fairly representative.

I did not let these men know they were being 'followed', in case this might bias my results, but each day I saw them at work, or talked with them as they went to work or came home, or politely asked about their health and activities from near relatives. For only seventeen man-days of work was I unable to learn what had been done by the individuals I was 'following'.

In deciding whom to follow each week I followed a plan formulated before I commenced close study, so that there would be no question of my observing only those individuals whom it was easiest to observe. Each week I followed men from three different categories, and in succeeding weeks I changed the categories so that all men were followed an equal amount, but the same categories were not followed at the same time. Thus if the five categories are termed a, b, c, d, and e, I followed in the first week men from d-e-c; in the second week, b-c-d; in the third, a-d-e; in the fourth, a-b-c, and so on.

The activities performed were classified as:

(A) Work on large communal gardens, building fences, clearing and planting.
(B) Work on lineage tasks, mainly making individual gardens, repairing fences, and planting, but some housebuilding and hunting.
(C) Work at home, usually performing craft activities by the older men, but also some idling by the youths.
(D) Sick at home.
(E) Visiting, or entertaining visitors.
(F) Ceremonials, participating or attending.
(G) Courts, settling or participating.
(H) Government work.
(I) Attending Mission services.
(J) Playing football.

The unit of measurement was the day, or half-day of work (see pp. 49 et seq.). The time spent by each individual at each of the various tasks during the nine weeks of close study and the week of preliminary study is shown in Table I.

The great diversity in individual figures indicates the variety of individual motivations to work and the changing nature of men's occupations from week to week. A calculation of the percentages of total time spent by each category is shown in Table II.

For the implications of these figures in analysing the economic values of the various categories in Siane society and Siane values in general, see Chapter 3, pp. 110-11. The figures for 'sickness', although probably representative for the whole clan, give undue weight to the fact that one 'big man' was sick for most of one week when he was being 'followed'. The figures for 'lineage work' are somewhat inflated because the periodic 'hunt' for flying foxes took place during the course of this study. On the other hand the figure is somewhat depressed because no housebuilding, another periodic activity, took place between June and October 1953.

Table 2 (p. 108), on which most of the textual analysis is based, is derived from the final column of Table II. This, in its turn, is calculated from the bottom line of Table I. Since the sample of individuals selected for study is fairly representative, summing the time spent by the various individuals gives the best estimate for an 'average clan' figure.

The calculations of time spent in the stone technology in Table 2 are primarily based on the use of the factors of $2\frac{1}{2}$ and $1\frac{1}{2}$ to convert amounts of time spent in clan work and lineage work respec-

TABLE I

Man-days Spent by Individuals of Antomona Clan, Emenyo Tribe, on Various Activities during Periods of Two or Three Weeks, 13 June to 17 October 1953

Individual		Days Spent in Each Category of Activity										
		A	B	C	D	E	F	G	H	I	J	Total
Youths	a	—	—	1·5	—	—	4·0	—	2·5	1·0	3·0	12·0
	b	—	4·0	1·5	5·0	3·5	1·0	—	1·0	0·5	1·5	18·0
	c	4·0	0·5	5·5	1·0	—	—	—	0·5	0·5	0·5	12·5
Total		4·0	4·5	8·5	6·0	3·5	5·0	—	4·0	2·0	5·0	42·5
Childless	d	—	—	2·0	3·0	—	4·0	—	1·0	1·0	2·0	13·0
men	e	3·0	9·5	—	—	—	3·5	—	1·5	—	—	17·5
Total		3·0	9·5	2·0	3·0	—	7·5	—	2·5	1·0	2·0	30·5
Unimportant	f	1·0	10·5	1·0	—	—	4·5	1·0	1·5	—	—	19·5
men	g	8·5	5·0	2·0	1·0	1·0	—	1·0	2·5	1·0	—	22·0
	h	3·5	0·5	3·0	—	6·0	3·5	1·0	2·0	1·0	—	20·5
Total		13·0	16·0	6·0	1·0	7·0	8·0	3·0	6·0	2·0	—	62·0
'Big men'	i	6·0	1·0	1·0	7·0	—	3·0	0·5	0·5	—	—	19·0
	j	3·0	1·0	4·5	3·0	2·0	1·5	—	1·5	0·5	—	17·0
Total		9·0	2·0	5·5	10·0	2·0	4·5	0·5	2·0	0·5	—	36·0
Officials	k	8·0	2·0	0·5	1·0	0·5	3·5	2·5	3·5	1·0	—	22·5
	l	9·0	1·0	3·5	—	—	1·0	2·5	2·5	—	0·5	20·0
Total		17·0	3·0	4·0	1·0	0·5	4·5	5·0	6·0	1·0	0·5	42·5
Total		46·0	35·0	26·0	21·0	13·0	29·5	8·5	20·5	6·5	7·5	213·5

tively. These factors were arrived at from the detailed figures of time spent in operations using axes (as against operations not involving axes) in clan and lineage work. Thus of the 46 man-days of clan work shown in Table I, 36½ involved axe work in garden fencing and clearing and 9½ days of planting did not. If steel axes cut the time needed for axe work to one-third, 109½ days or 3 × 36½ days' axe work would have been involved, together with the same 9½ days of other work—a total of 119 days' work. In round figures, this is 2½ times as long as for clan work. The 35 days of lineage work in Table I involved 8 days of fencing and garden clearing and 3 days of housebuilding—both tasks using axes—together with 3 days of planting, 11 of garden maintenance, and 10 of hunting. If the fencing, clearing and housebuilding took three times as long, this means that 35 man-days of work took 57 man-days (3 × 11 + 24) in stone-using time, or roughly 1½ times as much.

TABLE II

Time Spent on Various Activities by Various Categories of Males in Antomona Clan, Emenyo Tribe

(%)

Activity	Category of Worker					Total clan
	Youths	Men no child	Unimpor- tant men	'Big men'	Officials	
Clan work	9	10	21	25	40	22
Lineage work	11	31	26	5	7	16
Home work	20	7	10	15	9	12
Sickness	14	10	2	28	2	10
Visits	8	–	11	6	2	6
Ceremonial	12	25	13	12	10	14
Court cases	–	–	5	1	12	4
Government work	9	8	10	6	14	10
Mission	5	3	3	1	2	3
Football	12	7	–	–	1	4

Note: Figures are rounded and may not add to 100.

The central figure in all the calculations is the estimate that axe work took three times as long in stone-using times. This figure has a fair degree of reliability. It was given to me first by my most reliable informant, who unexpectedly said, when we returned from a day watching and timing gardening operations, 'That would have taken three times as long when we had stone axes.' His remark was the germ for much of the analysis in this book. I checked it

extensively by making spot checks, asking individuals whose work
I had watched how long they would have taken using stone axes.
The consensus was that stone axes took between three and four
times as long.

A further check on this figure was given by the agreement among
all Siane that, in the old days, no sooner was one garden cleared
and fenced than work had to start on the next garden. There was
also consensus that men went to work in clan gardens roughly
every other day, instead of roughly every third day as now. At
present ten to fifteen days of garden clearing work are spread
roughly over a month. Three times as much work, involving one
and one half times as frequent employment, would take over two
months. The fact that in 1953 five cycles of garden clearing were
needed to ensure continuous cropping indicates that two months
would be less than the minimum needed. In short, the factor three
is a conservative estimate.

In the calculations in the body of this work I use a conservative
estimate. To use a factor of four—probably an overestimate—would
have rendered the contrasts even more striking. Clan work would
have required 77 per cent of a man's time in the stone technology,
and lineage work 32 per cent, or over 100 per cent of a man's time
would have gone on mere subsistence. The alternative would have
been that production was substantially less during stone-using times,
and that people often went hungry. Occasional hunger as a result
of wars was described to me, and gardens were somewhat smaller
in stone-using times, but the general impression given to me (and
to early explorers) is that food was fairly abundant in those days.
Or again, the use of a factor of four in the calculations of capital
investment would make the reduction of capital stocks, following
the introduction of steel axes (Table 5) even more striking. It would
turn the slight increase in the use of capital relative to labour (see
p. 148) into a marked decline. It appears safer (and simpler) to use
the factor of three which was originally given to me.

Appendix C

DEMAND FOR EUROPEAN GOODS IN SIANE
1952-3

During the first ten months of the period of fieldwork, I kept records of all goods demanded by natives in payment for food, goods, or services supplied to me (see Ch. 7). Fixed exchange rates for goods, cash, food, and services were established during the first month and maintained until the end of record-keeping. All records show the number of units of goods or services, valued at threepence, that changed hands. Whenever a transaction was made, an entry was made on a rough check list. These entries were totalled at approximately two-week intervals. Each entry specified what clan the native came from (and for one clan the name of the individual also), and what he took. In the figures given, the goods demanded have been grouped into categories as explained in Chapter 7. The bi-weekly periods have been grouped into longer periods to provide adequate numbers of transactions to warrant talking about 'patterns of demand'. The figures are of numbers of transactions involving a demand for a specific category of good during a specific period.

TABLE III

Siane Demand for European Goods, 1952-3
(Units of 3d.)

Group	Period	A Native valuables	B Luxuries	C Novel European hard goods	D Soap	E Cash	Total
				Categories of Goods Demanded			
Feramana clan, Emenyo tribe	17 Dec.- 13 Mar.	177	30	9	20	41	277
	14 Mar.- 25 May	72	33	16	3	2	126
	26 May- 6 Oct.	11	64	12	12	4	103
		260	127	37	35	47	506
Antomona clan, Emenyo tribe	17 Dec.- 1 Jan.	47	—	—	—	85	132
	1 Jan.- 17 Jan.	111	13	10	18	25	177
	18 Jan.- 16 Feb.	152	28	—	12	54	246
	17 Feb.- 13 Mar.	120	38	5	26	5	194
	14 Mar.- 25 May	125	163	40	54	135	517
	26 May- 2 Aug.	57	126	23	23	153	382
	3 Aug.- 6 Oct.	148	109	71	73	122	523
		760	477	149	206	579	2,171
2 clans of Fowe tribe	17 Dec.- 6 Oct.	19	12	12	7	—	50
Rofaifo clan, Komunku tribe	17 Dec.- 1 Jan.	17	6	—	—	38	61
	2 Jan.- 16 Feb.	97	25	3	8	33	166
	17 Feb.- 23 Mar.	36	22	16	31	9	114
	24 Mar.- 6 Oct.	50	151	64	192	—	457
		200	204	83	231	80	798

| Group | Period | Categories of Goods Demanded | | | | | |
		A Native valuables	B Luxuries	C Novel European hard goods	D Soap	E Cash	Total
Waifo clan, Komunku tribe	17 Dec.-30 Jan.	5	24	—	—	104	133
	31 Jan.-23 Mar.	16	3	—	20	9	48
	24 Mar.-2 Aug.	20	82	13	27	—	142
	3 Aug.-6 Oct.	13	27	9	34	40	123
		54	136	22	81	153	446
Roanti clan, Komunku tribe	17 Dec.-6 Oct.	48	43	14	66	38	209
3 clans of Aranko tribe	17 Dec.-17 Jan.	7	—	—	—	39	46
	18 Jan.-28 Feb.	21	21	1	17	8	68
	1 Mar.-25 May	181	22	5	40	—	248
	26 May-6 Oct.	69	64	11	43	—	187
		278	107	17	100	47	549
4 clans of Ramfau tribe	17 Dec.-28 Feb.	60	2	—	—	21	83
	1 Mar.-25 May	49	—	14	—	7	70
	26 May-6 Oct.	30	13	4	9	40	96
		139	15	18	9	68	249
2 clans of Duma tribe	17 Dec.-6 Oct.	170	27	18	64	1	280
2 clans of Raya tribe	17 Dec.-6 Oct.	72	31	42	47	16	208
6 clans of Gai tribe	17 Dec.-6 Oct.	104	8	2	20	—	134

Appendix D

DEMAND FOR EUROPEAN GOODS BY ANTOMONA CLAN, EMENYO TRIBE, 1952-3

Records were kept of all transactions involving the exchange or goods or services for European goods for each individual of Antomona clan, as described in Chapter 7. In the tabulations below, the figures for individuals are given as totals for each of the following categories of person:

(1) Men returned from indenture 2 years previously (4 individuals)
(2) Village officials (2 individuals)
(3) Men newly returned from indenture—mostly youths (17 individuals)
(4) Youths who had not been indentured (22 individuals)
(5) Young married men without children (13 individuals)
(6) Unimportant men with children (18 individuals)
(7) 'Big men' (15 individuals)
(8) Women (54 individuals)

The transactions were classified by the type of article desired (as in Appendix C) and by the period during which the transaction occurred. Figures refer to transactions involving 3d. worth of goods or services.

TABLE IV

European Goods Demanded by Antomona Clan, Emenyo Tribe,
1952-3
(Units of 3d.)

Period	Category of Persons*	Category of Goods					
		A Native valuables	B Luxuries	C Novel European hard goods	D Soap	E Cash	Total
17 Dec.-	(1)	26	10	—	6	56	98
17 Jan.	(2)	24	—	—	3	4	31
	(3)	8	1	9	3	4	25
	(4)	9	—	—	—	1	10
	(5)	10	1	—	3	—	14
	(6)	12	—	1	—	1	14
	(7)	5	—	—	3	16	24
	(8)	64	1	—	—	28	93
		158	13	10	18	110	309
18 Jan.-	(1)	16	8	—	—	—	24
16 Feb.	(2)	16	1	—	4	—	21
	(3)	46	2	—	—	—	48
	(4)	23	7	—	—	42	72
	(5)	14	9	—	8	—	31
	(6)	—	1	—	—	6	7
	(7)	2	—	—	—	—	2
	(8)	35	—	—	—	6	41
		152	28	—	12	54	246
17 Feb.-	(1)	19	8	—	6	—	33
13 Mar.	(2)	—	1	1	4	—	6
	(3)	29	7	—	1	—	37
	(4)	30	11	3	5	—	49
	(5)	6	2	1	10	2	21
	(6)	6	—	—	—	—	6
	(7)	6	6	—	—	3	15
	(8)	24	3	—	—	—	27
		120	38	5	26	5	194

Period	Category of Persons*	Category of Goods					
		A Native valuables	B Luxuries	C Novel European hard goods	D Soap	E Cash	Total
14 Mar.-25 May	(1)	6	31	6	8	—	51
	(2)	12	1	1	8	—	22
	(3)	27	34	15	1	31	108
	(4)	26	59	14	25	48	172
	(5)	8	16	4	12	7	47
	(6)	16	9	—	—	26	51
	(7)	17	11	—	—	13	41
	(8)	13	2	—	—	10	25
		125	163	40	54	135	517
26 May-2 Aug.	(1)	—	10	—	—	3	13
	(2)	8	1	—	8	1	18
	(3)	13	38	5	6	60	122
	(4)	20	50	14	8	83	175
	(5)	8	4	2	1	5	20
	(6)	7	14	1	—	1	23
	(7)	—	3	1	—	—	4
	(8)	1	6	—	—	—	7
		57	126	23	23	153	382
3 Aug.-6 Oct.	(1)	—	3	16	4	—	23
	(2)	1	4	4	17	—	26
	(3)	62	49	47	39	22	219
	(4)	26	32	3	9	43	113
	(5)	6	1	1	4	10	22
	(6)	20	20	—	—	29	69
	(7)	6	—	—	—	2	8
	(8)	27	—	—	—	16	43
		148	109	71	73	122	523
Dec.-Oct. Total	(1)	67	70	22	24	59	242
	(2)	61	8	6	44	5	124
	(3)	185	131	76	50	117	559
	(4)	134	159	34	47	217	591
	(5)	52	33	8	38	24	155
	(6)	61	44	2	—	63	170
	(7)	36	20	1	3	34	94
	(8)	164	12	—	—	60	236
		760	477	149	206	579	2,171

* For key see p. 224.

BIBLIOGRAPHY

This bibliography lists the works cited in the text.

Anonymous (1955). Used Cars. *Consumer Reports,* 20: 4. The Consumers' Union of the United States.

Arensberg, C. M. (1937). *The Irish Countryman.* Macmillan, New York.

Armstrong, W. E. (1924). Shell Money from Rossel Island, Papua. *Man,* 24: 161.

Barnett, H. G. (1938). The Nature of the Potlatch. *Amer. Anthrop.,* 40: 349.

Barton, F. R. (1922). *Ifugao Economics.* Univ. Calif. Publ. Amer. Archaeol. Ethn., no. 15.

Bauer, P. T., and Yamey, B. S. (1957). *The Economics of Under-Developed Countries.* Cambridge University Press, Cambridge.

Bell, F. L. S. (1933). Report on Field Work in Tanga. *Oceania,* 4: 290.

Belshaw, C. S. (1950). Changes in Heirloom Jewellery in the Central Solomons. *Oceania,* 20: 169.

———— (1954). *Changing Melanesia.* Oxford University Press, Melbourne.

———— (1955). *In Search of Wealth.* Mem. Amer. anthrop. Ass., no. 80.

Benedict, R. F. (1934). *Patterns of Culture.* Houghton Mifflin, Boston.

Benham, F. (1938). *Economics* (4th ed.). Pitman, London.

Boas, F. (1921). *Ethnology of the Kwakiutl.* United States Bureau of Ethnology, 35th Annual Report. Washington.

Bohannan, P. (1955). Some Principles of Exchange and Investment among the Tiv. *Amer. Anthrop.,* 57: 60.

Carter, G. F. (1950). Plant Evidence for Early Contacts with America. *Sthwest. J. Anthrop.,* 6: 161.

Chatfield, C. (1947). *Food Composition Tables for International Use.* Food and Agriculture Organization, Washington.

Codere, Helen (1950). *Fighting with Property.* American Ethnological Society Monographs, No. 18. New York.

Duesenberry, J. S. (1949). *Income, Saving and Consumer Behavior.* Harvard University Press, Cambridge.

Eisenstadt, S. N. (1956). Ritualized Personal Relations. *Man,* 56: 96.

Evans-Pritchard, E. E. (1940). *The Nuer.* Clarendon Press, Oxford.

Firth, R. (1929). *Primitive Economics of the New Zealand Maori.* Routledge, London.

———(1939). *A Primitive Polynesian Economy.* Routledge, London.

———(1951). *Elements of Social Organization.* Watts, London.

Fisher, I. (1906). *The Nature of Capital and Income.* Macmillan, London.

Fortes, M. (1936). Culture Contact as a Dynamic Process. *Africa,* 9: 24.

———(1949). *The Web of Kinship among the Tallensi.* Oxford University Press, London.

Fortune, R. F. (1932). *Sorcerers of Dobu.* Routledge, London.

Frankel, S. H. (1953). *The Economic Impact on Under-Developed Societies.* Blackwell, Oxford.

Freeman, J. D. (1955). *Iban Agriculture.* Colonial Research Studies, No. 18. Colonial Office, London.

Gitlow, A. L. (1947). *Economics of the Mount Hagen Tribes.* American Ethnological Society Monographs, No. 12. New York.

Goodenough, W. H. (1953). Ethnographic Notes on the Mae People of New Guinea's Western Highlands. *Sthwest. J. Anthrop.,* 9: 29.

Gregory, T. E. (1935). Money. *Enc. Soc. Sci.,* 10: 601.

Herskovits, M. J. (1926). The Cattle Complex in East Africa. *Amer. Anthrop.,* 28: 230.

Hicks, J. R. (1939). *Value and Capital.* Clarendon Press, Oxford.

Homans, G. C. (1950). *The Human Group.* Harcourt Brace, New York.

——— and Schneider, D. M. (1955). *Marriage, Authority and Final Causes.* Free Press, Glencoe, Illinois.

Hunter, Monica (1936). *Reaction to Conquest.* Oxford University Press, London.

Keesing, F. M. (1941). *The South Seas in the Modern World.* Day, New York.

Keynes, J. M. (1936). *The General Theory of Employment, Interest and Money.* Harcourt Brace, New York.

Knight, B. W., and Hines, L. G. (1952). *Economics: An Introductory Analysis.* Knopf, New York.

Kuznets, S. (1953). *Economic Change.* Norton, New York.

———(1960). *Economic Growth.* Free Press, Glencoe, Illinois.

Leach, E. R. (1951). Structural Implications of Matri-lateral Cross Cousin Marriage. *J. R. anthrop. Inst.,* 81: 23.

Leahy, M. J. (1936). The Central Highlands of New Guinea. *Geogr. J.,* 87: 229.

Leahy, M. J., and Crain, M. (1937). *The Land that Time Forgot.* Funk & Wagnalls, London.

Lévi-Strauss, C. (1951). *Les Structures Elémentaires de la Parenté.* Presses Universitaires de France, Paris.

Malinowski, B. (1922). *Argonauts of the Western Pacific.* Routledge, London.

────── (1935). *Coral Gardens and Their Magic.* Allen & Unwin, London.

────── (1944). *A Scientific Theory of Culture.* University of North Carolina Press, Chapel Hill.

Marshall, A. (1925). *Principles of Economics* (8th ed.). Macmillan, London.

Mauss, M. (1951). *The Gift* (trans. I. Cunnison). Free Press, Glencoe, Illinois.

Mead, Margaret (1938). *The Mountain Arapesh: An importing culture.* Anthrop. Pap. Amer. Mus., No. 36, Pt. 3.

Murphy, J. J. (1949). *The Book of Pidgin English* (3rd ed.). Smith & Paterson, Brisbane.

Nadel, S. F. (1942). *Black Byzantium.* Oxford University Press, London.

────── (1951). *Foundations of Social Anthropology.* Cohen & West, London.

Norris, R. T. (1941). *The Theory of Consumer's Demand.* Yale University Press, New Haven.

Oliver, D. L. (1956). *A Solomon Islands Society.* Harvard University Press, Cambridge.

Parsons, T. (1937). *The Structure of Social Action.* McGraw Hill, New York.

────── and Shils, E. A. (1951). *Toward a General Theory of Action.* Harvard University Press, Cambridge.

Radcliffe-Brown, A. R. (1922). *The Andaman Islanders.* Cambridge University Press, Cambridge.

────── (1939). *Taboo.* Cambridge University Press, Cambridge.

Read, K. E. (1951). The Gahuku-Gama of the Central Highlands. *South Pacific,* 5: 154.

────── (1952). Land in the Central Highlands. *South Pacific,* 6: 107.

────── (1954). The Cultures of the Central Highlands of New Guinea. *Sthwest. J. Anthrop.,* 10: 1.

Richards, Audrey I. (1932). *Hunger and Work in a Savage Tribe.* Routledge, London.

────── (1939). *Land Labour and Diet in Northern Rhodesia.* Oxford University Press, London.

Riesenfeld, A. (1951). Tobacco in New Guinea. *J. R. anthrop. Inst.,* 81: 69.

Riesman, D. and Roseborough, H. (1955). Careers and Consumer Behavior. *Consumer Behaviour* (ed. L. H. Clark), 2: 1. New York University Press, New York.

Robbins, Lionel (1935). *An Essay on the Nature and Significance of Economic Science* (2nd rev. ed.). Macmillan, London.

Roberts, A. A. (1935). A Report on the Native Inhabitants of the Chimbu Valley. MS. Department of Territories, Canberra.

Roseborough, H. (1957). The Sociology of Consumer Spending. Unpublished Ph.D. thesis, Harvard University.

Royal Anthropological Institute (1951). *Notes and Queries* (6th rev. ed.). Routledge, London.

Sahlins, M. (1958). *Social Stratification in Polynesia.* University of Washington Press, Seattle.

Salisbury, R. F. (1956a). Unilineal Descent Groups in the New Guinea Highlands. *Man,* 55: 2.

———— (1956b). Asymmetrical Marriage Systems. *Amer. Anthrop.,* 58: 639.

———— (1956c). The Siane Language of the Eastern Highlands of New Guinea. *Anthropos,* 51: 447.

———— (1958). An 'Indigenous' New Guinea Cult. *Kroeber Anthropological Papers,* 18: 67.

———— (n.d.). Political Organisation in Siane Society. *Political Systems of Papua/New Guinea* (ed. K. E. Read). In press.

Schindler, A. J. (1952). Land Use by Natives of Aiyura Village. *South Pacific,* 6: 302.

Simpson, C. (1954). *Adam in Plumes.* Angus & Robertson, Sydney.

Stanner, W. E. H. (1934). Ceremonial Economics of the Mulluk Mulluk and the Madngella Tribes of the Daly River, North Australia. A Preliminary Paper. *Oceania,* 4: 156.

———— (1953). *The South Seas in Transition.* Australasian Publishing Co., Sydney.

Tax, S. (1953). *Penny Capitalism.* Smithsonian Institution, Institute of Social Anthropology, publication no. 16. United States Government Printing Office.

Thurnwald, R. (1932). *Economics in Primitive Communities.* Oxford University Press, London.

Tueting, Laura (1935). *Native Trade in S.E. New Guinea.* Bernice P. Bishop Museum occasional papers, no. 11, pt. 15.

United Nations, Department of Economic Affairs (1951). *Measures for the Economic Development of Under-Developed Countries.* New York.

Veblen, T. (1899). *The Theory of the Leisure Class.* Macmillan, London.

Vial, L. G. (1935). Exploring in New Guinea. *Walkabout,* 4 (12): 13.

—————— (1941). Down the Wagi. *Walkabout,* 7 (9): 16.

—————— (1941). Stone Axes of Mount Hagen. *Oceania,* 11: 160.

Vicedom, G. F. and Tischner, H. (1945). *Die Mbowamb.* Friedrichsen & de Gruyter, Hamburg.

Viljoen, S. (1936). *Economics of Primitive Peoples.* King, London.

Weber, M. (1947). *The Theory of Social and Economic Organization* (trans. A. M. Henderson and T. Parsons). Oxford University Press, New York.

Wedgwood, C. H. (1933). Report on Research on Manam Island, Mandated Territory of New Guinea. *Oceania,* 4: 373.

INDEX

151, 155, 208-9; Siane economic concepts, 4; Southern Massim (Papua), 207-8, 211; stocks, 140-53 *passim,* 189; technological change, 148, 206, 211-12; units, 148, 150, 152, (output) 150; working, 144

Cargo cult, 114, 121, 129, 159

Cash crops, 133-4, 137-8, 159-61

Cassowaries, 44, 90-1, 120, 145

Casuarinas, 10, 43, 48, 82, 160

Chickens, 44, 134, 158, 164, 169, 183

Clan: corporate group, 161; intermarriage, 13, 14, 25, 27; membership, 14, (maternal) 14, (paternal) 14, (women) 37-8; nomenclature, 14; political organization, 25, 28; relationships, 26-8, 37, 194, (kin) 86; social group, 12-15; sovereignty, 37; size, 13, 14, 15, 208; territory, 68-71; trade-partnerships, 86-7; unit, 15, (kinship) 13, 14, (religious) 15, 37, (warfare) 15, 25-7 *passim;* usufruct, 68-71, 138

Climate, 11, 45

Clothing, 43-4, 50, 52, 83, 127-30 *passim,* 146, 149, 152, 154-5, 171, 188, 195

Codere, Helen, 1, 200-1, 208

Coffee, 43-5, 134, 137, 159-61, 172

Conversions: food for valuables, 124-5, 133, 169-70, 182-3, 203; money, 130, 157, 168, 211

Cooking, 49-51, 58, 74, 76, 103, 187

Courtship, *see Awoiro*

Cowrie shell, 194

Crafts, *see* Skills

Credit, 92-3, 99-100, 116

Cucumbers, 42, 79-82, 88

Death: compensation, 35-6; gifts at, 97, 133; inheritance, 73; personalty at, 64-5; taboo, 170

Debt, 92-3, 156-7, 167-70

Demand (economic), 5, 151-3, 162-83, 205-10, 221-6

Dene tribes, 7-8, 71-2, 84, 112-14, 117, 121, 162

Detribalization, 156

Disputes, settlement of, 25-7, 30-2, 63

Dogs, 44, 90-1, 115, 120

Duma tribe, 173

Dwyer, M., 1, 112

Dyes, 42

Economy: activities, 105-7; definition, 3-4, 39; system, 82; values, 6, 120-1, 129-30, 184-212

Eisenstadt, S. M., 194

Emenyo tribe, Antomona clan, 43,

70-1, 73, 98, 103, 123, 165, 173, 175-83, 215-16, 221-6; Feramana clan, 69-70, 87, 172-3, 177, 221-6

Entertaining, 59, 61-2, 76, 88-9, 130, 192-3

Entrepreneurs, 136, 141-3, 148, 158; *see also* Capital

European goods: bride-prices, 116-17, 130, 132; categories of demand, 171-83, (luxuries) 115, 121, 124-6 *passim,* 130, 133, 174-8 *passim,* 180-3 *passim,* (valuables) 3, 115, 118-21, 130, 174-8 *passim,* 180-3 *passim;* money, 125-7, 130, 138, 154-8 *passim,* 164; payments, 164-6, (money) 168-70 *passim,* 176; presentations, 123-4, 128-30; sources, 115, 118, 119, 126-7, 162-6 *passim;* trade, 87-8, 106, 120-1; uses and effects, 118-19, 121-2, 131-2, 138, 154-8

Europeanization, 173-80

Face-paint, 171, 194-5

Face-powder, 71, 194

Family, 18

Feathers, 44, 72, 91, 100, 132-3

Fences, 46-7, 50-1, 54-7, 109, 143, 146

Firewood, 50, 51, 68-9, 71-2, 134, 169

First Fruits ceremonies, 32-3, 52-3, 63n., 74, 77-8, 80, 94

Firth, R. W., x, xi, xiii, 141, 149n., 163n., 186, 199, 201-2

Flutes, sacred, 17, 34, 61, 97, 114

Flying foxes, 32, 217

Fortes, M., 23

Fowe tribe, 112, 172, 173, 215, 222

Frankel, S. H., 140-3, 152

'Friends', 86, 98, 101-2, 106, 120, 128, 189, 192-4

Gahuku, 7, 47, 158, 163, 165, 197

Gai tribe, 173

Garden clearing, 51-7, 109, 144, 146, 154, 219-20

Geography, 8-12

Gerua, 17, 21, 32-4, 61, 65

Gimaiye (ceremonial presentations): capital, 152-5; commodities, 102-3, 105-6, 115, 162, 169-70, (nature) 102-3, 197; compared with *umaiye,* 88, 97-9, 101-3, 106; contributors, 100-1; definition, 86; European contacts, 128-33 *passim,* 156-7; luxuries, 90; relationships (inter-clan) 94-7, 101-6 *passim,* 190-2, (intra-clan) 127-8, 169-70, (with Europeans) 124, 126; rights, 103, 105, 189-92 *passim;* valuables, 100; *see also Umaiye*

Gitlow, A., 39

236 INDEX